KING DAVID
His Times and Our Life

KING DAVID
His Times and Our Life

Life Lessons with David

Tony Jordan

Copyright © 2016 by Tony Jordan.

Library of Congress Control Number: 2016915008
ISBN: Hardcover   978-1-5245-9446-6
                Softcover   978-1-5245-9445-9
                eBook   978-1-5245-9444-2

All rights reserved. No part of this book may be reproduced or transmitted in any form or by any means, electronic or mechanical, including photocopying, recording, or by any information storage and retrieval system, without permission in writing from the copyright owner.

KJV
Scripture quotations marked KJV are from the Holy Bible, King James Version (Authorized Version). First published in 1611. Quoted from the KJV Classic Reference Bible, Copyright © 1983 by The Zondervan Corporation.

NRSV
Scripture quotations marked NRSV are taken from the *New Revised Standard Version of the Bible*, Copyright © 1989, by the Division of Christian Education of the National Council of the Churches of Christ in the United States of America. Used by permission. All rights reserved. Website

GW Scripture is taken from GOD'S WORD®, © 1995 God's Word to the Nations. Used by permission of Baker Publishing Group.

GNB 'Scriptures and additional materials quoted are from the Good News Bible © 1994 published by the Bible Societies/HarperCollins Publishers Ltd UK, Good News Bible© American Bible Society 1966, 1971, 1976, 1992. Used with permission.'

Message Bible: "Scripture taken from The Message. Copyright © 1993, 1994, 1995, 1996, 2000, 2001, 2002. Used by permission of NavPress Publishing Group."

Any people depicted in stock imagery provided by Thinkstock are models, and such images are being used for illustrative purposes only.
Certain stock imagery © Thinkstock.

Print information available on the last page.

Rev. date: 10/03/2016

To order additional copies of this book, contact:
Xlibris
800-056-3182
www.Xlibrispublishing.co.uk
Orders@Xlibrispublishing.co.uk
748572

Table of Contents

1. David with "Warts and All" 1
2. Beginning at the end
   2Samuel 23.1-7 6
3. It's the Lyrics that count
   Psalm 23 10
4. God's seeds grow in fertile ground
   1Samuel 16.1-13. Mark 4 13
5. The return of the King Maker
   1Samuel 16.1-13 17
6. The Idea
   1Samuel 8:5 21
7. David's heart
   1Samuel 13.14 & 16.7 26
8. Jesus, the ultimate image of God
   Philippians 2.6 30
9. The loss of God's blessing
   1Samuel 15.1-35 33
10. Does God have a plan "B"?
    1Samuel 15.11 & 16.1-13 36
11. Diagnosing the illness
    1Samuel 16.14 -23 39
12. The cottage cheese expedition.
    1 Sam. 17.1-58 42
13. The position of the armies
    1Samuel 17.1-58 44

14.	David a Shepherd King
	1Samuel 16.11 & Ezekiel 34.1-31 47
15.	The necessity of leadership. 50
16.	Success and its pitfalls
	1Samuel 18.1-30 54
17.	The Escape
	1Samuel 19.1-24 57
18.	Dealing with Saul's illness.
	1Samuel 19.1-24 59
19.	Listening to advice
	1Samuel 19 1-24 62
20.	The nature of friendship
	1Samuel 20.1-42 65
21.	The use of Subterfuge
	1Samuel 20. 68
22.	The effects and consequences of fear.
	1Samuel 21.1-15 70
23.	The vulnerable city
	1Samuel 21 73
24.	Proof of the pudding is in the eating
	Psalm 34 76
25.	Another psalm from the Giant's den.
	Psalm 56 see also 57 80
26.	The Cave of Adullam
	1Samuel 22 84
27.	Alone
	Psalm 142 87
28.	The razor sharp tongue
	Psalm 52 1Sa 21:1-9 & 1Sa 22:6-23 93
29.	Principles to live by.
	1Samuel 23 97
30.	David's Prop
	Psalms 54 101

31.	An embarrassing encounter 1Samuel 24	104
32.	Don't spoil the Coronation day 1Samuel 25	106
33.	Resentment's Rush 1Samuel 25.33	109
34.	Claiming the future 1Samuel 26	114
35.	Living with the enemy 1Samuel 27	116
36.	Saul's descent into spiritualism. 1Samuel 28	118
37.	When God gets you off the hook 1Samuel 29	121
38.	David failed to do a risk assessment. 1Samuel 30	123
39.	Deliberate Death 1 Samuel 31 & 2 Samuel 1	127
40.	The Slain on Gilboa 2Samuel 1	131
41.	Saul lost his life because he lost his way 1Chronicles 10.13	134
42.	An elegy or a eulogy? 2Samuel 1	137
43.	Don't lose your crown 2Samuel 2	139
44.	Too Big for your Boots 2Samuel 2.22	143
45.	Dealing with People's Character defects 2Samuel 3	146
46.	A history lesson in character judging 2Samuel 4	149

47.	Crowned the Shepherd King of all Israel	
	2Samuel 5	*151*
48.	Whose people?	
	2Samuel 5	154
49.	Jerusalem, hark how the anthems ring	
	2Samuel 5	*156*
50.	Where could Israel meet with God?	
	2Samuel 6	*158*
51.	Accepting our mistakes	
	2Samuel 6.8 Numbers 6	*161*
52.	The Day of Rejoicing had come	
	1Chronicles 16	*165*
53.	God's refusal	
	2Samuel 7.1-29	*169*
54.	Ultimate honour	
	1Chron.17.16-19	*174*
55.	A Setback?	
	Psalm 60 2Samuel 8.1-18	*177*
56.	Expansionism	
	2Samuel 8	*180*
57.	Keeping Promises	
	2 Samuel 9	*182*
58.	Misunderstood	
	2Samuel 10	*184*
59.	Bathing Bathsheba	
	2Samuel 11	*186*
60.	Voyeurism	
	Job 31.1	*189*
61.	When the bad guy owned up	
	Psalm 51	*193*
62.	The unfairness of life.	*197*
63.	I will go to him	*199*

64.	An Inadequate response towards evil 2Samuel 13	202
65.	Don't beat up David.	205
66.	The sea-change Jesus brought Mark 9.42	207
67.	Knowing which way the wind is blowing 2Samuel 14	209
68.	You must choose right or wrong?	211
69.	When the chickens come home to roost 2Samuel 15	214
70.	A time to run? 2Samuel 15	216
71.	Post-mortem of the Rebellion Psalm 3 & 2Samuel 15.1-31	219
72.	Allegiances 2Samuel 15.14	222
73.	Keeping life in perspective 2Samuel 16.5 - 23	225
74.	Ahithophel's not so sweet counsel 2Samuel 17	227
75.	O Absalom, Absalom my son 2Samuel 18	231
76.	Acting defeated in the day of Victory 2Samuel 19	234
77.	Love's Excess 2Samuel 19.6	238
78.	Bring Back the King 2Samuel 19.9 – 40	240
79.	A War of Words 2Samuel 19.41- 43	244
80.	Conciliation or Compromise? 2Samuel 20	246

81.	Natural disasters 2Samuel 21.1 - 14	248
82.	Ritual Killing 2Samuel 21	251
83.	Goliath's Relatives 2Samuel 21.15	253
84.	Song of Victory 2Samuel 22.1-51 Psalm 18	255
85.	When mighty men make a man mighty 2Samuel 23	259
86.	Obsession with numbers. 2Samuel 24.1 - 25	263
87.	Extraordinary Means 1Kings 1.1-4	267
88.	The Snake Rock Conspiracy 1Kings 1.5-53	270
89.	Passing on the baton 1Kings 2.1-12	272
90.	Whose eyes are you looking through? Psalm 36	276
91.	The Song of the slandered saint (CH Spurgeon) Psalm 7	279
92.	David in the desert place Psalm 63	283
93.	God has a long nose Psalm 86 and others.	287
94.	I'm the Good Guy Lord Psalm 17 and others.	290
95.	The Charge to Solomon 1Chronicles 28.9	293
96.	The Writers and their message. 1Chronicles 29.29	297

1

David with "Warts and All"[1]

Like almost no other person in ancient history David's psalms enable us to feel with him in his searching of heart, his fears, his disappointments, and his hopes.[2] His one-time friend, Ahithophel, knew the importance of a person's state of mind. He knew David's inner thoughts would influence his performance in battle. He

---

[1] An alleged saying of Oliver Cromwell to his portrait painter, but like so many sayings it is of doubtful origin.

[2] "Generally, it has long been fashionable in Old Testament studies to dismiss the psalm-titles as entirely worthless for both authorship and 'biographical' allusions, they being as late liturgical/musical insertions. However, this attitude rests on no particle of respectable evidence and has much against it." *KAKitchen Old Testament in Context. Joshua to Solomon*

"Numerous fragments and in some cases substantial portions of manuscripts containing the Biblical psalms have been found in the Dead Sea area in the past thirty-five years. Perhaps the most significant of these finds was the Psalms Scroll (11QPsa) from cave 11 at Qumran, which has been dated by Sanders in the Herodian period between A.D. 30 and 50. In addition to the Psalms Scroll several other text portions containing psalm titles have been found in Qumran Caves 4 and 11, in the Nahal Hever region, and on Masada. As these texts are examined they are found to be in essential agreement with the MT in the assignment of titles to the various psalms they contain except for a few minor variations." *The Authenticity of the Psalm Titles, James Fraser 1984*

advised Absalom in the rebellion, *"I will come upon him while he is weary and discouraged, and throw him into a panic; and all the people who are with him will flee. I will strike down only the king,"*[3]

We might have a plan, a scheme, but if we become despondent and down cast with little faith then we are as good as defeated. Remarkably David knew the secret of overcoming the failures that inner thoughts can bring. He could say, *"From the ends of the earth, I call to you when I begin to lose heart. Lead me to the rock that is high above me. You have been my refuge, a tower of strength against the enemy."*[4] We too can enjoy the Lord and strengthen ourselves with the strength of God just as David did.[5]

These songs we know as the psalms were written in the poetic style of the era. For several hundred years before similar songs had been sung to heathen deities too[6.]

Let's journey with David through the vicissitudes of his life and share his joys, his triumphs, his pain and his setbacks as he transformed disparate people into the beginnings of a strong nation.[7] But do not think in terms of clean cut rights and wrongs. This is the building up of a nation where every people group in the area of Israel were seeking for their own security and sufficiency and aspiring for regional supremacy.

---

[3] 2Samuel 17.2 GW

[4] Psalm 61.2 NRSV

[5] Psalm 138.3 You answered me when I called to you; with your strength you strengthened me. GNB

[6] "The close affinity of many of the psalms with the style, forms and expressions in the Ras Shamra epic poetry from ancient Ugarit, dating from the fourteenth century B.C., demonstrates the antiquity of many of these odes.... Unless one's thinking is distorted by the unsound presuppositions of the Wellhausen school, it is reasonable to view the bulk of the psalms as pre-Exilic, some dating even from before the Davidic-Solomonic era. Unger's Bible Dictionary, 1974, p. 899

[7] Israel was already a nation in its own right but not strong nor a homogeneous unit, the Bible has long called them a people and Egypt recognised them as such two hundred year earlier. About 1207 BC

Today David would have been excommunicated from almost every church because of his adultery and polygamy. In most countries of the world he would be given life imprisonment or executed for his complicity in the murder of Uriah. He would have been questioned by the police's organised crime department, for his protection racket.[8] Worse still, if living today he would have been brought before a war crimes tribunal for killing prisoners in cold blood. Last but not least there would have been protests against him by the animal rights supporters for his crippling of war horses.[9]

Some Jewish Rabbis have sought to exonerate David from adultery, suggesting that Uriah had given his wife a conditional divorce while he was at war[10] and that Uriah was a bad apple anyway. This is not a good explanation, David had major faults adultery was one, Nathan did not excuse him.

Yet we as Christians enjoy, and more than enjoy David's psalms, we appreciate them, and share the emotion and the heart's cry of the songs as they appeal to God for help and praise him for his goodness. God spoke to him, and through him, and speaks through him to us this day.

There was no New Testament, and most of the writing prophets had not yet lived and the Geneva Convention was thousands of years from being written. Where was the Law of God? Were the ten commands still kept in the Ark of the Covenant? Almost certainly the Law of Moses was hidden away, without being open for general

---

[8] This is perhaps a little harsh. David was behaving more like a private security guard than a racketeer.

[9] "... the authors of Samuel create an epic account in which the most beloved King in Judahite memory is the most human and fallible character in the narrative. Rulers in the ancient Near East are never portrayed with emotion. They are immutable. Not so the Biblical David. He is 'human, all too human.'" Jacob Wright, "David, King of Israel" page 93.

[10] Whether or not the conditional divorce was practised in David's day or not Uriah was still alive. See Babylonian Talmud, Tractate Shabbath, folio 56a

viewing.[11] How much did the prophets and priests of God know? The Law clearly stated that when they appointed a king he should be a regular reader of it.[12] Samuel performed the ceremonies of a priest, yet he was of the tribe of Ephraim. Two of David's sons became priests, even though the law limited certain functions of the office to the tribe of Levi and there were Levitical priests in office for example in Nob to sacrifice.

Although his failings, to put it politely, are disappointing, David had a mighty spiritual experience and a tremendous understanding of who God is and what he can do. When we know God and his power we will not be the same again.[13] The writers of the Hebrew history showed David with all his weaknesses and his sins.[14] What are we faced with? A Genghis Khan? No, but perhaps an Oliver Cromwell. Though of course Cromwell was not for a monarchy.[15]

We must never dismiss a person from our thoughts and prayers as unworthy because of their present behaviour. God warned David and limited his plans because of his behaviour, but God did not cast him off. Even though it was not his conscience that drove him

---

[11] When Samuel gave a written memo about the role of a king he could have been quoting the law. 1Samuel 10.25 Samuel told the people the rights and duties of the kingship; and he wrote them in a book and laid it up before the LORD. Then Samuel sent all the people back to their homes. NRSV

[12] Deuteronomy 17.18 And it shall be, when he sits upon the throne of his kingdom, that he shall write him a copy of this law in a book out of that which is before the priests the Levites: 19 And it shall be with him, and he shall read therein all the days of his life: that he may learn to fear the LORD his God, to keep all the words of this law and these statutes, to do them: KJV

[13] Philippians 3:10 That I may know him, and the power of his resurrection, and the fellowship of his sufferings, being made conformable unto his death; KJV

[14] 1Ch 29:29 Now the acts of David the king, first and last, behold, they are written in the book of Samuel the seer, and in the book of Nathan the prophet, and in the book of Gad the seer, KJV

[15] Cromwell must have shared some of David's inner feelings when he said: - Men have been led in dark paths, through the providence and dispensation of God. Why, surely it is not to be objected to a man, for who can love to walk in the dark? But providence doth often so dispose.

back to God for mercy but the challenges of the prophets Nathan and Gad. These were no doubt brave men who would dare to rebuke an autocratic ruler. In New Testament times Paul was a persecutor and murderer before his conversion, then his life changed. But time after time we find that David failed both morally and ethically over a period of many years even while he loved God.

We must ask a question, "Why was David's weaknesses seemingly overlooked but not King Saul's?" Was it because David was more ready to ask for mercy, or was it due to the purpose of God? It was true that Saul was more ready to excuse himself and David more ready to acknowledge his fault and fall on God's mercy. It seems that Saul was two-timing God and David was out and out for the Lord. Yet it was not only the grace of God, but also the purpose of God to be fulfilled that Israel should become a strong nation, worshipping God alone. Was it grace or purpose? It was both. There was another matter as well, the main activity of Saul was to defend his country. David was in an attacking mode. If Saul managed a reasonable defence of his country[16] David went ahead with expanding the borders. This comes as a challenge to the whole Christian Church. Are we seeking to win people to Christ or are we defensive, just looking after our borders?

---

[16] 1Samuel 14.48 He did valiantly, and struck down the Amalekites, and rescued Israel out of the hands of those who plundered them. NRSV

2

Beginning at the end
2Samuel 23.1-7

Music in the soul of man.

What do we experience while singing with all our hearts a worship song to the Lord? Could it be a feeling of thankfulness and joy, with a heart contemplating the majesty of our Saviour and Maker?

When Handel composed the "Messiah" he said that he felt as if he was in the presence of God every moment. David too experienced the anointing of God upon him as he wrote songs.[17] One of the Psalms Scroll from the Dead Sea Caves say that he wrote 3600 psalms.[18] And well he could have done, many song writers such as Charles Wesley, Fanny Crosby and others have written thousands. David was open-hearted, prepared to be real, and truthful with himself, and share his feelings with others, and we love that. He told it like it was, he wore his heart on his sleeve. The Psalms are straight from the inner-being, poetic and powerful. They speak today to us

---

[17] "The Spirit of the LORD spoke through me. His words were on my tongue. 2Samuel 23.2 KJV

[18] And the Lord gave him a discerning and enlightened spirit. And he wrote 3,600 psalms; 4 Col.27 of 11QPs[a]

as much as they did three thousand years ago. No other songs have been sung so much. David is the music maker of all time.

Music is a mood changer, and it is medicinal. Our grandsons' pet dog would sing along as one played the saxophone. Animals are musical, from mice to monsters of the deep not just our feathered friends.[19] When David, and most likely other musicians as well, played for Saul it relieved his depression. Music, as millions know can soothe and calm the troubled soul. It worked for Saul. He became dependant on music, as modern man becomes dependant on pills to overcome despondency. But David's songs were more than nerve calming, peace giving music, they drew people to God, opened hearts to prayer and praise and filled people with truth and hope.

Music is God's invention. There came a time in the mist of prehistory when the discovery was made that there were sounds that pleased, soothed and brought joy to the heart of mankind.[20] God made this art form to be blessed even more than acting, painting and similar artistry. It is said that the Israelis excelled in music and in later years the Assyrian Sennacherib demanded male and female musicians from defeated King Hezekiah as tribute.[21]

Music brought prophets closer to the Lord

2Kings 3. *15 But now bring me a minstrel. And it came to pass, when the minstrel played, that the hand of the LORD came upon him.* KJV See also -

1Ch 25:3 *under the hands of their father Jeduthun, who prophesied with a harp, to give thanks and to praise the LORD.* KJV

---

[19] Music stimulates all parts of the brain. It results in the release of the neurotransmitters dopamine, endorphins, serotonin etc. Some churches seem to use it to seek to produce a feeling of euphoria which is not the same as a genuine spiritual experience of meeting with God.

[20] Genesis 4.21 *His brother's name was Jubal; he was the ancestor of all those who play the lyre and pipe* NRSV. It has been posited that music came before language to the human race.

[21] ANET pp287,288

Music was part of early Christian worship, the only time it speaks of Jesus singing is when He and the disciples left the Last Supper for Gethsemane.[22] It was a moment of deep emotion for the Lord as he was facing the cross. The letters of Paul and James encourage the new Christians to sing, and Paul put his preaching into practise when in jail.

Ephesians 5.19 *Speaking to yourselves in psalms and hymns and spiritual songs, singing and making melody in your heart to the Lord; KJV*

Acts 16:25 *And at midnight Paul and Silas prayed, and sang praises unto God: and the prisoners heard them. KJV*

Colossians 3:16 *Let the word of Christ dwell in you richly in all wisdom; teaching and admonishing one another in psalms and hymns and spiritual songs, singing with grace in your hearts to the Lord. KJV*

James 5:13 *Is any among you afflicted? Let him pray. Is any merry? Let him sing psalms.*[23]*KJV*

Many modern song writers have marvellously enhanced the worship of the Church and thousands of the old hymns of a hundred and more years ago still take us to the throne of God. The KJV says David played the "harp" most modern versions have the "lyre." It was often played with a plectrum though the verse says hand. 1Samuel 16:23 *Whenever God's spirit came to Saul, David took the lyre and strummed a tune. Saul got relief from his terror and felt better, and the evil spirit left him.* GW The lyre is first mentioned in Gen.4.21. Music was part of the "school curriculum" a thousand years earlier than David's time in some of the nearby countries!

Many Christian songs have been written from experiences in life that have changed and transformed people. Whether songs like

---

[22] Almost certainly the Hallel Psalms 113-118
[23] See also:- 1Co 14:26 *When you gather, each person has a psalm, doctrine, revelation, another language, or an interpretation. Everything must be done to help each other grow.* GW

"How Great Thou Art,"[24] written when the author Carl Boberg contemplated the majesty of God. Or "It is no secret," was said to be written as a result of the writer Stuart Hamblen's conversion, when he explained to the actor John Wayne that it was no secret what God could do. Joseph Scriven wrote, "What a friend we have in Jesus," to bring comfort and assurance to his mother. Even "Abide with me," being the dying author's prayer. Worship can never take the place of the Word of God but it must be a vital part of every Christian's daily life. A song can be much more than worship it can be a personal encouragement to continue following Jesus and a building up of faith, so get singing! But do not let music be an alternative to replacing the power and presence of the Holy Spirit in your life or the life of the church.

---

[24] See the article in Wikipedia regarding its origin and the translation by Stuart Hine.

3

It's the Lyrics that count
Psalm 23

Although we have spoken about music, not a single musical note of the psalms is known to us.[25] We have the lyrics only. Words have power, and anointed and inspired words have mighty power. These are words to which we have put our own tunes, whether Crimond, Brother James' Air or the many others for the 23rd Psalm and tens of thousands of other tunes and chants for the remaining one hundred and forty-nine. For two thousand years Christians have chanted and sung these ancient and powerful songs, their strength giving qualities is undiminished today. Every emotion of life can be found in the words. A mass of teaching on God's character is here in the Psalms, as well as prayers, desires and hopes and assurances for the inner man.

There are times in the Christian Church when the songs and hymns tend to concentrate on one particular theme of the Christian faith. Sometimes the greatness of God is emphasised to the detriment of other qualities such as the love of God, or testimonials of God's faithfulness to people to the exclusion of prayer songs. Teaching and

---

[25] It is often considered that the tune titles are occasionally at the introduction to the individual psalms.

encouragement by song can lapse for long periods of time too. David not only shared his inner feelings in the psalms he also showed his hopes, dreams and his certainties. He let people know he was in no doubt that God would come to his aid.

The New Testament Christians sang together. They would sing in the Holy Spirit and they would sing words that all could understand.[26] It was anticipated that non-Christians would be present. Furthermore, singing was not just for worship. Paul said sing to one another. It was not only for worship to the Lord it was to encourage one another. There are in the New Testament a number of songs, Mary's song, Zachariah's song plus others in the epistles and Revelation. The Puritan John Lightfoot added another important point: - *[Singing God's praise] is a work of the most meditation of any we perform in public. It keeps the heart longest upon the thing spoken. Prayer and hearing pass quick from one sentence to another; this sticks long upon it.*[27] Singing enables people to concentrate and remember what they are saying.

David could say, *"I was glad when they said unto me, 'let us go into the house of the LORD.'"* Psalm 122.1 KJV He was looking forward to worshipping the Lord. Christian worship must be no less exciting today than it was three thousand years ago. It cannot be that it becomes boring like Isaac Watts found the chanting of the psalms. Isaac was challenged by his father to write better songs, so he did. Often putting some of the Psalms into a Christian context, such as "Oh God our help in ages past" from psalm 90. Surprisingly he wrote most of his hymns between the age of twenty and twenty-two!

Today there must be a joy of Christian worship. To lose that, is to lose a generation of a people who can be challenged, directed

---

[26] 1Cor.14.15 so what does this mean? It means that I will pray with my spirit, and I will pray with my mind. I will sing psalms with my spirit, and I will sing psalms with my mind. Otherwise, if you praise God only with your spirit, how can outsiders say "Amen!" to your prayer of thanksgiving? They don't know what you're saying. GW

[27] Ritzema, E., & Vince, E. (Eds.). (2013). *300 Quotations for Preachers from the Puritans*. Bellingham, WA: Lexham Press.

and called to follow Jesus to the ends of the earth. This in no way takes from the greater importance of the Word of God. It must go alongside the preaching which too must have a lively living power to grab at the hearts of young and old.

4

God's seeds grow in fertile ground
1Samuel 16.1-13. Mark 4

The Westminster catechism[28] asks the question, *"What is the chief and highest end of man?"* In answering it they state, *"Man's chief and highest end is to glorify God, and fully to enjoy him forever."* David's songs let us know that he enjoyed his relationship with God. He was totally open with the Lord about his misgivings, failures, fears and joys as well as his anger at times. David's close relationship with God meant he enjoyed his company. He and God shared secrets, he could say, *"God-friendship is for God-worshippers; they are the ones he confides in."*[29] He knew that God had something good up his sleeve for him in Psalm 31.19 he says, *O how abundant is your goodness that you have **laid up**[30] for those who fear you, and accomplished for those who take refuge in you, in the sight of everyone!* NRSV.

---

[28] Written in 1646 and is widely used by the Presbyterian Church with alterations.

[29] Psalm 25.14 "The Message Bible." Could it be translated, *"sitting on God's couch"? Psalm 25.14 says, "The secret of the Lord is with them that fear Him."* KJV The word for secret is very expressive. It means to sit on the same couch or cushion! In other word it means an intimate friendship with God. See Amos 3.7 *Surely the Lord GOD does nothing, without revealing his secret to his servants the prophets.* NRSV Remember that John was on the couch next to Jesus to ask who was going to betray Jesus. See Gesenius

[30] Sapan – to hide away

...stening to God as well as talking to Him. He encouraged ... to pour their hearts out to God.[31] He enjoyed God, but with ...gard to the second part of the catechism's answer, "glorifying God," David did not achieve such high marks. We know that on one occasion God spoke highly of him.[32] Yet this might not be the same view everyone had of him and some with good reason too. We also, might have reservations about some of the acts and decisions that he made. Neither did God allow him to build the temple with blooded hands.

The Empires had disintegrated. Egypt, now in the time of their 21st dynasty[33] had declined in power from previous generations, a priestly race ruled over much of the country. (Joseph and Moses some centuries earlier had both married into priestly families). A hundred and more years before the Hittite empire had imploded, and the Assyrian Empire too had contracted in size and power. The Elamites that later became the Persian Empire were almost silent while David was around. It would seem previously the Philistines had policed the lands on behalf of Egypt, guarding their frontiers.[34] Now with retrenchment of Egypt's authority they were on their own.

It was the beginning of the iron-age,[35] people were developing new tools, and new weapons of war; iron was harder and a little lighter than bronze. The tin that needed to be alloyed with copper to make bronze was rare, and could have come from as far away as Cornwall, England. Iron was more abundant though needing higher temperatures to extract it from the ore.

As the Bronze Age was coming to an end, and the empires of the known world had collapsed, it left the smaller nations to fill the

---

[31] Psalm 62.8
[32] Later God would not allow him to build the Temple because he killed so many people.
[33] The Pharaohs ruled from Tanis. Their influence would be more cultural and for trading purposes during this time. (Dictionary of the Ancient Near East, British Museum.)
[34] The Great Harris Papyrus, see "Sea People of the Bronze age" Raffaele D'Amato, Osprey page 17
[35] Most of Goliath's armour was of bronze, but the spear head was of iron.

power vacuum. There are theories as to how this collapse happened, but no one complete answer seems to fit. The Sea people, of whom the Philistines were part, have been blamed but do not fully solve the puzzle.[36] Climate change, earthquakes, political infighting and plagues might have all played their part besides the invasion of the Sea People.

The region was multi-racial, some of the nationalities in David's lifetime were often of different appearances. The Hittites mentioned in the Bible could have been the remains of the former superpower, if so, they had a Chinese type appearance with pointed chins.[37] Then there were Egyptians and North Africans mentioned as well. From Sumerian sources it was said that the Amorites ate their meat raw and did not properly bury their dead. If this were so they would not be as fit as those who cooked their food.[38] Some nation groups were more cultivated than others. To further confuse things, peoples of different ethnic origins would fight alongside David. At various times Philistines and others joined with him in battle against his opponents.

People dressed differently too, the battle scenes from Egypt show the sea people dressed in various costumes. Although most of the peoples would have a Semitic based language the Philistines coming from Crete[39] would have an Indo-European based language. Though having lived along the coasts of Israel for a century or two, were now speaking the local languages. In war the Philistines had a feathered head dress, other sea people had helmets with horns.

---

[36] See the book "1177 the year civilisation collapsed," Eric Cline, Princeton U.P.
[37] They were known for their skills in warfare. See Jacob L. Wright, "David king of Israel." Page 82
[38] BBC Radio 4, 23.9.2009 See also Israel's troops who were hungry, 1Sa 14:31 After they had struck down the Philistines that day from Michmash to Aijalon, the troops were very faint; 1Sa 14:32 so the troops flew upon the spoil, and took sheep and oxen and calves, and slaughtered them on the ground; and the troops ate them with the blood. NRSV
[39] See Am 9:7 Are ye not as children of the Ethiopians unto me, O children of Israel? Says the LORD. Have not I brought up Israel out of the land of Egypt? And the Philistines from Caphtor, and the Syrians from Kir? KJV. Also Jeremiah 47.4 Caphtor – old name for Crete. The Philistines were known elsewhere as the Pelest, one of six groups of what were known as the Sea People.

There would be artisans working in different trades, building, weaving, carpet making, furniture making but there was one trade not in Israel at the beginning of this period. There were no smiths.[40] The Philistines were in control of the area they would not allow smiths who might make swords or other weapons for them to rebel. No doubt many people were labourers working in the fields.

A multitude of gods were worshipped.[41] Every nation had one or many gods. Yet there was at this time the small nation of Israel which had for hundreds of years been worshipping Yahweh, the sinless, holy God who loved and cared for his people, in total contrast to the sinning, self-seeking multitudes of gods worshipped through idolatry. Though this was far from the total picture as we see later in the story.

Then there was sin, showing itself in its myriad forms, from sibling rivalry, through jealousy, adultery, murder, rape, greed and hatred and from malice to genocide. Among all these evils of mankind virtue also shone, bravery, love, loyalty and generosity of spirit and faithfulness to name a few.

God's seed grows in fertile soil. The heart of David was prepared for the call of God; his heart was open for God to have access to him. And the land of promise was now open for Israel to be established with deeper roots than before as a nation united to one another and to God. One thousand years later Jesus came when the situation was just right, the scripture says, "In the fullness of the time."[42] We must have open and prepared hearts and minds for God to sow into our lives, producing not just a little personal fruit but a whole life of service for God that will change many people. But let us also be aware that there comes in a time when a nation is ready for God to prepare them for something greater than they have already. When it can be said, the fields are white unto harvest.[43]

---

[40] 1Sa 13:19 No blacksmith could be found in the entire land of Israel. In this way the Philistines kept the Hebrews from making swords and spears. GW
[41] Ugarit had seventy gods or goddesses. Their chief god was El.
[42] Galatians 4.4
[43] John uses "theaomai" when quoting Jesus, we need to take a good look at the harvest not just a glance. John 4.35.

5

The return of the King Maker
1Samuel 16.1-13

Samuel reappears – The last of the line of judges who rule Israel. He was a prophet as well as performing priestly duties, Abraham was also called a prophet[44] as was Moses.[45]

- The Hebrew word for prophet was Nebi'im it was taken from nebi which meant to bubble up or as the New Testament says *"Holy men spoke as they were moved by the Spirit of God."*[46]*KJV*
- They also used the word "seer" as in 1Samuel 9.9 miss off the "r" and you have the meaning. It was more about seeing visions. They were called "men of God" because God walked with them and they walked with God. Rabbi Avrohom Feuer said the source of the Seer's clear vision is not his eyes but his ears![47] Which as we know can be true.

---

[44] Gen 20.7
[45] Deut.18.15-17
[46] 2Pe 1:21 No prophecy ever originated from humans. Instead, it was given by the Holy Spirit as humans spoke under God's direction. GW
[47] Tehillim, Artscroll Tanach series, Introduction page xxvi

So Samuel, the deposed leader of Israel, came to Bethlehem, causing consternation in the village. It was not that he was inactive around the towns and villages of Israel but they sensed there was something different. Saul had now been ruling Israel for some years as their first king. But he was a man who did not often go to Shiloh to pray. He was not known for seeking God. When the youthful Saul and his servant (a young boy) went looking for their donkeys he did not seem to know where the prophet Samuel lived. His servant had to tell him and the young lad was the one who was prepared to give his money to Samuel even though Saul was wealthy. We read too in later years his daughter was allowed an idol among her possessions, and he named one of his sons after Baal. Before Saul became king the Holy Spirit came on him and he prophesied, the local people questioned whether he had a change of heart.[48] It must have been that he was not then seeking God either.

God said to Samuel, "How long will you mourn for Saul?"[49] It could be that Samuel was constantly in mourning garb, making it obvious to all and sundry that he was unhappy with the present country wide spiritual situation and Saul in particular. Yet too Samuel must have been concerned for his own sons' waywardness as well.[50] Leaders have a twin responsibility, one for their organisation, church or charity, secondly for their family. Far too many in leadership have bemoaned their failure to care for the family as they should have done. Samuel was one of the many. We need to pray much for our families, caring for their whole being is essential. I always remember our daughter saying, "You seem to care more for my soul than my body." She was right, but did not realise that the body and soul are almost inseparable and you cannot care for one without the other.

---

[48] 1Samuel 10.11 When all who knew him before saw how he prophesied with the prophets, the people said to one another, "What has come over the son of Kish? Is Saul also among the prophets?" NRSV

[49] 1Samuel 16.1

[50] 1Samuel 8.3 And his sons walked not in his ways, but turned aside after lucre, and took bribes, and perverted judgement. KJV

People have always been wary of previous rulers. This was the situation when Samuel said that he had come to sacrifice to the Lord at Bethlehem. The locals were not convinced that was all he had come for. Samuel found a young shepherd boy looking after a few sheep and in front of the villagers he anointed David with oil. Israel was one of the few countries that anointed their monarchs with oil at that time.[51] Change was coming and change is always difficult. The behaviour of Saul was the cause for this change. We too can fear change, yet it can bring freshness and new life. Are you ready to embrace rather than fear the factors that cause change in your life especially ones that are beyond your control? Paul was always ready to accept whatever happened in his life: - Philippians 4.11 *I've learned to be content in whatever situation I'm in. I know how to live in poverty or prosperity. No matter what the situation, I've learned the secret of how to live when I'm full or when I'm hungry, when I have too much or when I have too little. I can do everything through Christ who strengthens me.* GW

How did Samuel hear the voice of God? How was he able to hear God speaking to him? Mitzi was our small poodle. On a pebble beach by Lake Coniston we could sit and throw a pebble and out of the millions on the lakeside she would find the pebble we had thrown. There was a trace of scent from our hands on the stone and she would search it out. Samuel would know the heart of a man in contact with the Lord. God's heart could speak to him. There was a spiritual union. David had the scent of God on him and Samuel knew it. When his eyes said "Eliab is the man," God said to his heart, "There is no anointing on him." Psalm 89.20 *I found my servant David. I anointed him with my holy oil.* KJV

There was a dimension of the Holy Spirit that Samuel had experienced that most people of his day did not have, and of our day too. There was a further factor too he had a tender heart, he saw it would be sin to fail to pray for the people. 1Sa 12:23 *moreover as for me, God forbid that I should sin against the LORD in ceasing to pray*

---

[51] IVP Bible Background Commentary. Though some nations anointed their officials.

for you: KJV No wonder he could hear God speaking to him, even though there was deep hurt in his heart, he was still able to pray for those who had rejected him.

God told Samuel to start looking on the heart of people. If it was important for Samuel to do that it is important for us as well. How can we delve deeper into a person's soul? Every Church board would love to be able to do that when they are appointing a new minister. Every pastor would want to know the spiritual depth of the possible new deacon or elder. There is only one way to achieve the seemingly impossible, which is to be listening to him who searches the heart. It is a tough call. The early Christians could not agree on a replacement for Judas. They solved it by choosing a name at random, first asking for God to check the outcome. We are all far too confident in our own decision making ability to leave a matter to God to choose. Samuel had to look away from the person and look to God.

6

The Idea
1Samuel 8:5

There are new ideas that come from time to time and sweep across great swathes of a nation. They can be good, or bad, or just different from the prevailing view at the time. We have had many in Britain such as all people being equal, when all were not treated equally. During Richard II's reign Wat Tyler lead a revolt, John Ball the Lollard priest and a compatriot could say, "When Adam delved and Eve span, who then was the gentleman?" Unfortunately, the seeking for equality failed then. Hundreds of years later the French revolution came and with rather a bloody outcome succeeded. At this time in Israel came an idea the idea of kingship. For a century or two they had been content with judges, but now they were clamouring for a king to be like other nations.[52] John Bright suggested that the survival of Israel was now threatened by the Philistines, this could have been true and so they needed a more centralised leadership than previously.[53] Yet God would have seen them through.

---

[52] 1Sa 8:5 They told him, "You're old, and your sons aren't following your example. Now appoint a king to judge us so that we will be like all the other nations." GW

[53] The History of Israel, John Bright, SCM Press 1977 page 180

There can be a failure of existing leaders to see the present problems. In 1992 the existing American president, George Bush was seeking re-election, Bill Clinton's team hit on the problem. They used the slogan, "It's the economy, stupid." Clinton won, as there was an ongoing recession. During the 1978/79 winter of discontent in Britain the prime minister Jim Callaghan did not fully appreciate the hardship of the workers in a bitterly cold winter, he spoke light-heartedly to the press. The next morning one newspaper's headlines were, "Crisis? What crisis?" Which lead to his defeat by Margaret Thatcher. Leaders need to see the problems of the people they are leading if they are to lead.

If there was a major problem for the Israelites, it was security. No doubt poverty was an issue, as well as corrupt spiritual leadership, but the main concern was the safety of the people. The book of Judges speaks of the difficulties of gathering the harvest, and the lack of security for the inhabitants.[54]

These motivating forces among people can happen within countries, conglomerates, and churches. Even when they do not take a majority with them they can take over power, such as National Socialism in Germany leading to the Second World War. The missionaries in the Belgium Congo at the beginning of the 1960s spoke of the change among the national Christians as independence approached. So much so that often outward hostility was shown to them and later lead to the murder and rape of a number of them.

Books have transformed nations for good or ill, "Uncle Tom's Cabin," or "Mein Kampf" or Karl Marx's "Communist Manifesto," have all been instrumental in nation changing. There can be total philosophical and scientific revolutions in thinking. Nicholas Copernicus showed the world that the earth revolved around the sun, publishing on his death bed, "On the revolutions of the celestial spheres." Charles Darwin's,

---

[54] See J. David Pleins view in "The Social Visions of the Hebrew Bible." WJK page 103 states, "On the surface, Judges would seem to prefer a charismatic set of deliverers. Yet read more closely, the text is actually making a subtle argument in favour of the selection of a human king by the divine sovereign."

"Origin of Species" let people know the world was no recent invention. Sometimes ideas can have a subtler influence, without a single point of origin but similar ideas from different sources. The change in Israel was bloodless, Samuel asked God about them having a king, and he did what God said.[55] God is often prepared to give in to the request of people. Even if it is not always for their good.[56] King David came from the idea of men,[57] but with the guidance of God.

There is a chasm between an idea born from the mind of man and a truth from God that has been ignored for generations. Both have influenced the church over the centuries. It was the "Spirit of the age"[58] that influenced Israel, brought on by Samuel seeking to appoint his own sons, who were unsuitable for the task and the prevailing social problems not being dealt with.

From time to time both democracy and authoritarianism have affected the church. It has often been a yoyo experience even in the lifetime of an individual. The ultimate story is that of the supposed vicar of Bray. The song about him suggests he was prepared to change his religious and political views depending on who was in power at the time.[59] Kingship was part of God's plan for God's people to one day have the ultimate King of all kings.

Samuel had been involved in a revival of religion, men and women began turning to God.[60] Yet this faith in God had not passed

---

[55] 1Samauel 8:5 They told him, "You're old, and your sons aren't following your example. Now appoint a king to judge us so that we will be like all the other nations." GW

[56] Psalm 106:15 And he gave them their request; but sent leanness into their soul. KJV

[57] This seems to fit Arthur Hocart's and other anthropologists holding to diffusionism theory for kingship etc. but this is a one off case. It shows a tendency for, "They have one we want one too." desire.

[58] See Zeitgeist and the philosopher George Hegel, also William Hazlett

[59] Part of the song's chorus goes, "Whatever king may reign, I'll be the vicar of Bray sir."

[60] 1Samuel 7.4 So Israel put away the Baals and the Astartes, and they served the LORD only. GW

through to his sons. Israel was now going to choose a king where the weakness of Eli and Samuel would become constitutional law and they would have to accept the future generations of the kings as the legitimate rulers. It was no solution to the problem of wayward children. The real reason Israel wanted a king could have been to be like other nations. Often our solutions are not solutions. They are just different. The early church had a problem. The needy people were not being cared for equally. They solved the problem with another tier of leadership containing people that understood the complaint. It worked. We must always ensure that a problem is solved not just a different method employed that has the same weakness or even greater in the long term.

Many preachers have used the phrase, "The spirit of the age." meaning the pervading views of the present generation. Such a desire for a monarchy was the reason for Saul and then David becoming king. The New Testament has the phrase "this present world." KJV. The NRSV is better saying "present age."

- Galatians 1.4 *who gave himself for our sins to set us free from the present evil age, according to the will of our God and Father, NRSV*
- Titus 2.12 *and in the present age to live lives that are self-controlled, upright, and godly, NRSV*

Christians are children of the future not of the present only. When Galatians says, "set us free" from the present age it could almost be translated "take us out"[61] of the present age. We should never be subject to the whims of the age. Though, as has been mentioned, God can use the fickle nature of man's thoughts and dreams to his advantage.

Often Protestant Churches can be more influenced by the latest ideas of man. Though the Catholic Church is not immune to such as well. Whether it is the criticism and rejection of the inspiration of Scripture, or suggestions for a more Biblical style of leadership, such

---

[61] It is a middle rather than active though.

as rule by Elders or Apostolic leadership or Congregational decision making. We must be wary of falling foul of the latest idea of man, rather than a revelation from God. When a church has been blessed with growth a new fad will often come in. The successful minister will be asked what he has done differently from other churches and that will become the latest church innovation, be wary of fads and fancies those changes can damage rather than build the work of God.

7

David's heart
1Samuel 13.14 & 16.7

David's physical appearance, it would seem that Saul had the better outward appearance[62] Though there was no doubt that David was attractive. Unlike the Old Testament the New Testament never describes the appearance of people apart from one, Zacchaeus. The Old Testament is a little more forthcoming about how people appeared but not in great detail. We know David was a handsome person.

Although the English translations say *"Man looks on the outward appearance"* the literal translation would be *"looks on the eyes."* People seek to look deep into a person, God looks deeper still. David was handsome but perhaps not as tall as the others. *And he sent, and brought him in. Now he was ruddy, and withal of a beautiful countenance, and goodly to look to. And the LORD said, Arise, anoint him: for this is he.*[63] Again countenance is the word for eye. Another feature of David's appearance was that he could have been red-headed most likely from his grandmother Ruth (she was a Moabite).

---

[62] The Word Biblical Commentary suggests that in 1Samuel 16.11 that "QATAN" could be smallest as opposed to the youngest.
[63] 1Samuel. 16.12 KJV

It was his heart that counted – it was after God's heart. He was seeking after the Lord in the Psalms he speaks of the desire to seek the face of God.[64]

If we were to ask others of his generation what they thought of David we might have a different picture from them. Saul considered him to be ambitious and a grasper as well as a challenge to his throne. It would not be possible to ask the Hittite Uriah what he thought, but he would look on David not just as his murderer but also devious and untrustworthy. The prisoners who survived his merciless executions would have nothing but a fearful hatred of him. Because God said David would do his bidding it did not mean he was a perfect being. He certainly was not. Yet both the New and Old Testaments state he was after God's heart.

It was his heart that counted. Act 13:22 And *when he had removed Saul, he raised up unto them David to be their king; to whom also he gave testimony, and said, I have found David the son of Jesse, a man after mine own heart, which shall fulfil all my will.* KJV David was prepared to do what God wanted. It was not that David had a heart exactly like God, he was a person that God knew would do his will for the people of Israel.

God called both Saul and David to be leaders, but it was David that God said he was to be the shepherd of Israel. It was this addition dimension, caring as well as leading. Peter was told by the resurrected Jesus, *"Feed and care for my sheep and lambs."* He won far more for the Lord as a shepherd of people than he did as a fisher of men. David could shepherd people because he had the Lord as his shepherd. He would lead them through the dark valley as well as by the still water.

He had feelings too. The Psalms attributed to David leave us with the certainty that this was a man with feelings, going through the ups and downs of life. When he was let down by friends or attacked by enemies he felt it deep within. *His words were smoother*

---

[64] Psalm 27:8 When you said, "Seek my face," my heart said to you, "O LORD, I will seek your face." GW

than butter and softer than oil,[65] he commented with hurt in his heart. There were times when his bitterness broke through in his conversation with God. Vengeance at time was in his heart. Yet there were times when he felt the weakness and frailty of body and soul. In Psalm 63 he could call out to God. *O God, you are my God. At dawn I search for you. My soul thirsts for you. My body longs for you in a dry, parched land where there is no water.* NRSV

David had a personal desire to know God in a deeper experiential way. Julian of Norwich could say to the Lord, *God of thy goodness, give me thyself. For you are enough to me, and I may ask nothing that is less that may be full worship to thee. ... But only in thee do I have all.*[66] Paul could say, "That I might know Him and the power of His resurrection." KJV

David was always enquiring of God. *"Is this the first time I have enquired of God for him?"* Said Ahimelech. 1Samuel.22.15 KJV. This seems in contrast to Saul. In 1Samuel 9.9 it says that in the past people used to "enquire" of the Lord. It was the Hebrew 'DRSH' basically to beat, to tread, to trample down. So it came to mean to go to a place frequently, we must be ones frequently enquiring of God. David was prepared to act on God's advice.

He enquired too about God in general, Psalm 27.4 *I have asked one thing from the LORD. This I will seek: to remain in the LORD'S house all the days of my life in order to gaze at the LORD'S beauty and to search for an answer in his temple.* GW "to search" is 'DKR' to "split open," he wanted to investigate God. Some are just interested in their own personal problems, David wanted to know all about God.

There are people who have no strong feelings when going through hardships and hurts, but the vast majority of us do have emotions that fluctuate according to the situation. David was a man with soul, he went through life as we do, and his life was a roller coaster.

---

[65] Psalm 55.21. KJV
[66] Revelations of Divine Love. Translation of Julian's Middle English Long Text, Veronica Mary Rolf Orbis Books.

The call of David.

The Lord called him before the world had seen the fall of Saul. God had someone ready in the wings. He received an anointing from God as also Saul had previously received.

So often we feel that God positions people in leadership so that His will can be done without any consideration to the people concerned who are being lead. This is not so. Frances Ridley Havergal the hymn writer wrote a small book entitled, "My King." Using the scriptures from the Old Testament she referenced them to fit the kingship of Jesus. The first chapter starts with the text regarding Solomon. Huram the king of Tyre says of Solomon: - *"Because the LORD loves his people, he made you their king."*[67] Although this was no doubt a little flattery yet it was true. God cares for his people. Jesus made the point when speaking of the Sabbath day. He said that it was made for man, man was not made for the Sabbath.[68]

God has our interest at heart, there will be many times we feel that things that happen are not good, he is overruling situations so that they turn out for our good.[69]

---

[67] 2Chronicles 2.11 KJV
[68] Mark 2.27
[69] Romans 8.28

8

Jesus, the ultimate image of God
Philippians 2.6

Paul talking of Jesus said: - Col 1:15 *Who is the image of the invisible God, the firstborn of every creature: KJV* David could be said to have some Godlike traits in that he was a man after the heart of God, yet not close enough to be said to be in the ideal image of God. It is well known that most of us are far from the image we should be seeking be like. Was there in David a desire to be like God wanted him to be? There was no doubt he sought to do the will of God. Then this was a step towards being in the image of God. The way David behaved was not a way we would like him to have behaved. It is not only good to seek to do the will of God but also to do it in the right way.

The character of Jesus was prophesied as, "A bruised reed he would not break and a smoking flax he would not quench."[70] It is not just what we do but how we do it. We are all aware of the maxim, "The end does not justify the means."

Charles Wesley wrote for children, "Gentle Jesus, meek and mild, Look upon a little child." These are words which have been despised

---

[70] Matthew 12.17 – 20 KJV

and ridiculed in past years.[71] Often by preachers of note. We too can see Jesus throwing out the money changers from the temple and hear him firmly speaking to the religious leaders of the day, all that is true. Yet his kindness and condescension to all the needy and straying souls comes over far more forcefully in the Scriptures. It is not only what Jesus did but how he did it. Paul appealed to the Corinthian Church, *"I myself, Paul, appeal to you by the meekness and gentleness of Christ--I who am humble when face to face with you, but bold toward you when I am away!"* 2Cor.10.1 KJV It could perhaps be translated, *"by the meekness and mildness of Christ."* World leaders seem unable to have these qualities and lead. David, though kind and considerate to many individuals was often seen as harsh and indifferent to the pain of others. Today the doctor and nurse, the teacher and parent, even the boss can be seen to be concerned and sympathetic to the needs of others. But today's leader must be seen to be authoritarian, ruthless, almost heartless and must achieve results at all costs. Whether a football manager, managing director, prime minister or president they are all in the spotlight and must succeed. Unfortunately, this style of leadership has passed into the church, not totally or completely but too far and is too deeply entrenched.

Yet even David had limitations, he spoke of his nephew in the following words: - 1Ki 2:5 *Moreover you know also what Joab the son of Zeruiah did to me, and what he did to the two captains of the hosts of Israel, unto Abner the son of Ner, and unto Amasa the son of Jether, whom he slew, and shed the blood of war in peace.* KJV Earlier he said: - 2Sa 3:39 *Today I'm weak, though I'm the anointed king. These men, Zeruiah's sons, are too cruel for me. May the LORD repay this evildoer as his evil deeds deserve."* GW.

David spoke often of God's care for him. He spoke about his prowess that God gave him when in battle. Rarely did he declare that he had

---

[71] In the Preface to Androcles and the Lion, George Bernard Shaw wrote: ' "Gentle Jesus, meek and mild" is a snivelling modern invention, with no warrant in the gospels.

a deep love for God, as in Psalm 18.1 he used the word "RACHAM,"[72] to love deeply. He often spoke in the Psalms of the "lovingkindness" of God to him, which is translated from "KHESED." Time after time David will speak of his trust in God. There must always be not only our confidence in God but also affection for the Lord as well. Could it be that our trust in the Lord will see us through to do his will, but our love for him will help us to do his will his way as well?

David experienced the joy of the Lord. Psalm 4.7 *You have put gladness in my heart more than when their grain and wine abound*, NRSV. He enjoyed God, "I was glad," he said, "When they said let us go to the house of the Lord."

---

[72] Racham in the qal form as opposed to piel which is to have compassion.

9

The loss of God's blessing
1Samuel 15.1-35

David was brought in because Saul had lost out 1Sam.16.14 *But the Spirit of the LORD departed from Saul, and an evil spirit from the LORD troubled him. KJV*

Although it seemed to happen in a moment there was a downward spiral that led to this incident, there was a time when Saul lost out by sacrificing when it should have been left for Samuel.[73] It was disrespect for God's Word, a lack of trust, and a failure in personal holiness. Saul's fear of the situation became to him greater than the fear of God – when that happens a person is in trouble. Years later when David remembered what happened at this time to Saul he was fearful in case the Spirit of the Lord departed from him too, see Psalm 51. There are many examples where the people were more afraid of their situation than of God. Yet some courageous positive examples too. The three Hebrew boys facing the furnace of fire did not flinch. The proverb puts it clearly, *"A person's fear sets a trap for him, but one who trusts the LORD is safe."*[74]

---

[73] 1Samuel 13.13 Samuel said to Saul, "You have done foolishly; you have not kept the commandment of the LORD your God, which he commanded you. The LORD would have established your kingdom over Israel forever, GW

[74] Proverbs 29.25 GW

We can sympathise with Saul. Not long into his reign he was being deserted and left to fight with few troops. Samuel was slow to come.[75] There are times when it is difficult to keep a cool nerve. The Bible then says Saul acted rashly, in forcing a fast on his troops.[76] Again Saul seemed reluctant to destroy the captured animals of the Amalekites.[77] After this last incident Saul pleaded with Samuel to worship with him, which he did reluctantly, but never to visit him again.

Saul wanted Samuel to worship with him so that he looked okay in the eyes of the people. It was not because he personally wanted to worship God. Saul originally thought of himself as unimportant, now he was concerned how he looked in the eyes of others. He again spoke of God being Samuel's God rather than his own God. *Then Saul said, "I have sinned; yet honour me now before the elders of my people and before Israel, and return with me, so that I may worship the Lord **your** God."* 1Samuel 15.30. NRSV. You can look out of your eyes, or out of other people's eyes, or out of God's eyes, from each of them you will see differently. Put God's glasses on, he has the right angle on every situation.

There are one or two clues as to the reason for Saul's demise. He was no longer small in his eyes. He confessed to being afraid of the people, yet it might mean that he also thought it was unnecessary to do what God asked him to do. Like the great kings he built a monument to himself[78] and was now great in his own eyes. Finally, there was an emphasis on the sacrificing or outward acts rather than obeying God. There is the suggestion that he did not seek the will of God and might have been also worshipping other gods too. In

---

[75] 1Samuel. 13.11 Samuel said, "What have you done?" Saul replied, "When I saw that the people were slipping away from me, and that you did not come within the days appointed, and that the Philistines were mustering at Michmash, KJV

[76] Modern versions generally have the complete text from the Septuagint see NRSV 1Samuel 14.24.

[77] 1Samuel 15.14

[78] 1Samuel.15.12 Samuel was told, "Saul went to Carmel, where he set up a monument for himself, NRSV

the famous words of the prophet Samuel, *"God would rather have obedience than sacrifice."* Are we concentrating on the outward acts of worship rather than the inward work of God in our lives and obedience to Him?

Samuel made a promise to always pray for the country that had rejected his leadership.[79] These words of Samuel have always been a challenge to me, when people that came to Christ through our church ministry decided to leave to go to another church, they had rejected our church why should I continue to pray for them? Now the scripture says that Samuel was mourning for Saul. A minister who had long been in his church when he retired said to another that he was broken hearted to see how the church had become so secular under the new pastor. It happens so often that the next generation relies more on the natural than the spiritual. Samuel was grieving because obedience to God had taken second place in the life of Saul and so in the life of the nation. Leadership demands giving direction not acquiescing to the demands of those being led. There can be no compromise with that which is not of God. Yet there is a foolish leadership model, that of Rehoboam. He felt he had a divine right not to listen to genuine needs of the people of God.[80]

The hymn writer William Cowper wrote, *"Where is the blessedness that once I knew when first I saw the Lord?"*[81] The Ephesian Church lost out when Jesus could challenge them, *"I have this against you: The love you had at first is gone."*[82] If you have lost the blessing of God get it back!

---

[79] 1Sa 12:23 It would be unthinkable for me to sin against the LORD by failing to pray for you. I will go on teaching you the way that is good and right. GW

[80] 1Kings 12.14 And spoke to them after the counsel of the young men, saying, My father made your yoke heavy, and I will add to your yoke: my father also chastised you with whips, but I will chastise you with scorpions. KJV

[81] Cowper suffered from depression. This might not have been his true state at the time of writing but his feelings.

[82] Revelation 2.4 GW

10

Does God have a plan "B"?
1Samuel 15.11 & 16.1-13

Saul was made king by God then later rejected because he failed to do that which God asked. There are always alternatives for God. John the Baptist was blunt with the people of Israel when they were about to reject his message. Luke 3:8 *Do those things that prove that you have turned to God and have changed the way you think and act. Don't say, 'Abraham is our ancestor.' I guarantee that God can raise up descendants for Abraham from these stones.* GW

In accepting that God's will is sure and certain and knowing that it will be fulfilled, we as individuals, can still miss out. I don't want someone else to do the work that God would like me to do.

Jesus made clear to the whole of Jerusalem that God wanted something better for them. Luke 13.34 *Jerusalem, Jerusalem, the city that kills the prophets and stones those who are sent to it! How often have I desired to gather your children together as a hen gathers her brood under her wings, and you were not willing!* GW God works with the willingness of people. There may be exceptions, such as Jonah, but God loves working with people not in spite of them, though he will do that! Mark 16:20 *And they went forth, and preached everywhere,* **the Lord working with them,** *and confirming the word with signs following. Amen.* KJV

When God has a calling for us, and a ministry to accomplish, we must not fall short of His plan for us. Sometimes we need encouragement to do it. Mordecai had to challenge Esther, Esther 4:14 *For if you altogether hold your peace at this time, then shall there enlargement and deliverance arise to the Jews from another place; but you and your father's house shall be destroyed: and who knows whether you are come to the kingdom for such a time as this?* KJV God's will, will be done, it is just that He has a choice of people after all there are a few billions of us to choose from.

It is not the plan, it is the people, it is alternative people he can use to achieve the results He has in mind. If Abraham wished to return to his homeland he could have done so. Hebrews 11:15 *If they had been thinking of the land that they had left behind, they would have had opportunity to return.* NRSV Abraham was looking to the future he had not spent his time contemplating the past. We are not backward looking people; our life is our future. It is that which God has for us, we are staring ahead with excitement. Philippians 3:14 *I run straight toward the goal to win the prize that God's heavenly call offers in Christ Jesus.* GW

There is a challenge to us to make sure that we fulfil the plan and purpose that God has for us. Jesus could say to the Philippi Church, Revelation 3:11 *I am coming soon! Hold on to what you have so that no one takes your crown.* KJV Jesus said, "Keep what you have got." Don't let go of the ministry that you have from God. The crown was the "stephanos" - a wreath for the victor at the games. It meant for them joy - It meant achievement and success. Paul could say "*I have fought a good fight, I have kept the faith.*" KJV Keeping hold is vital. There is a story told of a girl in love with a young soldier in the English civil war. He had been sentenced to death and was due to be executed at the curfew bell. She climbed up the bell tower and clung on to the bell tongue and would not let go to stop it ringing. When Cromwell returned he pardoned him after hearing how his girlfriend would not let go of the bell's clapper. Although the legend really comes from an earlier period of the wars of the Roses in the fifteenth century. This is where the saying, "Hang on the bell Nellie," comes from. Although the scripture speaks of God keeping hold of us, there is the sense that we must keep hold of what he has given to us. 1Co 15:2 *In addition, you are saved by this Good News if you hold on to the doctrine I taught you.* GW

God is not a cheat. The Scripture says on several occasions that God regretted what he had done. As in Genesis 6.6 speaking of the evil nature of mankind. The word used, and the further explanation in this verse, shows the disappointment and sadness of the Lord. Similarly, with Saul, God says: - *"I regret that I made Saul king, for he has turned back from following me, and has not carried out my commands."*[83] When the scriptures clearly state that God does not change his mind such as in Romans 11:29 *God never changes his mind when he gives gifts or when he calls someone.* GW. Or here in 1Samuel 15.29 *the Glory of Israel does not lie*[84] *or change his mind, because he is not a mortal who changes his mind."* GW He is the unchanging God, unfortunately we change at times. Saul had a heart change that was not for the good. It was not just the disobedience; it was that Saul had stopped following God. His actions displayed the direction of his heart. God had not changed, Saul had. God will not cheat on us, he sticks to his word. We must be true to our commitment to follow him. There is also some good news with this if we repent from going bad ways God removes his threat to us. After the prayer of Moses, the Scripture says: - *And the LORD changed his mind about the disaster that he planned to bring on his people.*[85] Samuel like Moses also prayed but in anger, there was no answer.

---

[83] 1Samuel 15.11 NRSV
[84] "shaqar" is used several times in the Hebrew Bible and could be translated occasionally as "Cheat."
[85] Exodus 32.14 NRSV

11

Diagnosing the illness
1Samuel 16.14 -23

The origin of Saul's illness was evil, and there was no remedy without repentance. The Hebrew suggests his rages could happen in a moment.[86] One-minute okay the next he was in a furious rage and melancholic. The phrase "from the Lord" has worried many people. When God removed his Spirit from Saul he became prey to anything going.

It could have been that David was just one of many that played for King Saul, as later he did not seem to know him well, or at least his family origin. Yet Jessie had provided food and wine for Saul as well as providing a musician son. It could have been that many families did likewise, and so Jessie would have been one of many families providing the same service for the king.

David was the music maker, Saul needed the music, we can be the source and supply of a blessing to others, or we can be the absorber of all good things without giving in return. An orchestra will be practising for hundreds of hours to satisfy not only their director and conductor but to please an audience who may only listen for an hour or two and go away satisfied and refreshed with an evening's

---

[86] See 1Samuel 18.1

entertainment, but without a life changing experience. Let's be music makers that make a difference! There is music that satisfies the soul.

The rejection of all things spiritual by modern man has caused a majority of people to be against the teaching of the possibility of a person being possessed with an evil spirit. There has been a seeking to laugh such explanations off as medieval beliefs, suitable for the ignorant and illiterate. Further complications have been caused by some immigrant Churches in the Western World and their attempts at exorcism, which have sometimes been coupled with heathen as well as Christian practices. Modern man has no difficulty in understanding that a cancer is a living organism connected to a body but is acting against the best interests of the person, and that its agenda is different to the host body, and that it will destroy that person unless it is eradicated or checked in its progress. Likewise, in the mind of man there can be something with a different agenda. (The Scripture does not suggest that they are totally controlled by evil but that the evil spirit will influence them.)

When things go wrong, and our personal weaknesses begin to control us we have a chance to change. Saul sought to deal with the symptoms rather than the source of the problem. We must be prepared to return to the scene of our sin and correct the problem. Saul could have put the matter right. Instead he lived seeking to control the consequences and the symptoms of his actions. Don't let failure become fatal. Go back and put it right. Deal with the cause not the consequences.

Yet at one time Saul seemed to have a conversion experience. 1Samuel 10.9 *As he turned away to leave Samuel, God gave him another heart; and all these signs were fulfilled that day. NRSV.* He had an anointing from God, the same as the prophets. God was with him. Saul was given a wide open mandate to lead his country. But like Samson he never recognised the day that God's Holy Spirit left him, nor did he appreciate the day he received the anointing. Or shall we say he never realised the depression he had was when his heart became disobedient and later jealous of David. It came in twenty-four hours of letting go of God. 1Samuel.18.10 *the next day an evil spirit from God rushed upon Saul, and he raved within his house, while David was playing the lyre. NRSV* We must never hang on to sin, let it go immediately. God wants us to change he can never use us as he should if we are without his presence with us. God takes all sorts of people, timid Timothy, brash Peter, determined Paul, then he changes them. Some were ambitious, some were weak, some were doubters, and God does the changing when we make ourselves available.

The experience of the Holy Spirit was a one-day wonder to Saul, not a day never to be forgotten. John Newton the writer of Amazing Grace said, "That tenth of March is a day much remembered by me; and I have never suffered it to pass unnoticed since the year 1748 the Lord came from on high and delivered me out of deep waters." Never let the day God revealed himself to you depart from your memory.

God has always been in the changing business. Jesus transformed his disciples by his teaching and their experience while following him plus the Holy Spirit's power. We might think that we are good enough, God has a different assessment of us! There is a good chance that God wants you and me different from how we are now at this very moment.

12

The cottage cheese expedition.
1 Sam. 17.1-58

Only a century or two ago the armies of Europe would often have their women and children with them as they travelled, but kept a distance away from the main battlefield when the fighting was to take place. We can imagine young teens taking an avid interest in the state of play, David would be the same.

The world of David was different to ours, but we must never underestimate their culture. Ebla in Northern Syria was considered to have, long before David's time, a population of a quarter of a million people. Later Nineveh was described as a vast city. The majority of the cities were smaller walled ones, and some would have minimal defences. The attackers had grappling irons and battering-rams for attack. The defenders had stones and rocks etc. to throw down on the attackers. They made treaties with equals but the defeated paid taxes.

The Philistines were one of the groups of the Sea People that had fled Crete and perhaps other lands too, they were warlike but also built temples and palaces and had subjugated much of Israel. They had access to iron manufacturing technology which they removed from Israel.[87]

---

[87] 1Sa 13:19 *Now there was no smith found throughout all the land of Israel: for the Philistines said, Lest the Hebrews make them swords or spears*: KJV

The size of the Goliath....Six cubits and a span. This is not a fairy tale story, Egyptians recorded people of similar height in the area of Canaan. Also seven-foot female skeleton has been recovered from the locality.[88] A cubit was generally the distance from finger tips to elbow though there were variations, 16" (0.4m) to 18" (0.46m). This made Goliath about 8'-5" (2.56m) to 9'-3" (2.8m). They talked about a nation of giants too, as well as his brothers. His armour of bronze scales weighed 125lbs. or 57Kgs. (History records others having heavy armour with which to go into battle.) The armour was a little more than the weight of a sack of coal. He was a walking tank. Early drawings shown some with the mailed armour down to their ankles, though Goliath had shin guards. There was a chink in the armour, David's stone found it. (When you are fighting your Goliath remember that there will be a chink in his armour.)

With the query as to why Saul did not know, or admit to knowing David it has been suggested that Saul's illness affected his memory. (1Samuel 17.15 *David would go back to Bethlehem from time to time, to take care of his father's sheep.*) NRSV This might explain part of it, in that it could have meant that he was occasionally at the palace. It could also be that he was one of a number of musicians. There is also the matter of protocol, it may have been the case that the king would not acknowledge the servants. *17.55 And when Saul saw David go forth against the Philistine, he said unto Abner, the captain of the host, Abner, whose son is this youth? And Abner said, "As thy soul lives, O king, I cannot tell."* KJV He was asking about his family as much as who David was. God has often used the energy and excitableness of youth. The majority of Jesus' disciples seem to have been relatively young. God can use what you have, whether the energy of youth or the wisdom of old age! And also the in-between ages too.

---

[88] See IVP Background Commentary in location.

13

The position of the armies
1Samuel 17.1-58

The armies were sixteen or so miles south-west of Jerusalem and about ten to fourteen miles from Bethlehem. David could have made it there and back in a day although it was unlikely. He had to bring back tokens from his brother to prove to his parents that they were alive.[89] 1Samuel 17.18

Where was the champion of Israel?

Saul was as tall as any of the people in Israel, David's brothers seem to have been taller than David. He would have been under twenty years of age, otherwise he would have been called up. God does not always use the obvious to do the job. The accusation of the brothers that he had come for a little excitement would have almost certainly been true.

Don't let a challenge go unchallenged

Forty days was far too long to keep hearing the challenge of Goliath. David's questions were really an offer v26,30,31. Paul let the woman with the python spirit trouble them only for a day or two. Act.16.

---

[89] Jewish commentators have suggested that this was to do with the conditional divorce of soldiers.

There comes a time when if no one else is meeting a need then we must step in. David stepped in when no one else would or could. Nearly all the orphanages in Britain were started by Christians, Schools and hospitals were too. Is there something today that is challenging us that we should respond to the challenge?

The possibility of heart failure

1Samuel 17.32 *David said to Saul, "Let no man's heart fail because of him; thy servant will go and fight with this Philistine."* KJV That is of course spiritual heart failure. Often we can suffer anxieties as adults that we never would have had in our youth. Though practising Christians don't usually have so many physical heart attacks! David had already killed a lion and bear in hand to hand combat. Notice that there were major wild animals at this time in Israel. *"If you have raced with foot-runners and they have wearied you, how will you compete with horses? And if in a safe land you fall down, how will you fare in the thickets of the Jordan?"* asked the prophet.[90] Life can be so easy and comfortable for many of us, we could not cope in a famine land, or a war zone.

Whose armour are you wearing? And in whose name are you going?

Saul's armour left David useless, the strategy of David was sensible. He was to attack before Goliath could get in certain killing range with his javelin.[91] As children we used string with a knot to give our hazel nut javelins a much longer throwing distance. Keep you distance from a Goliath, and have a long range weapon yourself. The giant had a weak spot and David aimed for it. The sling was made of leather and one strap was released at the vital moment. David was a crack shot, as are many people who are practised with slings today.

---

[90] Jeremiah 12.5 NRSV.
[91] The Word Biblical Commentary quotes that it might have been an Anatolian javelin for long distance throwing. The IVP Background Commentary suggest that it was a scimitar and that the spear was for distance throwing.

Thousands of years ago children on Balearic Island were not allowed to eat till they had hit the target with their slings.[92]

1Samuel 17.45 *Lord of Sabaoth (hosts)* 1Samuel 1.3 is the first use of this title, but see Joshua 5.14 David saw through the visible to the invisible. In the New Testament the centurion could say to Jesus, *"My servants do what I tell them. You can do the same with your servants,"* David knew he was not alone, one visible soldier among the many invisible ones.

The five stones have been the preachers' favourite ever since Bible times. Listen to St. Augustine: -

"So our Divine David at the temptation to meet our ghostly Goliath chose five stones out of the brook. The five books of Moses. What was solid out of what was fluid. What was permanent out of what was transitory. With one He overthrew Satan…" Others have suggested it was one stone for each of Goliath's brothers, I think he had some common sense and used the stones as possible back up!

---

[92] See Wikipedia under Slings (weapons) The earliest known reference in the word is in Judges 20.16

14

David a Shepherd King
1Samuel 16.11 & Ezekiel 34.1-31

When Chris, one of our church deacons, was preaching on this passage. He pointed out when David's brothers accused him of wanting to see the battle. He could have replied rather sarcastically, "What battle? I can't see any fighting."

Saul and his troops were waiting and hoping that Goliath would go away. Unfortunately, they don't go without a fight. David was a king in waiting, he was prepared to take on the giant. It was an era when kings were fighting men. David was a fighting youth.[93]

Where is the King? He's keeping the Sheep. (1Samuel 16.11) Ezekiel outlines the good shepherd, David fitted the bill. His was not a large flock 1Samuel 17.28 *Eliab, David's oldest brother … became angry with David. "Why did you come here," he asked him, "and with whom did you leave those **few sheep** in the wilderness?* GW So the taunts came from his brothers as well as Goliath. He was despised by those who should be backing him up to the hilt. As the minister of a local church in the suburbs of a city I was often asked, when introduced to a Christian, "How many are in your Church?" Non-Christians

---

[93] The last king of England to lead his troops into battle was George II in 1743. Richard III was the last to die in battle in 1485

almost never asked the question. The numbers game is a despising game. The hymn "Blessed be the tie that binds," was written by John Fawcett a Baptist pastor in Wainsgate, Yorkshire. Although a small chapel, and his salary was only £25.00 per year he was able to influence the king of England.[94] A small rudder changes the direction of mighty ships. You can influence the world by being you.

The contrast between a shepherd and a king. Jesus is the Shepherd King. Kings get, shepherds give. Jesus referred to Himself as the Good Shepherd – giving as only the Good Shepherd can. *"The good shepherd … he gives his life for the sheep."* Kings number, shepherds name. David in his later years made that mistake. Kings are protected, shepherds protect. "If I were a king then would my servants fight" said Jesus. See Luther's hymn.[95]

Jesus the Servant King, also see Isaiah 42.1-9, 49.1-13, 50.4-11, 52.13-53.12. These Servant passages are all connected to the coming Messiah.

Jesus the Priest king, Hebrews 5:6 *As he says also in another place, Thou art a priest for ever after the order of Melchisedec.* KJV Other kings died seeking to take the place of the priest, Saul had lost the blessing of God. Jesus is the sacrifice and the sacrificer.

When does the battle in our life become the Lord's battle?

17.47 KJV And all this assembly shall know that the LORD saves not with sword and spear: for the battle is the LORD'S, and he will give you into our hands.

Sometimes we provoke a situation that God is not involved in, then when the things don't turn how we were hoping we want Him to

---

[94] How he came to write, "Blessed be the tie that binds our hearts in sacred love." And why he turned down a lucrative Baptist Church in London is another story.

[95] A safe stronghold is our God, … With force of arms we nothing can, full soon were we down-ridden; but for us fights the proper Man whom God himself hath bidden. Ask ye who is this same? Christ Jesus is his name, the Lord Sabaoth's Son; he, and no other one, shall conquer in the battle.

finish the job for us. That is wrong. King Josiah generations later went out to fight the Egyptians who were on their way to a battle in Carchemish. He was told to keep out of it, and mind his own business, he didn't and lost his life.[96] In verse 45 David had named the Lord as his deliverer. He had not provoked the fight; it was a danger to his community. It is the name of Jesus that we can call upon that makes the difference. When we are called to battle the forces of darkness.

---

[96] 2Chronicles 35.20-25

15

The necessity of leadership.

Little is known about the everyday people in the Bible or in history in general, it is the leaders whom we know more about. It may be that they were wicked or good, wise or foolish, failures or successes but more is written about them, much more. The slave girl who was kidnapped and made to work for Naaman then helped him find healing has barely a sentence or two in the Bible, and we do not know her name. Many such individuals have changed the direction of history yet it is the leaders who have the limelight.

There are different types of leaders and different styles of leadership. Also there are different peoples that need to be lead. Some will lead a country and others will lead a group of downtrodden people to stand against inequity. Many are good in times of peace but not suitable when their country is at war. Within the Christian Church there are international leaders that all Christians have looked up to. Then there are local and national ministers who by their very nature command respect giving direction and guidance. Some of these leaders emerge and others are chosen by their denominations.

We are well aware of the advice Jesus gave his followers who would seek to lead in Mark 10.42-45: -

Jesus called the apostles and said, "You know that the acknowledged rulers of nations have absolute power over people and their officials have absolute authority over people. But that's not the way it's going to be among you. Whoever wants to become great among you will be your servant. Whoever wants to be most important among you will be a slave for everyone. It's the same way with the Son of Man. He didn't come so that others could serve him. He came to serve and to give his life as a ransom for many people." GW.

This was a revolutionary style of leadership that Jesus taught. Both Saul and David were referred to as captains, but as noted before only David as a shepherd of his people. People in charge can be autocratic wanting total control, some are democratic sharing decision making. There are some today that leave their subordinates to choose their own direction as long as it is to the benefit of the organisation.

Paul wanted to ensure that the Corinthians knew he was not seeking to control the Christians there, he said: - 2Co 1:24 *It isn't that we want to have control over your Christian faith. Rather, we want to work with you so that you will be happy. Certainly, you are firmly established in the Christian faith.* GW

Peter put it this way in 1Peter 5.2-4: - *Be shepherds over the flock God has entrusted to you. Watch over it as God does: Don't do this because you have to, but because you want to. Don't do it out of greed, but out of a desire to serve. Don't be rulers over the people entrusted to you, but be examples for the flock to follow. Then, when the chief shepherd appears, you will receive the crown of glory that will never fade away.* GW

The emphasis is on leading by example. There is no thought of control, nor of authoritarian leadership, a little of a paternalistic style in leadership but not much.

This latter type of leadership is best illustrated with Paul speaking of the leading role of women in the church. To Timothy he states that he would not allow a woman, as the KJV puts it, "Usurp authority."[97]

---

[97] This word 'authentein' is used only the once here in 1Timothy 2.12 can mean to domineer, acting on their own authority. See TDNTT under "Women". Used elsewhere of a self-appointed killer! Thayer.

But to the Romans he speaks of Phoebe being a succourer (KJV) of many,[98] which is a term for a woman in authority who is caring for others. One Paul rejected, the other he respected.

Jesus, as well as Paul and Peter without exception spoke against a controlling form of leadership. Speaking of Jesus Peter said: - 1Pe 2:21 *God called you to endure suffering because Christ suffered for you. He left you an example so that you could follow in his footsteps.* Paul said, 1Co 11:1 *"Imitate me as I imitate Christ."* GW. By contrast king Saul was very controlling in 1Samuel 18.2 it says that he refused to allow David to go home.

David was prepared to use the successful and the fearless to achieve his aims. 1Ch 11:6 *Now, David said, "Whoever is the first to kill a Jebusite will be made a general and a prince." Zeruiah's son Joab was the first to go into Jerusalem, so he became the general.* GW There was reward and incentive to produce leaders. Yet the early church used failures such as Peter to leadership roles.

The Motivating Force. Did David from the very beginning see a vision of a strong country and sought to engage people with his vision? His first call was to survive, to overcome, to constantly seek God. Then gradually the vision grew and he could see the possibility of the end product. God gave him the promise of kingship and you cannot have that without a kingdom.

Yet there was a greater motivation in the life of David. He speaks of it in Psalm 69.9 *It is zeal for your house that has consumed me;* NRSV or as the KJV states, **"*has eaten me up.*"** He saw a vision of the house of God where people came to worship the Lord. Amid all the idolatry and corrupt worship of Yahweh he set out to provide a purer faith and a more joyful exuberant praise of God by God's people. He had a twin aim and not all persons that were with him were with him in totality. Furthermore, he found that some having an initial spurt of faith later became apathetic or even changed their minds. David said in Psalm 101.3 *I will not set before my eyes anything that*

---

[98] Phebe was called a 'Prostatis' a woman in authority caring for others, only used in Romans 16.2. Paul is requesting they give her top class treatment.

is base. I hate the work of those who fall away; it shall not cling to me. NRSV He wanted to keep his eye on the ball and noted that some had left the Lord. Backsliding is not a new phenomenon. There was time when David was settled he realised that his ambition for God was unfulfilled. 2Samuel 7:2. *So the king said to the prophet Nathan, "Look, I'm living in a house made of cedar, while the ark of God remains in the tent."* GW. The writer of Hebrews commented how sin sticks to us. *Therefore, since we are surrounded by so great a cloud of witnesses, let us also lay aside every weight and the sin that clings so closely, and let us run with perseverance the race that is set before us.*[99]

---

[99] Hebrews 12.1 NRSV See Job 41.17 about the crocodile's scales.

16

Success and its pitfalls
1Samuel 18.1-30

David had success in all his undertakings; for the LORD was with him. Jonathan and David became inseparable friends, "close buddies" is too weak a phrase. It has been suggested that Jonathan was wanting to keep him close to have him under control, a form of Machiavellianism. This is not so, but it is true of Jonathan's father, King Saul.[100] It is great to have someone you can confide in, who will never betray you, and never seek to up-stage you. Some have questioned whether Jonathan would readily step aside for David, but not all the heir apparent wish to fulfil the roll that others feel they are destined for. Richard Cromwell, Oliver Cromwell's son, was not too troubled when Britain did not wish him to continue after his father died. David could pay genuine tribute to Jonathan after his death. If you are going to be a great person you must have good friends.

The Covenant of Friendship. Jonathan was cutting a covenant. This was no ordinary friendship. He was handing over his prince's garment to David.[101] He was prepared to say like John the Baptist,

---

[100] 1Samuel 18.2
[101] See IVP Bible Background Commentary in location.

"He must increase, I must decrease." There will always be someone who could achieve more than we are able to. That is not the issue. Have they the call and the anointing of God on their life? David had that and Jonathan knew it.

An affection can be built up between politicians and their constituents, between teachers and pupils and between ministers and their congregations. John Fawcett in the eighteenth century was going to leave his chapel. The congregation came to say goodbye. They were broken hearted as he and his family prepared to leave. It was not long before he was taking his furniture off the cart and staying with the people who loved him and he them.[102] Make an unwritten covenant of friendship!

Originally Saul had affection for David. In 1Samuel 16.21 the scripture says, *"And David came to Saul, and entered his service. Saul loved him greatly, and he became his armour-bearer."* NRSV The word for love is AHAB, used many times, in many different occasions as well as for Jonathan's love for David too, also God's love for people and places. The difference was that Saul loved David for what he was receiving from him, it was not the same with Jonathan. He loved David for who he was, not what he could do. Much of David's life is affected by his friendships, both good and bad. We can learn from his life and search our heart for the reason for our choice of friends and colleagues.

The Jealous Eye. 1Samuel 18.9 NRSV *So Saul eyed David from that day on.* AWAN, a Hebrew word to look with suspicion. The Pharisees took a look at Jesus to see if he would heal on the Sabbath day. *And the scribes and Pharisees watched*[103] *him, whether he would heal on the Sabbath day; that they might find an accusation against him.*[104] It was the critical look. If we are trusting God then we will never trouble about what others are planning against us, it is in God's hands. Success can produce enemies as well as false friends.

---

[102] It was said that this was when he wrote, "Blessed be the tie that binds,"
[103] *paratereo to watch insidiously*
[104] Luke 6:7 KJV

Beware of the jealous eye on you as well as ensuring we do not become envious ourselves of others! Jesus spoke of the evil eye; it is usually translated "envy" in modern versions.[105] It is not only what comes out of our mouths but that which enters our eyes too than can become sinful.

When the medicine ceased to work. 1Samuel 18.10 *The next day an evil spirit from God rushed upon Saul, and he raved within his house, while David was playing the lyre, as he did day by day. Saul had his spear in his hand; NRSV*

The root cause of an illness has to be dealt with. Saul had only sought to deal with the symptoms and now it was reaching a critical stage. Do we have a weakness in our life that needs surgery not just a sticking plaster? Jesus put it plainly, Mt 5:29 *"So if your right eye causes you to sin, tear it out and throw it away. It is better for you to lose a part of your body than to have all of it thrown into hell. GW.* Jeremiah said that sometimes more than sticking plaster is needed to heal a wound,[106] just as some would say, "Have a nice day." When much more help is needed than a passing wish. J. John the evangelist tells the story of a psychiatrist. Before he discharged a patient he would check them out by overflowing a sink with running water. The psychiatrist would then hand them a mop and bucket then ask them to clear up the water. If they turned off the water tap and pulled out the plug in the sink before trying to mop up the water, they were discharged. Because they had dealt with the source of the problem. We sometimes leave the origin of the problem and just try to clear up the symptoms.

---

[105] Mark 7.22
[106] Jeremiah 8,11 They act as if my people's wounds were only scratches. 'All is well,' they say, when all is not well. GNB

17

The Escape
1Samuel 19.1-24

David's first love, Michal put her life on the line for David and loved him in spite of her father's attitude to David. (Her possession of a household idol showed that the worship of God was not absolute at this time, 1Sam.19.13). There is always a time when we must think for ourselves. Both Jonathan and his sister, Michal were able to have thoughts independent of their father. Always take into account the thoughts of your friends and family, but you will be accountable yourself. You cannot blame another for your actions.

It was at this time David wrote Psalm 59

He likened the guards to be like a pack of dogs[107] – he claimed his innocence – then he called on God, see verse 9 & 17. God was his Strength, fortress and loving God. In verse 9 of the psalm he says he will wait for the Lord. It Is the same word that was in 1Sam 19.11 *Saul sent messengers to David's house to keep watch over him, planning to kill him in the morning.* NRSV Saul's guards were watching for David. He was watching for the Lord – are we watching for the Lord? In verse 17 he was in a position to start singing! He

---

[107] Dogs often roamed in packs and in some European countries today they have killed people it must have been the same in David's day.

goes from anxiety to confidence. We will too when we weigh up the options.

After several attempts had been made on his life David made his way to Samuel. It was here that Saul tried to capture him and each occasion was thwarted by the Holy Spirit coming on the attackers and Saul too. This is a remarkable thing. Men opposed to God and His will can become subject to Him. (1Samuel 19.18-24) They have a temporary change of nature. As earlier when Jonathan spoke with his father.

Don't be fickle and changeable in your thoughts. We must be open minded for the truth and able to correct our misunderstandings, we have a right to change our minds. But we cannot be constantly changeable in our attitude to people like Saul was. The common sense of Jonathan and the Holy Spirit coming on him was not sufficient to overcome, in the long term, the effect his jealous heart had on his life decisions. We can have an overwhelming controlling emotion that captivates and controls our lives. It might not be jealousy, as there are many emotions that stop us from thinking coolly and calmly, destroying rational thought. Some scientists have held to their theories long after sufficient evidence has proved them incorrect. They have ceased looking for the truth and sought to bolster their own views. If someone is good for a position in church, though we are not enamoured with them, we should not stand in their way. Likewise, we must seek the truth at all costs or we are living not only a lie but also failing to live righteously.

David had no choice but to leave, it was a decision that would hurt his heart. Years later Michal would be restored to him. But what a heartbreak? There may come a time when we have to make choices that cause us hurt. They must only be made in life and death situations, not just so that we may further ourselves in this life.

18

Dealing with Saul's illness.
1Samuel 19.1-24

As we mentioned before the Bible states that the cause of Saul's illness was spiritual. The attack became possible because Saul had let his guard down. In Samuel's question, "What is this bleating of the sheep I hear?" (1Samuel 15.14) The result was that the Spirit of God left him and he was open for Satan to reach him. Depressive illness can be physical and though it has similar effects it cannot be put down to spiritual causes. If there is anything we can do to correct our lives spiritually then this should have a good effect on our mental well-being as well.

Natural depression can be caused by failure to reach objectives. Elijah thought that Israel would turn to the Lord when he called down fire from heaven. They didn't, and he felt he did not wish to live. Sickness and over-work can also affect us, remember the Roman Governor thought that it had happened to Paul, *"Much learning has made you mad."*[108] Bereavement which Isaac had experienced, etc. Bi-polar depression (when a person suffers with highs as well as lows) has natural causes. The results of continued

---

[108] Acts 26.24 KJV

depression can lead to tragedy. It is important that we recognise it in ourselves and others.

Saul's depression was the result of lack of obedience to God and a failure to genuinely repent with a desire to hold his position at all costs. 1Samuel 15.24-31. Therefore, obedience, and if we fail true repentance, will put the matter right. In the case of natural depression some matters can be put right with medicine and therapies and prayer.

The cause of Saul's anger.

Saul's rage was going to lead to murder if not stopped. Jealousy of course was the reason for this (1Samuel 18.7). *Anger is cruel, and fury is overwhelming, but who can survive jealousy?*[109] His first outburst was when David was playing the Lyre[110] The NIV said Saul was prophesying the NRSV. says raving. The same Hebrew word was used for both because often the prophets became rather carried away. The latter translation seems to fit the context better. The jealousy of Saul made him keep an eye on David. Jealousy stops you looking at and enjoying the good things all around. We are unaware of the length of time that passed before David was taken from the palace to the battle front in the hope of a quick end, but that was where he was at home. (David too used this method to kill Uriah).

The effects of jealousy

Ecclesiastes 4.4 *Again, I considered all travail, and every right work, that for this a man is envied of his neighbour. This is also vanity and vexation of spirit.* KJV

Matt.27.18 KJV. *For he knew that for envy they had delivered him.*

1Cor.13.4 GW *Love is patient. Love is kind. Love isn't jealous. It doesn't sing its own praises. It isn't arrogant.*

---

[109] Proverbs 27.4 GW
[110] 1Samuel.18.10

We are challenged by two men in the Bible who were not jealous – John the Baptist could say, *"He must increase I must decrease."* Jonathan while talking with his father could say, *"I know that one day he will be king,"* when speaking of David, yet though this position would have been his, he was willing to give it up for the will and plan of God. Some have no desire to be the leader, they are happy to be lead. Great leaders usually have someone to be their adviser and support with being in the limelight. Enjoy the position you are comfortable with, rather than seek to be the top dog.

If a spear could be driven into the wall of Saul's palace it might not have been much of an elaborate affair (1Sam.19.10,20.25). So it might have been made of wood. Then again it could have been made of stone but lined with wood. Saul certainly did not look after it very well if he was prepared to throw spears at it.

19

Listening to advice
1Samuel 19 1-24

Saul's son gave his father good advice.

There was a difference in temperament between father and son. We need people that are of a different temperament to us. They see things in a different light. Some ministers will gather around them people that agree with them. "Yes" men and women, that will not give a contrary suggestion. People that do not contest the status quo, nor any decisions that are made.

Jonathan was prepared to challenge his father. He had not only a friendship with David, but a conscience and a sense of justice as well. It is good to look at decisions and plans from different angles. There are other viewpoints in life besides ours. Sometimes it is, like this case, the difference between right and wrong. Sometimes it is a choice between a wiser direction to go than the one being contemplated.

Paul and Barnabas went to Jerusalem to consult with the other apostles.[111] It was not a case of who was the leader. It was a case of truth and concern for practical church needs. Church is not a

---

[111] Acts 15

one-man band. We always ran our church so there was consensus by the leadership not just a majority for a plan. It saves a great deal of dissention and discord; it is often better to leave a decision till a future date than to force something through.

A wife's courage.

When Saul ignored the warnings of Jonathan he was outwitted by Michal, his daughter. It was her wisdom, her courage that saved David. I have always been sorry that David was not prepared to wait for Michal, till they could be together again.

Bad men always seem to have subservient people who will do their bidding. We might be the least important in our organisation but morality must always play a part in our work. Right and wrong is a choice that goes down to the bottom rung of the ladder. Saul's messengers became messengers of evil, Michal stopped them from being part of the crime, but they will be judged on their attempted actions not on their success or failure to achieve their master's bidding. Jesus put our sin and failure not just down to our actions but to our inner thoughts.

The Final barrier.

God the Holy Spirit stepped in. Cowper wrote, "God moves in a mysterious way, his wonders to perform."[112] God sure does! There are times, as the three Hebrew boys stated, God may or may not step in when we are in trouble. God had a purpose to perform and he overrode the evil passions of a king, not for the first or the last time.

Was Saul among the prophets? He was there in body but not in spirit. Once again he experienced the Spirit and power of God but it was a momentary effect that it had on his life. It is amazing that God will bless wayward people as well as good people. This could have meant a whole new life for Saul, but like many of us he let the blessing pass. When God the Holy Spirit comes do not miss out because you might be in doubt about some of the manifestations.

---

[112] It is said that he wrote this after he was thwarted in a suicide attempt.

Down through history some of the more extreme elements of revival have often been ignored by many church historians. Were there weird goings on in ancient revivals? Yes, there were. Were there excesses in the Welsh revival? Sure, things happen. They got the jerks in the American Pine Ridge Camp revival. And all unusual things happened in the Pentecostal revival as well. When you read the reports of those who were critical of what happened at the time of these revivals, it puts Saul lying naked and prophesying into perspective.[113] God the Holy Spirit always works outside the box we have made for him. Give the Holy Spirit place to work in your life without inhibitions.[114] When I was filled with the Holy Spirit at fourteen years of age my prayer life came into being. I burst out with languages unknown to me as I prayed by my bedside. Get all you can from God and keep hold of him too.

---

[113] See the history of the Tongues Movement by GH Lange., which was negative, or the Cambuslang Revival by Arthur Fawcett which was positive but reported observations of others at the time.

[114] If you then, who are evil, know how to give good gifts to your children, how much more will your Father in heaven give good things to those who ask him! Matthew 7.11 KJV

20

The nature of friendship
1Samuel 20.1-42

There is a friend that sticks closer than a brother.[115] The usual Hebrew word for friend (REA) can mean a neighbour as well it is used in the majority of Old Testament texts. This Proverb makes the difference between a companion and a trusted friend who loves you (AHEB). This friend would die for you, give preference to you. Such was the friendship of Jonathan and David. For example, 1Samuel 18.3 *Then Jonathan made a covenant with David, because he loved him as his own soul.* Finally saying that their relationship was "passing the love of women." Christian friendship should be like that! 1Samuel 20.8 says that they regarded it as a sacred covenant before God. As has been said, a friend is another self. 1Samuel 18.3

Kidner brings out some qualities of a real relationship.[116] Constancy as above, candour Prov.27.6 counsel Prov.27.9 & tact Prov.25.17. He points out that the strongest Hebrew word for friend is ALLUP meaning a bosom pal, as in Proverbs 17.9 *One who forgives an affront fosters friendship, but one who dwells on disputes will alienate a **friend**,* where it is used to seek to build up that friendship and

---

[115] Proverbs 18.24
[116] Tyndale commentary on Proverbs page 44, 1969 edition

not destroy it. Watch your friendships work at them! David knew about both sorts, for Ahithophel sadly let him down yet Hushai was faithful. Psalm.41.9 & 55.14

The Cost of the Friendship Covenant.

It was a covenant of friendship between Jonathan and David that was made in the sight of God v.8. There was a lifelong cost to it. Hardly ever would they see one another again. Yet there was a later opportunity for David to keep his side of the covenant, and he almost missed it. In seeking to decide on a true friend ask yourself questions.

- "Would this friend of mine stay with me if I were in a dangerous situation or would they run?"
- "If I had a disaster that was not of my own making would they help me out?"
- Then ask, "If I were at fault would they seek to correct me and put me on the right path again?"
- There is a further question, "Does this person have a major flaw in their character, such as a bad temper?" See Psalm 101.6 *But I have my eye on salt-of-the-earth people-- they're the ones I want working with me; Men and women on the straight and narrow-- these are the ones I want at my side.* (Message Bible.) David wanted to choose friends and colleagues who he could trust.

If I could answer, "Yes," to the first three and "No" to the last one, then I know I have the possibility of a true friend and they demand my unspoken covenant of friendship too. Remember no one has reached perfection yet, all of us are seeking more of a likeness to Jesus, and we have a little way to go. Friendship covers more than just two people it must also cover related persons too. Jonathan made sure it covered his family as well. He perhaps already had children whereas David did not seem to have any, although he was married.

When Proverbs speaks of the faithful wounds of a friend, it again does not use the usual Hebrew REA for "friend" but AHEB. God's

Word translation is as follows: - Proverbs 27:6. *Wounds made by a friend are intended to help.* Yet neither David nor Jonathan needed to call on that quality of friendship. The quality they needed to call on was simply that of standing by one another when times were difficult. The scriptures note that David wept the most,[117] or wept the loudest, at their parting, which could have endangered them. Perhaps David wept the louder because he could see further into the future.

---

[117] NRSV translation of 1Samuel 20.41. K&D suggest he wept loudly

21

The use of Subterfuge
1Samuel 20.

The commandment states "You shall not bear false witness against your neighbour." Were they breaking the rule when Jonathan was to say that David had gone to his father's house? Not at all. Samuel had the okay from God to say that he was going to sacrifice, when really he was going to anoint the new king.

Corrie ten Boom and her father and sister were hiding Jewish men and women during the Second World War. They lived in Holland. The Gestapo called at their house and the secret residents managed to hide in a cellar which was accessed from under the table. A carpet was laid over the trap door. The table had a cloth that went down to the floor. When asked where the Jews were hidden Betsy said they are under the table. One of the Gestapo soldiers flung the cloth covering the table up. There was no one there. Betsy laughed. Eventually the Germans left, not having discovered the lodgers.[118]

Afterwards they discussed whether they should tell lies to protect the Jews in their house. The answer is simple. Which is the lesser evil, to have handed over Jews for the gas chamber, or to deny that

---

[118] See The Hiding Place by Corrie ten Boom.

you have any Jews? No right minded person would have any trouble answering that question.

David asked Jonathan to check out the litmus paper test. What colour would Saul turn if he was missing? *If he says, 'Good!' it will be well with your servant; but if he is angry, then know that evil has been determined by him.*[119]

Anger can be a problem with a "controlling person," and Saul sought to control people. It is a device used by bullying individuals to keep others under them in line. There is also the almost indistinguishable line of demarcation, whether they are in control of their anger or that it has control of them. All parents will put on an outward appearance of being cross to seek to correct their children. (Even if inwardly they are laughing at the antics their youngsters have been up to.) The military often make use of this tactic, shouting at new recruits and humiliating them in front of others. It is not a Christian option when dealing with adults unless under extreme circumstances.

Now the Bible says God is angry with the wicked every day.[120] When Jesus went to the money changers in the temple he was prepared to show his anger at the misuse of the temple precincts. There is legitimate anger because of what is happening to the weak and vulnerable. Anger is illegitimate, and sinful, when it is used to obtain our own way and purposes. Anger is wrong when it is the result of an uncontrolled temperament, God has given us the promise of the help of his Holy Spirit. There is no excuse for unnecessary anger.

---

[119] 1Samuel 20.7 GW
[120] Psalm 7.11

22

The effects and consequences of fear.
1Samuel 21.1-15

Early in my ministry a man spoke to me about the onset of his agoraphobia.[121] He was walking down the town's main street when a sudden fear came over him he felt unsafe, and that he must get home. He gave in to it, this was the beginning of his fear. We can all suffer attacks of fear. To constantly be afraid is timidity. David gave in to fear, the fearless became fearful. The situation in David's case was that he had a reputation that the Philistines might not like, "King of the land."[122] He therefore pretended madness. ***Fear is about what might happen rather than what has happened.***

It is sometimes a wonder that people who should be afraid are not, and those who shouldn't be afraid, are. On the battlefield Goliath was not afraid, but Saul was!

Saul's fear of people. 1Sam.15.24 Now Proverbs says, *"The fear of man brings a snare"*[123] The Hebrew for Snare here means a noose. It was used in Job 40.24 as a ring in an animal's nose. If you fear

---

[121] Agoraphobia, though often described as fear of open spaces, is a fear of being where they do not have control of a situation, which might lead to panic.
[122] 1Samuel 21.11
[123] Proverbs 29.25 KJV

people, you can be dragged anywhere. It dragged Pilate down, he let Jesus be crucified for "Fear of the Jews."

Saul's fear of the fight.

Saul should have been the one to fight Goliath. Was it the fear of physical injury or possibly death? As a result, it meant that like Barak he was upstaged, Judges 4.8. Learn to face the inevitable head on without wavering. God is not in the dodging business. That does not mean you go looking for fights!

Saul's fear of David.

1Samuel.18.12,29 etc. This fear became an obsession. It must have finally taken over Saul's thought life and total happiness was gone. The thought of David haunted him. It was not only jealousy but fear that destroyed him. This was totally different sort of fear. It was the fear of being outclassed. That someone was greater than him, and that it would be recognised by others. It is often the reason why someone is not promoted. Some leaders in the past would have people killed because of their abilities, not least Herod the Great, who was prepared to kill his own sons, as well as the children of Bethlehem.

Ahimelech's fear of taking sides

1Samuel.21.1 Had Ahimelech really no bread or was he wanting to stay on the side-lines? Was he trying to be a spectator like the elders of Bethlehem? 1Samuel.16.4 "Why O, why did you tremble Ahimelech? You were the priest of God. Had you a vision of the slaughter to come? Or did you realise you had to take sides?" In fact, everybody seems to be trembling in these episodes of David's life.

Later Ahimelech lost his life anyway. There comes a time when our peaceful existence has to be forfeited and we have to face our fears. Never be afraid to side with the right side. Even if it costs you your life. This was a fear of making a moral choice. Decision making can be difficult but it is necessary, which side is the right side? The right side to be on is the right side.

David's fear of Achish

Though David said he was meeting others he wasn't. He was alone, seen by a servant of Saul, his whereabouts was betrayed. Where better to go than to Saul's enemy? Very much alone and afraid he went to the Philistine city of Gath. David realised he had made "From a frying pan into the fire" decision. There are times when we fail in our choice of direction – God will see us through. He will not make us to be total fools, only we can do that to ourselves. 1Peter 5:7 *Casting all your care upon him; for he cares for you.* KJV David appears to have been safe while he was with Samuel, the power of God the Holy Spirit overcame Saul's soldiers. Could he have stayed there as long as needed to? There are times when we have to stay rather than move, many ministers have moved to another church because of problems when they were safe in the will of God where they were.

23

The vulnerable city
1Samuel 21

2 Corinthians 10.4,5 *Casting down imaginations, and every high thing that exalts itself against the knowledge of God, and bringing into captivity every thought to the obedience of Christ;* KJV Much of the fighting of a Christian takes place in his mind. In 1682 John Bunyan wrote a book called the "Holy War." It was the siege by Diabolus on a city called Mansoul with five gates. The names of the five gates were the eye gate, ear gate, nose gate, feel gate and mouth gate. It was about the fall and then the regaining of the city by Emmanuel. Fear grasps hold of the mind and can influence every area of it. Mark 4.40,41 *He asked them, "Why are you such cowards? Don't you have any faith yet?"* GW The disciples acted with cowardice[124] in the storm. Then they had a greater fear, the fear of the Lord when he stilled the storm. They "feared a great fear." This time it was the right one, it was the fear of God. Giving way to fear results in cowardice. It kept Joseph of Arimathaea from confessing Christ till the last moment. It kept the disciples locked up without being behind prison bars after the crucifixion.

---

[124] 'deilos' – fearful and faithless tend to go together. There is a sense cowardice.

Overcoming fear

Esther was afraid yet she went ahead with the plans because Mordicai challenged her... "Do not think you will escape." So she went ahead in spite of what could have been an overwhelming fear.[125] Nehemiah was afraid and so was Paul (1Cor.2.3) Moses too, (Heb12.21 & Deut.9.19) Do not worry about the fears you have, worry about giving in to those fears. *"God never was a chocolate manufacturer, and never will be. God's men are always heroes. In Scripture you can trace their giant foot-tracks down the sands of time"* Said the famous missionary C.T. Studd.[126] Paul said, *"I can do all things through Christ"* KJV Philippians 4.13 When we have a true fear of God all other fears take second place. If we must have an obsession it must be that we fear God. Someone said, "Don't take care, take risks."[127]

It was at this time David wrote Psalm 34 and it is full of references to the fear of God. The title of it says "David changed his behaviour." He must have realised his mistake. Verse four of the psalm says, *I sought the Lord and He heard me and delivered me from all my fears.* KJV. In verse six he says, *"This poor man cried and the Lord heard him."* KJV. In verse eighteen he admits to a broken heart - so he lets God deal with it. He was on the run from a king whose country he saved, having to leave his wife and friends behind. Then taking his parents to another country and living in a country he had fought against! "Broken", it was the word for being lame, a broken heart, stops us from doing anything.

Medicine and God's answer. A phobia is a persistent and unduly strong fear of a certain object or situation. Two popular treatments for it are psychoanalysis and cognitive behavioural therapy, besides pills and potions! In the first they seek to uncover repressed feelings etc. when fully understood by the patient the fear can be overcome or become manageable dealing mainly with the past. The latter

---

[125] Esther 4.14
[126] "The Chocolate Soldier" by CT Studd.
[127] Donald Coggan, quoted by Andrew White (Vicar of Baghdad)

technique deals with the present, they believe that the phobia is a learned response and so can be unlearned.

God has an answer – *Perfect love casts out fear* (1John 4.18 KJV) Talking therapies are not to be ignored, neither are pills. But if we can seek to solve our own fears and phobias with the Lord's help it saves the health service money and makes us stronger.

Titanic Survivor Eva Hart related the experience of what took place after the big ship sank. Twenty lifeboats were launched, but many people chose not to board one. Consequently, few of the rafts were filled. When the Titanic slipped from sight Lifeboat Number fourteen rowed back to the scene. It paddled through the darkness, chasing cries and seeking to rescue those in the water. The other lifeboats remained distant because they feared if they rowed back to help, too many swimmers would converge on their boat and cause it to sink. Unfortunately, we sometimes act more like those in the other nineteen boats. Fear stops us being involved in the plight of others.

Martin Luther made this interesting observation in his *Table Talk*. God and the devil take opposite tactics in regard to fear. The Lord first allows us to become afraid, that he might relieve our fears and comfort us. The devil, on the other hand, first makes us feel secure in our pride and sins, that we might later be overwhelmed with fear and despair.

24

Proof of the pudding is in the eating
Psalm 34

David was on a learning curve. When we defend ourselves we must hide behind God. He was using his wits, which we need, but we must be careful of going beyond the limits of what is right and wrong and what is endangering others. David wrote this psalm having learned a lesson. We can often advise better when we know the mistakes we have made and are able to tell others how to escape the same trap.

The Psalm is an acrostic using all except one letter of the Hebrew alphabet. The title says it was written when David went to Gath running away from King Saul. He had just been to get Goliath's sword. Unbelievably he walked into Gath, Goliath's home town, asking for political asylum with the sword of Goliath by his side. The Psalm here is very polite to David, *"changed his behaviour"* could have read, "Acted the Idiot" Though for a very good reason, his life was at stake.

When we act the fool – A fool is described as a person who lacks judgement or sense. Paul said he acted the fool when he sought to justify himself speaking about his achievements.

2Co 11:23 *Are they Christ's servants? It's insane to say it, but I'm a far better one. I've done much more work, been in prison many more times, been beaten more severely, and have faced death more often.* GW

2Co 12:11 *I have become a fool. You forced me to be one. You should have recommended me to others. Even if I'm nothing, I wasn't inferior in any way to your super-apostles.* GW

We act the fool in many different ways David did it by pretending madness to escape a dangerous situation. When he behaved as if he was mad, it was degrading. It must have been difficult and lonely in enemy territory. David was living by his wits without taking God into account.

This psalm begins with praise, it is amazing, David could praise the Lord when down and when up. He had let himself and God down but he overcame what could have been a period of self-despising. Mrs Cowman, the writer of "Streams in the Desert," went through a dark period in her life. She felt one of David's psalms impressed on her and years of praying turned to praise and praise turned to victory. Paul & Silas had great victories too when they praised the Lord in prison, (Acts 16). The crowd heard the disciples praising on the day of Pentecost. It is said that Theodore the martyr (4th Century) repeated the first verse of this psalm while he was tortured. Get praising!

David's praise turned to testimony. He was sharing what God had done for him and once again he calls on others to join him and experience what he has experienced.

William Gurnall said, "God expects to hear from you before you can expect to hear from him. If you restrain prayer, it is no wonder the mercy promised is retained." Someone said being delivered from your troubles is wonderful but deliverance from fears is even greater because you always have more fears than troubles. David was aware of the angels; Hebrews says - Hebrews 1:14. *What are all the angels? They are spirits sent to serve those who are going to receive salvation.* GW. If we had seen the angel hosts in our danger times we would have lost all fear.

Experience God for yourself. Then David says, mixing his metaphors, "Taste and see that the Lord is good." The word "taste" here - ta'*am* - means properly to try the flavour of anything. "Good" is the same word that is used for God seeing that creation was good in Genesis, God is attractive and beautiful, for all peoples. It was the last verse that St. Columba in the sixth century copied before he died. When writing a previous psalter, he caused a war because he wished to keep the copy for himself. We can understand him wanting to have his own copy, today we purchase as many copies as we wish for ourselves, just not as well illustrated as his, and perhaps not as well read as his either.

We can sample what God is like or we can have the full experience. God is not just a theory He works wonders and does not expect anyone to just take his word for it! Christianity is reliable, reasonable and real. Tasting? John 1.46 "Come see," John 4 "Come see a man." Our family came to Christ through a Scotsman who came to live in England. When he preached he often used to say about salvation, "It's better felt than 'telt'."

Many have sampled God's goodness. Go a step further, take him don't just taste him Job 12.11 But just as your tongue enjoys tasting food, your ears enjoy hearing music. "It is the difference between looking at the notes on a music score and hearing the music itself" – Francis Collins.

"Tasting stands before seeing, and trusting before knowing, for spiritual experience leads to spiritual knowledge, and not *vice versa*. David is desirous that others also should experience what he has experienced in order that they may come to know what he has come to know, viz., the goodness of God." - Keil.

Fear of God comes to David's mind, because he had just been afraid of people now he realised that God was the one to be feared. Some fail to do things because they fear the earthly consequences, others because they fear the eternal consequences. It should be because we want to keep our relationship with God right.

Seek peace and go after it he says, he knew what wars and battles were like, and as Winston Churchill knew too, "Jaw, jaw was better than war, war."

Verse fifteen tells us how to catch God's eye. Someone said the humbler a person is the less we notice him but the more God notices him.

"His ears are open unto their cry." As Peter has it, *"His ears are **into** their prayers"* *1Peter 3.12*; "To show that though their prayers are so faint and feeble that they cannot enter into the ears of the Lord of Hosts, yet that he will bow down and incline his ears *unto,* nay, *into* their prayers, their breathings." Lam.3.56 - *John Trapp.*

It may be sometimes we are the cause of our own broken hearts. As in the case of David in Psalm 51. But our broken hearts can also be caused by others. In verse 18 "contrite" is literally crushed to powder. David wanted others to experience the recovery that he had experienced. It is the sign of true conversion – you share Jesus.

King to be, David, gave this testimony: -

v4 he takes fear away.

v.6 he gets you out of trouble

v.7 delivers from danger

v.10 provides all you need

In the time of Moses, they had a taste of heaven, it was bread from heaven. Ex 16:31 *And the house of Israel called the name thereof Manna: and it was like coriander seed, white; and the taste of it was like wafers made with honey.* KJV

There are some tastes that are acquired, some tastes you like as an adult but not as a child. There are some like honey – that all seem to Like. Yet the experience of knowing God is better than any other taste it is for all ages, and all types without limitation.

25

Another psalm from the Giant's den.
Psalm 56 see also 57

David wrote this psalm at about the same time as psalm 34. It gives us a little more insight into the situation that he was in. Did they keep the sword of Goliath when he went to ask for asylum? It would appear that he ended up in prison and only escaped by feigning insanity, 1Samuel 21.13 says that David either beat on the door or scratched or even just spat on the door. Was it the palace door or city gate or prison gate?

David was praying, "Dear Lord get me out of my own mess," 1Sam.21.10-15. So when he was in Gath he was taken into custody. In Psalm 142.7 David asks God to get him out of prison. He seems to know what prison is like. Though he could have felt imprisoned while constantly on the run from Saul. If it was an actual prison no wonder, he acted mad. It is not just lions that eat people. V.1.

Two strange bedfellows, Fear and Faith, first he said he was afraid v2 then he said he wasn't v4. Doubt and faith can abide for a while, but in the end one has to win. (Hebrews 3: 12 *Take care, brothers and sisters, that none of you may have an evil, unbelieving heart that turns away from the living God.* NRSV)

There are different types of fear,

- Fear of failure, as in the case of the one talent man in the parable that Jesus told.
- Fear of unpopularity, Pilate wanted to keep in with the crowd.
- Fear of the unknown, as when Jacob left home.
- Fear of Danger phobetron; KJV translates as "fearful sight." That which strikes terror, a terror, (cause of) fright. Luke 21.11 fear and flight are connected phobos originally meant flight (as in running away)

David was being listened to. v.5 *All the day long they wrest my words: All their thoughts are against me for evil.* KJV Remember when they said about Jesus "He said that he would destroy the temple in three days."

David was being watched, v.6 *They stir up strife, they lurk, they watch my steps. As they hoped to have my life.* NRSV In a similar way the Pharisees watched Jesus intently to see what he would do that they could fault. As when he was at Bethany.

The account God keeps. Tears were often kept in bottles;[128] it was a practice the Egyptians had too. Malachi.3.16 says there is a record of godly conversations. In Revelation 20.12 God has a record of our works which might or might not be a blessing to us. David could say God kept an account of his wanderings. The NRSV has tossings as in a disturbed sleep.[129]

David Trusted God's Word. V.4 &10 There was something too: - v.12 *Thy vows are upon me, O God:* says the KJV. Many modern versions put it as David's vow. It would be nice to feel God had made a special vow to David. Even if the translation of the AV and the "Message" are wrong. The Lord has made a vow to us and he will never let us down.

---

[128] This is a normal wine skin here in Psalm 56.8. David was crying a lot of tears!
[129] See Word Biblical Commentary. It is a moving to and fro.

From a quote book: -

- You can expect from me everything save fear or recantation. I shall not flee, much less recant. I will go to Worms if there were as many devils there as there are tiles on the roofs of the houses - Martin Luther
- I have looked in the faces of many angry men, and yet have not been afraid above measure - John Knox
- Courage is that quality of mind which enables men to encounter danger or difficulty with firmness, or without fear or depression of spirits. The highest degree of courage is seen in the person who is most fearful but refuses to capitulate to it - J. Oswald Sanders
- Lord, the task is impossible for me but not for Thee. Lead the way and I will follow. Why should I fear? I am on a Royal Mission. I am in the service of the King of Kings - Mary Slessor, beginning her remarkable missionary career in Calabar (now part of modern Nigeria)
- When you're accustomed to standing before God, kings don't matter much. Big potentates are just small potatoes when you have been standing in the presence of the Most High - Vance Havner
- Courage is being the only one who knows you're afraid - Anonymous

In 1934, Adolf Hitler summoned German church leaders to his Berlin office to berate them for insufficiently supporting his programmes. Pastor Martin Niemoller explained that he was concerned only for the welfare of the church and of the German people. Hitler snapped, "You confine yourself to the church. I'll take care of the German people." Niemoller replied, "You said that 'I will take care of the German people.' But we too, as Christians and churchmen, have a responsibility toward the German people. That responsibility was entrusted to us by God, and neither you nor anyone in this world has the power to take it from us." He was unafraid of that evil man, later spending a considerable time in prison.

David was wanting to make sure that God had a memory of all that he had gone through. Nehemiah too wished for God to remember all he the good he had done and the bad that others had been involved in. Thinking back over my life it might be good if God does not remember everything, let us say like Nehemiah, "Remember me for good." We will leave the behaviour of others in God's hands. Though Paul did not hesitate to ask for God's help in certain problems with people. 2Ti 4:14 *Alexander the coppersmith did me much evil: the Lord reward him according to his works.* KJV

26

The Cave of Adullam
1Samuel 22

They were rough, tough, needy and troubled, they were a handful that joined David. Often David found he was not fully in control. They stayed together at Adullam It was not far from the site of Israel's victory over Goliath. Adullam means justice of the people.

The Church is like David's cave at Adullam, made up of all sorts. We had a move of God in our church. People that came to the Lord included bouncers and boxers, murderers and minders. It was a time when people found a new way to live, repentant yet rejoicing.

In Britain there is a sweet made by Bassett's called Liquorice Allsorts, there is a story how they came to be. In 1899 Charlie Thompson, a sales representative, was said to have dropped a tray of liquorice sweet samples he was about to show a client in Leicester, England. They had been in their separate compartments the fall resulted in mixing up the various varieties of the liquorice sweets. Before he could re-arrange them, the shop keeper was attracted to the new creation. He ordered the mixed sweets and as a result the company began to mass-produce the Allsorts as their popularity grew. They took off as Liquorice Allsorts. Christian Churches should be Christian Allsorts made up of all different types of people to have all of the same class, intellectual level or ethnic origin is not a complete church.

One of the last temptations Srewtape tried on the new Christian was to get him to go to another church that had more people of his type attending.[130] After I had completed a funeral for one of the ladies at our church, a friend of the deceased was telling me of the professors, surgeons and lawyers at her church in the city centre and how intellectual their minister was. Then she added that he was so deep that sometimes she could not understand him. We need an "all-sorts church." David could cope because he was a "man's man." If we cannot be on equal footing to all people, showing respect to all, then we cannot be part of the Christian Church.

The company Jesus kept was called into question, Matthew 9.11 *When the Pharisees saw this, they said to his disciples, "Why does your teacher eat with tax collectors and sinners?"* NRSV The quality of education of his disciples was questioned, Ac 4:13 *Now when they saw the boldness of Peter and John, and perceived that they were unlearned and ignorant men, they marvelled; and they took knowledge of them, that they had been with Jesus.* KJV The knowledge of Jesus the Saviour was questioned, John 7:15 *And the Jews marvelled, saying, "how does this man know letters, having never learned?"* KJV.

Paul had to put the Corinthians in their place on one occasion, 1Co 1:26 *Brothers and sisters, consider what you were when God called you to be Christians. Not many of you were wise from a human point of view. You were not in powerful positions or in the upper social classes.* GW.

After the day of Pentecost and Peter visiting Cornelius the Christian Church became international in character and in worship.

Someone wrote: -

> If you come to God as a boaster comes.
> In the pride of your own way,
> Then the God of Grace will hide His face,
> And send you empty away.
> If you come to God as a Beggar comes,
> With the plea of your bitter need
> Then the King of Kings will give good things,
> And make you rich indeed.

---

[130] The Screwtape letters by CS Lewis

How did David feel? If psalm 142 came to him then he felt as if he was on his own. In one verse of that psalm he could say that no one cared for his soul. The first days in the cave alone would have been bleak, homesick for Bethlehem would be an understatement, but he could not go there. Slowly the family came and joined him. Yet he might have written the psalm a little later because we can be among friends and family yet feel as if we are carrying the burdens alone. David would be grateful for every person that came to him at Adullam yet he would experience the loneliness of leadership.

It was the joining of a family again. No longer were the brothers at loggerheads. They were one with David, either out of love or necessity. Most likely necessity, because he took his father to Moab. Believing his enemy's enemy was his friend.[131] It was perhaps also because one grandmother was a Moabite too.

See psalm 57 as well as this psalm. When David was praying to God in the cave, He was low, in danger he said it was like fighting lions. Sometime later when people were coming to him from Benjamin, Gad and Manassah while David was at Ziklag the writer of Chronicles could refer to the people as the Army of God.[132] What a transformation. The ragtag army was developing. Just like the vision of John in Revelation, from a small group of ignorant and unlearned disciples came a host beyond number.[133]

---

[131] 1Sa 14:47 So Saul took the kingdom over Israel, and fought against all his enemies on every side, against Moab, and against the children of Ammon, and against Edom, and against the kings of Zobah, and against the Philistines: and whithersoever he turned himself, he vexed them. AV. See 1Samuel 22.3 David went from there to Mizpeh of Moab. He said to the king of Moab, "Please let my father and mother come to you, until I know what God will do for me." NRSV

[132] 1Chronicles 12.22

[133] Revelation 7:9 After these things I saw a large crowd from every nation, tribe, people, and language. No one was able to count how many people there were. They were standing in front of the throne and the lamb. They were wearing white robes, holding palm branches in their hands, GW

27

Alone
Psalm 142

Even if you feel you are alone and no one cares for you, you are not alone. Famous people film stars, singers, and sports personalities have often said that they often feel alone. Those in the Bible said it too. I remember living in a bedsit in North London with little money. It was my first pastorate; the evenings were lonely. One song I had on a record had the words, "I'm not alone although I'm often lonely." It did not bring me much and perhaps not any comfort. The theory of the presence of God I knew and appreciated, but loneliness is hard to bear just the same.

David said it when he had to live in a cave Psalm 142.4 *Look on my right hand and see - there is no one who takes notice of me; no refuge remains to me; no one cares for me.* NRSV. The right hand was the side a friend or advocate stood; look he said there is no one there. There is no one that has taken any notice of me, no one that has come looking for me.

The apostle Paul found it too. 2Ti 4:16. *At my first defence no one came to my support, but all deserted me. May it not be counted against them!* NRSV

Job knew it. Job 19.13-15 *"My brothers stay far away from me. My friends are complete strangers to me. My relatives and my closest friends have stopped coming. My house guests have forgotten me. My breath offends my wife. I stink to my own children.*GW

The Hebrew word for soul (nephesh) means, *"what you are to yourself."* Not how you appear to others. Many people have smiled pleasantly on their way to commit suicide. Most of us can put on a good show but God deals with us as we really are. He deals with the heart.

In a survey of the quality of children's lives they asked subjective questions to the children, such as did they feel happy? God asks you the question too.

Do you feel happy about yourself?

Is there a feeling that you would like to achieve more?

Would you like to be more cheerful?

Do you feel guilt for some of the things you have done?

Do you have a complaint that you would like to bring to God?

A preacher once asked the congregation to take off their masks by moving their hand over their face. What face have you got on? A brave one? A stiff upper lip one? Or are you one of those who lets people know how you are by the look on your face?

No one cared what I was like deep down, said David. Every Christian should care for the wellbeing of others. It is why we give to the needy; it is why we send to the missionaries. Because we need to let people know that we care for their soul!

Job had a flash of inspiration. Job 19.25. *For I know that my Redeemer lives, and that at the last he will stand upon the earth*; NRSV

If only they had known about Jesus. (Jesus had to die alone, he knew what it was like). Paul said in the next verse to the previous quote in 2Timothy *"Only the Lord stood with me."* The hymn writer Weigle wrote: -

No one ever cared for me like Jesus,
No other friend so kind as he.
No one else could take the sin and darkness from me.
O how much he cares for me.

Charles Weigle wrote this after a sad experience – he was an evangelist, one day he arrived home and his wife left him a note saying she was leaving him. She did not want to be the wife of an evangelist. For years after this he did not write any songs, five years later he met her in the street. That night or soon afterwards he went down to the lake walked to the end of the dock and considered throwing himself off. God spoke to him, he went home and the words of the song came to him as fast as he could write. Although he wrote a thousand songs this was his most famous.

God is in the soul caring business; Jesus is known as the good shepherd. Every Christian should be in the soul caring work. Jesus died for us. The shepherd is not a sheep dog, they just round sheep up, the shepherd cares, heals, searches out, he is looking for you!

There is a spider that builds its nest in the branch of a small tree or bush. In this delicate enclosure the baby spiders are hatched. If the nest is disturbed in any way, the little spiders will all rush out in fright. At once the mother goes to their side. She is alerted to their potential danger in a unique manner. Each of the young ones has a thin silky strand attached to it, and all of these threads are joined to the body of the mother. When an enemy threatens the babies, they naturally scurry off, giving their lines a sharp tug. The adult spider instantly feels this. Within seconds she pulls them back to the nest where they are protected from harm.

Mary Slessor, was a missionary to what is now Nigeria. She would often rescue babies who were in danger and dying, and often the infants filled her home by the dozens. How to care for them through the night became a problem, especially when one of them stirred and cried. Mary learned to tie a string to each little hammock, she lay in bed at night, and pulled the strings as each baby needed soothing.

The prophet Hosea says that we are linked to God with cords of love, cords that cannot be broken. The gentle cords of His eternal love bind all our hearts and hurts to Him.

It is the real "you" that God deals with, not the surface "you" or the outward "you" nor the show off "you", but the genuine, real "you". That is why Jesus came, to take away the guilt and the power of sin - give us a fulfilled and happy life. Will you let him be the one He is seeking you out, he has noticed you and he will stand by your side now and always, even when you are in the wrong.

George Matheson was only fifteen when he was told he was losing what little poor eyesight he had. Not to be denied, Matheson continued straight-away with his plans to enrol in the University of Glasgow, and his determination led to his graduating at age nineteen. But as he pursued graduate studies in theology for Christian ministry he became blind. His sister joined ranks beside him, learning Greek and Hebrew to assist him in his studies. He pressed faithfully on. But his spirit collapsed when his fiancée, unwilling to be married to a blind man, broke their engagement and returned his ring. He never married, and the pain of that rejection never fully left him. Years later, as a well-loved pastor in Scotland, his sister came to him, announcing her engagement. He rejoiced with her, but his mind went back to his own heartache. He consoled himself in thinking of God's love which is never limited, never conditional, never withdrawn, and never uncertain. Out of this experience he wrote the hymn: -

> *O love that will not let me go,*
> *I rest my weary soul in thee;*
> *I give thee back the life I owe,*
> *That in thine ocean depths it flow*
> *May richer, fuller be.*

A prisoner of circumstances. V7 *Bring me out of prison, so that I may give thanks to your name. The righteous will surround me, for you will deal bountifully with me.* NRSV

He was not at that moment in control – others seemed to be pulling the strings. There is an overall providence. God is above them all.

There is no circumstance that can keep you down – Paul said often knocked down never knocked out. It was not the result of David's wrong doing it was a result of the jealousy of King Saul. It was like prison for him. There was going to be an end to this situation one day! Yet some of the most exciting times of his life and some of the most wonderful Psalms were written when he was in those caves and fleeing for his life.

The fainting man. v.3 *When my spirit is faint, you know my way. In the path where I walk they have hidden a trap for me.* NRSV

Jonah knew about it. *Jonah 2:7 "As my life was slipping away, I remembered the LORD. My prayer came to you in your holy temple.* GW

Others too experienced exhaustion. Psalm 107:5 *Hungry and thirsty, their soul fainted in them.* KJV

Esau slipped up when he was exhausted Genesis 25:29 *Once, Jacob was preparing a meal when Esau, exhausted, came in from outdoors.* GW The smell of food lost him his birth right.

There were three problems David had – One, he was worn out. Secondly, there was no one to help. Thirdly, there were enemies about.

The solution to "burn-out". It is no good saying it has happened to others but it wont to us, we must know the way out of the dark. It is to be built up with a time of waiting on God. But not being idle, it is meditating and seeking the Lord, reading His word, having times of prayer till you have been refuelled. Get the strength of God not your own strength.

Isaiah 40:29 He giveth power to the faint; and to them that have no might he increases strength. 30 Even the youths shall faint and be weary, and the young men shall utterly fall:

Isaiah 40:31 But they that wait upon the LORD shall renew their strength; they shall mount up with wings as eagles; they shall run, and not be weary; and they shall walk, and not faint. KJV

David put it this way: - Psalm 61.2 *From the end of the earth I call to you, when my heart is faint. Lead me to the rock that is higher than I; for you are my refuge, a strong tower against the enemy. Let me abide in your tent forever, find refuge under the shelter of your wings.* KJV

28

The razor sharp tongue
Psalm 52 1Sa 21:1-9 & 1Sa 22:6-23

This Psalm considers the possibility of evil, its strength, and source and its effect.

There was trouble looming, there was a problem in the country. Jesse was afraid of Saul when Samuel came to anoint David. Now the priests were scared. This was not a peaceful country. It was run by fear, fear of Saul's reprisals. David had been on the run for three days or so, as Nob was near Gibeah,[134] where Saul's palace was thought to be, he must have been to other places seeking for a safe place to hide.

There could not have been too much worship of God or Saul, who was always afraid of people's reactions, would not have dared to kill eighty-five priests of the Lord. David though, was a regular at the house of God long before he was in trouble.[135]

---

[134] It was about 3 miles north of Jerusalem. This is not accepted by all historians.
[135] 1Samuel 22.15 Is today the first time that I have inquired of God for him? By no means! Do not let the king impute anything to his servant or to any member of my father's house; for your servant has known nothing of all this, much or little." NSRV

Careless talk costs lives; said the WWII posters. Doeg could have saved the lives of many people by his silence. Gossip wounds. The untameable part of the person, said James, is the tongue. David said the tongue was a sharp razor. The writer of Proverbs had much to say about talk including: - Proverbs 16.27 *A scoundrel plots evil, and his speech is like a scorching fire. A perverse man stirs up dissension, and a gossip separates close friends.* NRSV It is not what you know, or what you say, it is to whom you say it. Will they gossip about it? Will they act upon it?

Doeg was an Edomite at an Israelite place of worship, but was he really there to keep a look out for David coming? It was a place David frequented. It was said that Doeg was keeping an oath. It could be that he was genuinely worshipping the Lord and delivering sacrificial animals. Little is known of their god or gods it could be that they too worshipped Yahweh.[136]

Saul tried to defeat David when he had no need. He was seeking a pre-emptive strike. Even though Jesus knew the wickedness of Judas he did not seek to pre-empt his attack on him. Don't knock anyone down because they might attack you! David prayed that the wicked would fall into their own net. Leave it with God.

In verse one of psalm 52 the word boast is used, it could be more "self-satisfaction" Doeg was feeling please with himself.

The love of evil can be addictive. People can enjoy doing wicked things; in the New Testament it covers the speaking about it, or drawing attention to it, being the cause of it without being seen. Provocation is a terrible thing as in the case of Jezebel. Evil was seen in the Nazi Party; Himmler was responsible for the death of over ten million people yet he was able to sleep at night. Then after the war many committed equal evil upon innocent German civilians in retaliation. Evil crosses countries and continents, times and generations.

---

[136] See "An Edomite Joban Text. With a Biblical Joban Parallel,." by Victor Sasson *Zeitschrift fur die Alttestamentliche Wissenschaft* 117 (Berlin, 2006),

It was the final end of the wicked that was seen by David not the in-between time of prosperity. Sometimes we need to look further ahead than we are doing.

Saul and his supporters were living in the strength of possessions, but not in the strength of God. He did not seek to obtain his followers by claims of justice but by the wealth they could acquire by going his way. "Can David give you these things?" Was his challenge. We must always have our support from God alone. But some see something deeper in Psalm 52.7 more than just wealth, the word can be translated "craving or desire" this is the source of evil. Fame and Fortune were on offer and so many of us have carvings for these. Let us always check the motive of our actions and those of people we follow.

While seeking his own safety David put others in danger. The deaths of the priests and their families was due in part to David. He felt responsible for the massacre and had attempted to mitigate the problem for Ahimelech when he saw Doeg by telling a lie. Ahimelech would have been safer putting his lot in with David there and then. But he had a responsibility to all people and that was greater than personal safety. It was the book "Uncle Tom's Cabin," that had been said to be partly responsible for the American Civil War, and so Harriet Beecher Stowe must have felt terrible for the death of so many people yet the final outcome was good. We sometimes wonder how can so many people die so tragically, did they fulfil the purposes of God? The answer can only be in the eternal realm. We want our lives to count for God. After a tragic mining disaster in Durham, England, Bishop Handley Moule went to see the grieving families. He showed them one of the old bookmarks that were woven in those days. On one side it said God is Love. On the other was a tangle of coloured threads. We see the tangled threads of life at the moment. One day we will see the other side saying, "God is Love."

The present pain of grief is only known by those who go through it. Often the grieving have said to me in almost identical words, "I never knew it felt like this." Every day millions are discovering the same pain of bereavement, due to war, disease, old age and accidents. Abiathar was the lone survivor of a massacre of men, women and children of the priestly families. David could offer him safety but the trauma was his that God alone could deal with.

Yet the real cause of the massacre was just words, the order of Saul. Words just words but with such evil consequences. Jesus said all sorts of evil things come out of our mouths. It was said that Henry II said, "Who will rid me of this troublesome priest?" So off went some knights to kill Thomas a' Beckett. Words can make alive and words can kill.

29

Principles to live by.
1Samuel 23

We have talked about friendship and fear and how that David, though fearless in fighting, gave in to fear. In these episodes of David's life there are bright spots and dark spots.

David's men felt that they were not strong enough to help a beleaguered town. God knew otherwise. When someone is in trouble we must ask, "If we do not help who will?" Christians are here to help the downtrodden and the disenfranchised. If we don't who will? The writer of Proverbs put it like this: - *If you faint in the day of adversity, your strength being small; if you hold back from rescuing those taken away to death, those who go staggering to the slaughter; if you say, "Look, we did not know this," does not he who weighs the heart perceive it? Does not he who keeps watch over your soul know it? And will he not repay all according to their deeds?*[137] No Christian has a right to pass by on the other side.

Sir Nicholas Winton was born of Jewish parents in Britain. In 1938 he went to Prague and rescued 669 Jewish children from certain death by the Nazi regime in Czechoslovakia. Fifty years later his wife discovered a list of all the children he had rescued. Only then

---

[137] Proverbs 24.10,11,12 NRSV

the world found out the story. The queen knighted him and the rest is history. One man, what a story? Don't say you cannot and don't say you did not know. David was not the only one to check more than once that God said, "Do it." They did it and rescued a city.

Relationships based on favours are rocky relationships.

The town of Keilah were in debt to David and his warriors. He and his men had saved them from destruction, yet they were about to let David down. They were not prepared to return the favour; they were cowardly in their actions. Paul made use of personal debt when he wrote to Philemon v.19 *"you owe me your own self!"* Yet David found it did not work too well for him. "He has returned me evil for good," he said about a later experience.

Do a deed because it needs to be done**.** Jesus amplified this when He said *"Ask a person to a meal who cannot return the favour."* No one is in debt to you, you are in debt to them![138] Paul put it this way: - Romans 13:8 *Pay your debts as they come due. However, one debt you can never finish paying is the debt of love that you owe each other. The one who loves another person has fulfilled Moses' teachings.* GW. Jonathan owed David nothing yet sought out his friendship 1Samuel 23.16. Write off all debts that you think you are owed by others. Once I supported a person who was wanting a position of importance. A year or so later he let me down. I remonstrated with him reminding him of the help I gave him. His reply was simple and truthful, He said, "I never asked you to." That was right he hadn't asked for my help, we do things, and should not expect favours in return, we do them for the Lord and because they are right.

1Samuel 18.1 used the word "*knit together."* David summed up his relationship with Jonathan in 2Samuel 1.26 in the time of Jonathan's death. *I am heartbroken over you, my brother Jonathan. You were my great delight. Your love was more wonderful to me than the love of women.* GW

---

[138] Romans 1.14 I have an obligation to those who are civilized and those who aren't, to those who are wise and those who aren't. GW

Relationships that strengthen you in God. 1Samuel 23.16 *Saul's son Jonathan came to David at Horesh. He strengthened David's faith in the LORD.* GW This is the relationship that counts. Does the person that I am with draw me closer to God? Do they direct me in the right direction? Do they increase my faith? Once the people of Keilah had all they needed from David they would desert him. Some can suck us dry till we have almost no energy either spiritual or physical left.

If David was strengthened by Jonathan it implies that he was in need of encouragement. How did he strengthen him? Perhaps by reminding him of the past presence of God in Jonathan's own victory (1Sam.14.) Or of David's victory over Goliath. Of the yet to be fulfilled promise of Kingship for David. The Hebrew word (CHAZAQ) 'strengthen' means to bind fast. Get friendships that bind your hands to the hand of God. It was a word used to repair ruins as in 2Kings 12:8 *And the priests consented to receive no more money of the people, neither to **repair** the breaches of the house.* KJV Jonathan gave David a telescope to look to the future fulfilment of the promises of God. He showed him a view of the future hope that was still to be. Maybe too they sang one or two of David's psalms.

Paul spoke of personal encouragement by others as bringing good news. *Outwardly we have conflicts, and inwardly we have fears. Yet God, who comforts those who are dejected, comforted us when Titus arrived. We were comforted not only by his arrival but also by learning about the comfort he had received while he was with you.*[139] We sometimes say it is faith not feelings that count. Yet emotions are part of us. We not only trust God but we also love God. God uses our emotions to speak to us. Sorrow to correct us, joy to lift us up, love to encourage us. There must always be an opportunity in any church service to deal with our emotional response to God. We say people are downcast when they are sad, we might say when we are humiliated, "I feel so small." Paul said the same about himself. God can be touched

---

[139] 2Corinthians 7.5-7 GW

with how we feel. Hebrews 4:15 *For we have not a high priest which cannot be touched with the feeling of our infirmities;* KJV It was the sorrow of the Hebrew slaves in Egypt that reached God, not so much their prayers.[140]

---

[140] Ex 3:7 *And the LORD said, I have surely seen the affliction of my people which are in Egypt, and have heard their cry by reason of their taskmasters; for I know their sorrows;* KJV That was why he sent Moses.

30

David's Prop
Psalms 54

But surely, God is my helper; the Lord is the upholder of my life, NRSV says David in verse four. Upholder or prop suggests Strong's Hebrew Dictionary. He had no hang up saying he needed a prop to help him through life.

The Ziphims were the inhabitants of Ziph. Which was a little further south of Keilah the city that David had rescued from the Philistines. 1Sam.23.19 *Then some Ziphites went up to Saul at Gibeah and said, "David is hiding among us in the strongholds of Horesh, on the hill of Hachilah, which is south of Jeshimon."* NRSV.

They put the law of the land before the law of God. It was the mistake that many made in the past, especially in times of persecution. If the law of the land is against the law of God, then God's law comes first. David might have been on the wanted posters dead or alive, but he had not done anything to deserve death. Therefore, that law could be defied, because he would not have received a fair trial. Acts 4.19 *But Peter and John answered them, "Whether it is right in God's sight to listen to you rather than to God, you must judge;* KJV. Peter set the record straight. Are you to listen to man or God? We believe that Jesus Christ is the Head of the Church and we listen to him first and foremost.

At one time Saul and David were living together in the palace, now David was hiding from him. Yet David said the Lord is the one I lean on, he props me up. It was God he knew would eventually show him to be in the right.

Paul could write, 2Tim.1.15 *You are aware that all who are in Asia have turned away from me, including Phygelus and Hermogenes.* NRSV John experienced something similar, 3John 10 *So if I come, I will call attention to what he is doing in spreading false charges against us. And not content with those charges, he refuses to welcome the friends, and even prevents those who want to do so and expels them from the church.* NRSV

David's friendships came from unexpected sources, such as Jonathan, his enemy's son! Jonathan had no jealousy, unlike his father. He had no high ambition that would hurt him. They both had a similar agenda, the growth of the fledgling nation of Israel.

In the New Testament brotherly love is often mentioned. It was the love of brothers for one another. (Philadelphia!) The growth of the Gospel is helped by brotherly love. Paul was most likely a difficult character, yet still had friends. It is not living in one another's pockets, but is digging deep into our pockets when the other is in need.

It was said that Julius Caesar, when being stabbed by Brutus his friend, said, "You also Brutus?" and made no attempt to defend himself. Later in Psalm 55.12-14 David relives the horror of the treachery of Ahithophel. See 2Samuel 15:31 *And it was told David, "Ahithophel is among the conspirators with Absalom." And David said, "O LORD, I pray thee, turn the counsel of Ahithophel into foolishness."* KJV

After all the hurts and problems, he turned to the Lord and asked Him to deal with it. Psalm 55.22 *Cast your burden on the LORD, and he will sustain you; he will never permit the righteous to be moved.* NRSV See Psalm.54.5 in CEV it says, *"Be my faithful friend."* (*In your truth* KJV)

The people of Keilah were failing to support David in his time of need. The Ziphites were a step down from that, they were prepared to betray him and no doubt obtain a reward as well. No wonder he asked for wings of a dove to fly away. One missionary was being encouraged to leave the area where he was in Columbia. He replied that the safest place was in the will of God. Do not fear the place where you are if you are doing the plan God has for you. That is where the Lord has the angels stationed.

31

An embarrassing encounter
1Samuel 24

Close encounters.

The use of 'feet' in the authorised version is a direct translation of the Hebrew. It says Saul uncovered his feet when he went to the cave. It is a euphemism that meant he went to the toilet. We might say bathroom for toilet. David was hiding in the very cave where Saul was going to the toilet. It would seem unless there was another exit to the cave this was an exceptionally dangerous place to hide as well as being rather revolting, which could have been the reasoning behind choosing such a hiding place.

True Relationships will let you keep your conscience.

David's conscience was more tender that his soldiers, 1Sam 24.5 *But then David's conscience bothered him* GW, the moment you compromise your conscience to keep a relationship you are on rocky ground. David would not kill Saul, he stuck to his belief and also kept his comrades on his side too.

The use of the word "father," when David was speaking to Saul, and Saul calling him "son," is a touching tribute to a time past. For David was his son by marriage. But note the difference, when

Jonathan and David made a promise to one another is called a covenant. Saul demanded from David an oath he was showing superiority of position. There was no return gesture from Saul, he had nothing to give.[141] It was a promise David partially broke. It is interesting that many of the clay tablets sent from one king to another in this era address the recipients similarly as a son to a father. If they were addressing equals, they would refer to the other person as brother.[142]

The problem of retribution and vengeance.

David had grasped that, though Saul was disobedient to God, he had not yet been deposed by Him. It was not in his hands to interfere with God's plans either. Yet in the case of Nabal David behaved as though he could act with impunity. All people are equal before God yet David was not treating Nabal as an equal to Saul. Another sin would have been added to David's list if it had not been for the quick action of Abigail. Vengeance is a matter that is in the hands of God. We must never attempt it. Romans 12.19 Psalm 94.1

The keeping power of God.

- *Will God keep us from Physical danger?* Someone said, "I am immortal till I have finished the work God has given me to do." Very often he protects us but it is not a long life we are promised but a fulfilled life.
- *Will God keep us from Moral danger?* Jesus taught us to pray, "Lead us not into temptation but deliver us from evil." There is no doubt we have been delivered from times when we might have fallen.
- *Will the Lord keep us spiritually?* Jesus promised this, "None shall pluck them out of my hands." There is nothing that can separate us from the love of God!

---

[141] 1Samuel 24.21

[142] In these letters, (royal letters) the kings involved often referred to each other as relatives, calling one another "brother" or "father/son," even though usually they were not actually related, see Armarna letters. 1177 BC The Year Civilisation Collapsed, E.H Cline, Princeton. Page 54.

32

Don't spoil the Coronation day
1Samuel 25

Perhaps our greatest sins are when we retaliate against another that has sinned against us.

When we are accused of something that might or might not be true we often become defensive. Paul one time admitted he did that. He felt that others were being given more credit than they deserved and he was being ignored. So he did a little boasting himself. *2Co 12:11 I have become a fool. You forced me to be one. You should have recommended me to others. Even if I'm nothing, I wasn't inferior in any way to your super-apostles.* GW.

There are times when we can become insular. We feel that having been hurt previously, we keep our distance, and do not allow our self to become close to people to avoid the possibility of being upset again. This is not the way. We can never love if we do not make ourselves available to all and sundry, and that includes those who will give us grief.

David was about to take the worst option of all, vengeance. He was doing nothing when Saul was trying to kill him, yet was going to kill a host of innocent people just because he had been insulted by Nabal and had not been paid for protecting the man's flocks.

Overreaction is common to us all. I always try to leave things a day or two if I am upset about a matter. This has an advantage; we can look at things from another person's view point. We can consider whether we are taking things to heart more than we should. And ask ourselves, "Have we made similar mistakes?" There is a further big advantage if the matter can cool down, we can seek to see the best way to solve the problem.

Though some matters can be dealt with after a period of time, there are situations that require immediate intervention. Abigail knew this was one of those times. There was technically no reason for her to intervene. It was the request of a worker for her help. Abigail means a "father's joy," she brought a great deal of that to others as well, their lives were saved. There have been times when I have failed to act with haste and it can become more difficult to repair broken relationships and other problems later on. Wisdom is to know which situations require involvement straight away, and those that are best left to let tempers cool. Often people can see more clearly when the mist of anger has cleared. Abigail did not need divine revelation when to act, it was obvious haste was the order of the day.

The wisdom of Abigail 25.29

"Bound in the bundle of the living in the care of the Lord your God." NRSV God has you padded with cotton wool. If you are dropped, you won't break she was saying. It is common in Eastern countries to bundle valuable things together so that they can be taken around with you. Perhaps we could say God has you in his hand luggage. Keil says it is not talking about eternal life, but Jewish people often put this on their grave stones. Whatever it actually refers to, it is being protected like a delicate object for transportation. In some countries (such as India) they might say – The lover is bound in, "The Bundle of Love."

The keeping power of Jesus is often neglected, we so often want to challenge people to continue in the faith and love of God, rather than assuring people of the infinite love of God who will look after them. "None shall pluck you out of my hand," said Jesus. Colossians 3.3 *You have died, and your life is hidden with Christ in God.* NRSV

The Jews often referred to the dead believers being hidden beneath God's throne – see Revelation.6.9. The actions of Abigail had a similar effect to those of Jonathan. While she kept David from making a terrible mistake, Jonathan kept him trusting God for the final outcome.

The two points here are: -

- We must let the encouragement of others bind us to God and we must encourage others.
- We must appreciate that we are bound in God's protection.

33

Resentment's Rush
1Samuel 25.33

There is an emotion that usually turns to sin within seconds. It is a sin that destroys individuals, families, churches, workplaces and whole countries. It is not one of the so called seven deadly sins. Nor is the emotion listed as one of the six basic emotions of life. But it is up there with the big ones.

1Samuel 25:*10 But Nabal answered David's servants, "Who is David? Who is the son of Jesse? There are many servants today who are breaking away from their masters.* NRSV

The emotion that turns to sin is called resentment. The Bible calls it Bitterness.

A psychologist said: - *The inability to overcome resentment probably constitutes the single most devastating impediment to repairing a disintegrating intimate connection, family rift, or severed friendship.*[143] He understated it.

David was faced with two trigger points that initiate resentment. The first injustice - he had looked after Nabal's workers and kept

---

[143] Mark Sichel.

them safe. yet there was nothing in return. Secondly he had been insulted. Nabal called him a runaway slave.

David was not the sort to let the grass grow under his feet. His resentment was only going to last an hour or so. There was no cooling off period with David. He was dealing with it immediately. Just not in the right way. Most let it fester for years and it affects their life later. Some are abused and bullied when young and they take it out on others as they grow older. So reproducing a whole cycle of bitterness and resentment all over again. Because they did not deal with their resentment when it happened.

We might categorise David's emotion initially as resentment, that led to anger then hatred and then to vengeance. Can we use the word "resentment" when it is a feeling that is just an hour or two old? One definition is: - *Resentment refers to the mental process of repetitively replaying a feeling, and the events leading up to it, that goads or angers us.*[144] Yet we can say to someone, "I resent that comment you have made about me." Which is an immediate response to a negative comment about ourselves. Bitterness is often the Bible word that means resentment.

In the story of Ruth Naomi was saying that she was resentful towards God and perhaps to people as well because of her life experiences.[145] Call me Mara she said when returning to Bethlehem. The emotion David felt in his spirit did result in anger, but it was because he had been insulted. We can be angry without sin but David had sin in full measure over this insult.

It has been suggested that resentment can only be held against a superior.[146] Yet these feelings of being badly done by, or being defamed, causing a resentful feeling within us are caused by people from all walks of life. David's ill feeling toward Nabal was overcome by Abigail's generosity to him and his men and her obeisance to

---

[144] Mark Sichel in Psychology today March 2011
[145] Ruth 1.20 Ruth 1.20 And she said unto them, "Call me not Naomi, call me Mara: for the Almighty has dealt very bitterly with me." KJV
[146] Robert C Solomon, see Wikipedia under resentment.

him. There is a better way to overcome our feelings of resentment. It will not always be that we are compensated for hurt feelings.

The Damage of Bitterness. When Abner had been defeated in the civil war in Israel he called out to Joab: - *"Is the sword to keep devouring forever? Do you not know that the end will be bitter? How long will it be before you order your people to turn from the pursuit of their kinsmen?"* NRSV 2Samuel 2.26. Abner knew the long term damage that resentment would cause. It was said that one of the causes of the rise of Hitler and Nazism in Germany was the underlying resentment against the treaty of Versailles after World War 1.

If resentment can cause the world to go to war then it can cause devastation in families, workplaces, churches and individuals.

Nelson Mandela put it like this: *"Resentment is like drinking poison and then hoping it will kill your enemies."*

Ezekiel speaks of Edom holding a grudge for many years. Ezekiel 35.5 *Because you cherished an ancient enmity,* NRSV *"I'm doing this because you've kept this age-old grudge",* (The Message Bible). This is something that can last for centuries within the folklore of a country.

The Hebrew words for bitter or bitterness such as mara have connection with the taste of the herbs or wormwood as well as gall and snake venom.[147] When we come to the New Testament, the Greek "pikros" for bitterness has a different angle on it, as well as bitter it has the idea of being sharp or pointed.

We often need help to overcome resentment. The writer to the Hebrews saw that resentment was a dangerous emotion and that it would affected more than the one person with it. Hebrews 12:15 *Looking diligently lest any man fail of the grace of God; lest any root of bitterness springing up trouble you, and thereby many be defiled;* KJV It is a situation that could need others to help you through it. It is the work of a pastor or an overseer as well as the

---

[147] See Job 16.13 or Job 20.14

victim of ill treatment. It is not the attitude to say, "They have a problem leave them to it." We must help people through a feeling of bitterness or resentment. The grace of God must be applied in liberal quantities. Abigail was able to correct an injustice and "grovel" at David's feet. The vast majority of cases will not be corrected like that, and people will often have to live with the cause of their bitterness. The grace of God is sufficient to see us through. "My grace is sufficient."

In Hebrews 12.15 the word translated "fail" means to be left behind, see Hebrews 4.1. God wants us to be sure that we are not straggling at the back. Resentment is not initially a sinful emotion, but it becomes one when it affects our actions and thoughts resulting from it. Sarcasm toward others or violence can result from failing to deal with it. It could be the number one killer of a life of blessing. It nearly destroyed David, someone saw that he was going to have a problem to deal with it and the came to his aid, and so saved many lives.

The writer of Hebrews gave us the way to overcome without getting compensated for the cause of our resentment. Hebrews 12. *Think about Jesus, who endured opposition from sinners, so that you don't become tired and give up.* GW The KJV says "consider him." The Greek word means to think over and over again. One look at all Jesus went through will not do it. We forget too quickly.

Resentment towards God. If we can be resentful to people our biggest problem is when we are resentful to God. When Hezekiah thought he was dying in the prime of his life he became resentful. Afterwards he said: - Isaiah 38. 17 *Surely it was for my welfare that I had great bitterness:*[148] *but you have held back my life from the pit of destruction, for you have cast all my sins behind your back.* NRSV

- Hezekiah was facing death bitterly. When God gave him another 15years the bitterness left.
- A minister felt resentment towards God when he went blind. He said Jesus didn›t know what it was like. Then he

---

[148] mar mar could perhaps be translated, I was bitterly bitter.

remembered that Jesus was blindfolded with evil people all around, Jesus knew.
- A grave stone at a Cemetery near where I live said, «Justice was her life, but there is no justice in death.» - death can be bitter.
- In the story of Ruth, Naomi was saying that she was resentful towards God and perhaps to people as well because of her life experiences. Call me Mara she said when returning to Bethlehem.

Life does not seem to be fair. Lazy people succeed, bad people often get away with evil things. Some say they get closure when a person that has harmed them is gaoled. Not so. We believe that God will work all things together for good.

34

Claiming the future
1Samuel 26

In these chapters we see desperation in David's and Saul's life. David's life situation was imposed upon him. Saul's difficulty was considerably self-inflicted. We may have reached such depths ourselves. "I cannot stand it anymore," or "I will go out of my mind," are sayings that we use. In periods like this we often say rash things and do things we later greatly regret. Some in intense loneliness marry unwisely. Others give up jobs, move to another part of the country and suffer the consequences of foolish decisions. Perhaps calling in the wrong people to help. These experiences can lead to illness and breakdowns etc.

The possibility of losing what God has given you

David said to Saul, *Your Majesty, please listen to my words. If the LORD has turned you against me, let him be satisfied with an offering. But if mere mortals have turned you against me, let them be cursed by the LORD. They have prevented me from having a share of the LORD'S inheritance. 'Go and serve other gods,' they tell me.*[149] David did not want to lose the heritage that the Lord had promised him. If you are losing out on the promises of God for your life. If

---
[149] 1Samuel 26.19 GW

your relationship with God is at stake because of a personal fault, then conquer it. But if it is the fault of others, curse it. The ministry we have from God should be kept and guarded with our life. The message of Jesus to the Philadelphia church was: - Revelation 3:11 *I am coming soon! Hold on to what you have so that no one takes your crown*, GW.

Saul had repeated his search for David, and would have done so again and again, it was only because David entered Philistine territory that he stopped his hunting.[150] The Ziphites would not get their bounty, try as they might.

Temporary changes of heart happen to many people. Saul had a momentary rethink but it did not last. It is the change of heart that lasts which is of God. Jesus spoke of the temporary nature of some individuals in the parable of the sower. Their decisions were able to be influenced by the environment in which they were in. In Saul's case he was constantly brooding about David, so it clouded his judgement. Then it just needed one person to reignite his passion against David. We too can be guilty of such weaknesses. Jealousies, disappointments, and a thousand other thoughts need to be banished from our minds. If we do not dismiss them every time they cross our thoughts, they will control our lives.

The seeds sown by the wayside Jesus said were seized by the wicked one. It was the word, "harpazo," it was not stealing by stealth, it was robbery with violence. Whenever we have a different agenda to God's agenda our good thoughts are taken from us with violence. Saul, not long after calling David his son, start again with more intrigues to capture and kill David. His mind told him he was wrong but his emotion had taken over his will.

---

[150] 1Samuel 27.4 When Saul was told that David had fled to Gath, he no longer sought for him. NRSV

35

Living with the enemy
1Samuel 27

David's double life.

For the second time David went to Gath the city of Goliath. He did not feign madness but pretended to be on the side of the Philistines when he was still an Israeli at heart. We might find this surprising yet many tribes will change sides even today, the Afghan tribes have been doing it for generations changing sides when it suited them even after bitter fighting with one another. Looking back on it in the cold light of day it was not much safer nor very upright of David either. The Christian double life is composed of several possibilities.

- A. The hypocrite who acts in public the Christian part
- B. The secret disciple who pretends to be the Philistine.
- C. Seeking a worldly solution to a spiritual problem.

Someone said that secrecy destroys discipleship or discipleship destroys secrecy. David's actions caused him to lie, to massacre whole villages and behave in the same way as a Philistine. Living with the enemy caused him to behave like the enemy. When undercover police behave like the criminals they are investigating it is said that they have gone native. With all the evil that David and his men did we can say that they went native.

Is it possible, that we as followers of Jesus, but living among people who do not practise Christian ethics, could go native? It is unfortunately so, many a person, church or Christian charity have not behaved as they should have done. When a long time later David was called a man of blood by the prophet it was surely true. What will we be known for? A bully? A grasper? A misery? It could be any of those things if we do not daily examine our own hearts, motives and actions. Sometimes I have followed another car and then realised I was breaking the speed limit. I was following a law breaker, not my own speedometer. Measure your life with the yardstick God has given you, not how others behave.

36

Saul's descent into spiritualism.
1Samuel 28

The law regarding spiritualism is clear. Lev.19.31. *Do not turn to mediums or wizards.* NRSV *Lev.20.27 Isa.8.19. Deut.18.10. There shall not be found among you...anyone who practises divination, a soothsayer, or an augur, or a sorcerer, or a charmer, or a medium, or a wizard, or a necromancer.* NRSV

- Divination. Compare Ezekiel 21.21 like throwing the dice only arrows instead
- Soothsayer, either reading the clouds or an incantation.
- Augur, compare Gen.44.5,15 (Joseph's cup) Reading the tea leaves?
- Sorcerer, using herbs for magical purposes.
- Charmer, one who ties knots
- Medium, wizard or necromancer consulting spirits or the dead.

Saul had destroyed all known mediums, now he himself turned to one. The complete change from a self-effacing believer, to an arrogant destroyer, then to a pathetic mouse of a man must have been sad to chronicle. The change from believer to unbeliever is usually a subtle and almost unseen one. It must be distinguished from a temporary belief. The removing of the Holy Spirit from Saul was more to do with his kingship than his salvation. It was finally that Saul was receiving no answers to his prayers at all 1Samuel 28.5. The shock to the medium of Endor was considerable when her actions produced real results she might have been a fraudulent medium in normal life! No new information was available to Saul except that it was his last day on earth!

It is commonly believed that Samuel appeared by a sovereign act of God. This may be so, but nothing more than the words of the woman are there to say it was Samuel. Nothing more than was generally known about Saul & David apart from the fact of imminent death was discussed. Therefore, all this could have been no more than many fortune tellers are capable of. See 1Chronicles 10.13

Very often people in high positions, royalty, politicians, even bishops have been known to practice spiritualism. (It has been said that President Regan's wife used the horoscope to advise him when to hold meetings etc.) Henry II of England would take confession before setting sail and take advice from an augur regarding the time to travel. There must always be a clear line between Christian prophesy and fortune telling etc. and any spiritual gifts must be seen to come from above without any shadow of doubt at all.

David was seeking to cope with the present, Saul with the future and was delving into places God didn't want him to look by means not open to him. If God is silent then there is no need for us to know what he does not want us to know.

Our desire to secure the future.

The Lord limits our vision to see the future, years ago when horses pulled carts on the roads their vision was limited to see only what was at the front of them by blinkers so that they did not scare at what was happening at their side. There are parts of our lives that are closed to us. We put our life into the Lord's hands and trust him for the future. Ignore people who claim to know your future, God is in control of it. Yet on occasions some people had a glimpse of it.

- Peter did - John 21:18 *I can guarantee this truth: When you were young, you would get ready to go where you wanted. But when you're old, you will stretch out your hands, and someone else will get you ready to take you where you don't want to go."* GW
- Paul did - Ac 9:15 The Lord told Ananias, *"Go! I've chosen this man to bring my name to nations, to kings, and to the people of Israel.* GW He was not told that he would be in chains though.

David Duplessis was told that he would take the Pentecostal message to the historic churches by Smith Wigglesworth. Rick Warren was prayed and prophesied over about his ministry at Saddleback Church, California.[151] It would seem the exception not the rule though.

Often God leaves you in the fog.

Elisha experienced the fog of not knowing. 2Kings 4.27 *When she came to the man of God at the mountain, she took hold of his feet. Gehazi went to push her away. But the man of God said, "Leave her alone. She is bitter. The LORD has hidden the reason from me. He hasn't told me."* GW

Our future is in God's hands, to try to manipulate it as Saul, or to try to rush it as some of David's followers attempted will not do. We must deal with the present in a positive and righteous way. David sometimes shined through during this period at other times he failed badly.

If there is no indication as what to do keep on doing what you are doing.

There is a query as to who had the urim and the thumim. 1Samuel 23.6 David's priest had an Ephod, but it doesn't say about the stones. See 1Samuel 28.6 Saul seemed to have them with a priest.

---

[151] The Purpose Driven Church page 26.

37

When God gets you off the hook
1Samuel 29

Was there a Philistine "God Believer?" Achish said, "As the Lord lives." He used the title Yahweh not just Elohim. We know that there was widespread use of the Name Yahweh, and much corrupt practises using the name too within and around Israel.[152] Yet it might have just been possible that here was a Philistine believer. Achish was also prepared to say of David that he was like an angel of God. He seems to have had a form of belief that was a lot deeper than the polytheistic religions around.

"El," the word for God was used by many nations around Israel. The important matter is, how did David describe God, and how did the nations around describe their view of their god. Today many peoples and religions will use the term "god" but it is the description that matters. Christian have a simple definition besides the fact that God is spirit. It is this "God is Love." We of course believe him to be the eternal, omnipotent, omniscient, and omnipresent God, but it is his character that separates him from all the gods of the world. What separated David's "El" was the explanation of the character of his God from all the god of the neighbouring countries and nations.

---

[152] See references to the name in the writings in the city of Ugarit etc.

It was not only his character but also what God did for David that made him totally separate no wonder David could say, "Taste and see that the Lord is Good!" That one word "good" made all the difference.

I wonder how David could have looked Achish in the eye? He was being praise by Achish for his support and uprightness while David was up to his tricks. Always living a lie as well as speaking lies must have had a cost, causing a corrupted conscience. Seek always to have an open life that can be viewed by all because God views it anyway.

Many a fish has managed to get off the hook. David nearly ended up fighting with the Philistines against Saul. What a conundrum, how was he to get out of that? Are you in a place that you have got yourself into and need to escape from. If God did it for David, I feel sure he can get you out of a tight spot too. Any fish that has been caught once should be wary of an easy meal that is proffered to him. It was a dangerous place that David was in, not so much physical but spiritually and morally.

38

David failed to do a risk assessment.
1Samuel 30

Exhaustion, disillusionment, and extreme sorrow all wrapped up in one bundle. They would see the smoke rising from the ruins as they approached. A feeling deep in their gut that the worst had happened would come in an instant, then their anxiety would turn to reality as they saw the utter destruction.

After the time of grief came the time of a portioning blame. Could David have found an excuse not to go with Achish? Should he have left more troops behind? We often spend much of our lives on post mortems, and the older we are the more failures we have to go over what went wrong. The government officials always say after a failure, "We have learned lessons from the enquiries." The trouble is we so often fail in another area. After a decision by the men to postpone the stoning of David they went and did something about it.

After the total success of the operation, when all the kidnapped sons, daughters and wives and animals were recovered, the stoning of David was permanently put on hold. Yet he could say with Paul, "All things work together for good."[153] Out of this came a principle

---

[153] Romans 8.28

that is good for today. The exhausted soldiers who stayed to look after baggage were given the same status as the fighters at the front. Though they would not be able to tell their grandchildren the exciting stories of that occasion. There will always be some that are stronger physically, emotionally and intellectually than others. If we work to the limit of our capabilities, then we cannot be called into question. The praying person at home has the same status as the missionary in the jungle. One of the people praying for CT Studd the missionary in Africa knew the day he died because the burden of prayer left them on that day. Some prayer warriors have days written in their diaries when they knew their prayers had been answered. Yet these thing were not confirmed till long after the occasion.

The second good thing was that David had so much of the spoils of war that he could be generous with all whom he wanted to be friends.[154] Within a few days he had gone from almost total defeat to magnificent victory. He would never have had all those animals if Ziklag had not been burned. We might not all have such a transformation of our situations and certainly not as quickly. But God is in the alteration business, perhaps he wants not only to alter our situations but our character as well.

Have you been ready to blame someone, and have you contemplated stoning them? Not literally but metaphorically of course. It might be better to stick with the leader you have. David made a blunder, he had not done a full risk assessment of his venture. A Columbian church sent their children on a trip in a coach that was unsafe and many of the youngsters died when it caught fire. The pastor was arrested and others charged as well because the bus was not roadworthy. I remember the time forty odd years ago when we sent Sunday School children to the sea side, our church had little money. Because they were the cheapest, we used a company that locally were nick-named, "The Collapsibles." It could have so easily been us in the same situation, I could not believe my eyes when at the half way point, as the children went to the toilet and to have a

---

[154] The area covered with his generosity was quite a large area. Ziph is not mentioned as one of the recipients., I wonder why?

sandwich, the driver got out and started filling the hydraulic fluid reservoir up because of a leaking brake system. Today I would have demanded another coach. All of us have been foolish in our decision making at times.

But David achieved this because he strengthened himself in the LORD his God. Two things David received from God, one was strength, the other direction. Sometimes his strength increased from encounters with people such as Jonathan. This time he took the direct route. He had said to God before, "With your strength you strengthen me." He also sought God's advice. As mentioned before it seemed that Saul had a urim and a thummim yet David went to the priest and asked for the ephod. It would seem that he put it on. He wore one at a later date.[155] Although originally made for the high priest[156] many priests now were wearing the ephod. Saul had access to the Urim and the Thummim, we do not know whether there were additional sets, if not David must have had another means of obtaining direction from God. We are here to obtain the same two things from the Lord.

Isaiah knew of that strength; this is what he prophesied: - Isaiah 40.28 *Have you not known? Have you not heard? The LORD is the everlasting God, the Creator of the ends of the earth. He does not faint or grow weary; his understanding is unsearchable. He gives power to the faint, and strengthens the powerless. Even youths will faint and be weary, and the young will fall exhausted; but those who wait for the LORD shall renew their strength, they shall mount up with wings like eagles, they shall run and not be weary, they shall walk and not faint.* NRSV

When it speaks of "renew" it could mean an "exchange" (halap) It was used in Genesis 35.2 *So Jacob said to his household and to all who were with him, "Put away the foreign gods that are among you, and purify yourselves, and **change** your clothes;* NRSV

---

[155] 2Samuel 6.14. Later David made some of his sons priests even though they were not of the tribe of Levi.
[156] Exodus 28:4-14; Exodus 39:2-7

God is in the exchanging business to swap your strength for his! My grandmother used to send me to the Co-Op to exchange the accumulator. It was an old fashioned battery that the wireless ran from before they had electricity. They were full of acid, health and safety hadn't been invented then. We may be exhausted, but we can go and swap our strength for God's strength.

Isaiah promised direction from God too. Isaiah 30.21 *You will hear a voice behind you saying, "This is the way. Follow it, whether it turns to the right or to the left."* GW There is no better thing to do than follow Jesus. He has lead me all the way.

39

Deliberate Death
1 Samuel 31 & 2 Samuel 1

In Saul's final moments we find suicide, euthanasia and murder. We are dealing today with the possibility of death provided by the health services of many countries, whether abortion and perhaps euthanasia.

Euthanasia

David would not condone a mercy killing. Was it just because Saul was king? or was there a general principle involved? 2Sam.1.16. I was told, though I cannot find any historical reference to it, that some of the elderly warriors of the North American Indians used to peg themselves out when they were old. They tied their ankle to a peg in the ground near to the enemy camp. Then they challenged the young warriors from that encampment to attack them. Nevertheless, be that true or not they often left their elderly to die when they moved on to other hunting grounds. The term to die with dignity as applied to Euthanasia is a false one. It is every bit as dignified to fight death or allow it to take its course. It is not wrong to give drugs to relieve pain that may shorten a person's life. but it is not ethical as Christians to unnecessarily shorten an individual's life.

Biblical Considerations

Samson asked God to take him with the Philistines and God obliged.[157] Paul and Jesus could be said to have walked towards their death. Moses took his last walk up the mountainside and he knew it was the final journey he would make. Deuteronomy 32.50

At the beginning of the fourteenth century Raymond Lull the Franciscan from Majorca returned to take the gospel to the Moslem people of North Africa even though he was threatened with death if he returned he did return. (It seems he survived by the skin of his teeth.) Captain Oats, returning from Scott's fateful journey to the South Pole, left the tent knowing his weakness was slowing down the return of his team mates. As Titus Oats went out into the wild wasteland of snow, Scott recorded that Titus said that he would be a little while.

These people walked down a road knowing where it could them. Their death was so that others might live. Christians can reach a time when they feel that their purpose in life is completed. Simeon said, Luke 2:29 *"Now, Lord, you are allowing your servant to leave in peace as you promised.* GW

We can therefore reach a point, not one of despair, but of fulfilment and have an attitude that prepares us for death. Many have sacrificed their lives for the life of someone else and most of us just reached the end of the road.

In Saul's case and another leader, they asked for the inevitable to be hastened see Judges 9:54 *Then he called hastily unto the young man his armour bearer, and said unto him, "Draw thy sword, and slay me, that men say not of me, 'A woman slew him.'" And his young man thrust him through, and he died.* KJV These shortened their lives by their own request to avoid pain and humiliation. Who would not have also taken the same decision? The end was not in question.

---

[157] Judges 16.30

Abortion

We may ask the question, "Does the command, 'You shall not murder,' apply to the unborn child?" John the Baptist and Jeremiah were called while in the mother's womb. The scripture talks of God fashioning people in the womb, Job 31.15 Note too Samson is described as, "A Nazarite from his mother's womb." Judges 13.5,7.

Jeremiah uses the same word for kill in Jeremiah 20.17, when talking of death in the womb, as it used many other times in the Bible for example Psalm 34.21 Ex.16.3 Compare too, the law in Exodus 21.22-23

The Big Question, 2Kings 5.7 *When the king of Israel read the letter, he tore his clothes and said, Am I God, to give death or life?* NRSV He asked if he were God considering that life and death are in his hand.

There are two reports of the death of Saul and they can be reconciled if we consider that the armour bearer only in his panic thought that Saul had completed the job. Alternatively, the Amalekite could have lied saying that he killed Saul thinking he would get better treatment from David.

Assassinations

David would not kill Saul. He considered that the position was by divine appointment. It is interesting that the Greek word in Luke 22.2 translated *"to put him to death"* could be translated *"To take away"* which is very similar to the army phrase, "to take out". The chief priests and the scribes were looking for a way to take Jesus out, for they were afraid of the people. The people who attempted to kill Hitler with Bonhoeffer had questions of conscience. The American CIA were said to have made several attempts on the lives of one or two world leaders.

The world has more than once been put into turmoil when national leaders have been assassinated. For example, the cause of WWI. Perhaps we could say that pre-emptive assassinations are never acceptable. Just as we could say a pre-emptive war could be wrong. But if a war that is ongoing could be stopped by the assassination of a leader and save thousands of lives could that not be justified? Bonhoeffer said, "When a man takes guilt upon himself in responsibility, he imputes his guilt to himself and no one else. He answers for it... Before other men he is justified by dire necessity; before himself he is acquitted by his conscience, but before God he hopes only for grace."[158]

Is Cremation okay for a Christian?

There is little comment in the Bible as to how we should deal with the bodies of the dead. But here in this passage we find that they did burn Saul's body, (1Samuel 31.12).[159] Amos also refers to burning bodies in Amos 6.10.[160] It would appear from resent archaeological digs that the Philistines would sometimes cremate their dead. Many of the early Christians, and later ones, were burned and most of them were burned alive!

It was not until the end of the nineteenth century that cremations were allowed in Britain, in 1944 the body of the former archbishop of Canterbury, William Temple was cremated.[161] This let people know that Christians were not against the practice and today the majority of the people who die in England are cremated. The body will be destroyed whether by worms or fire, let us be concerned about our living and then our dying will not be a problem.

---

[158] Ethics see quote in Wikipedia under Dietrich Bonhoeffer
[159] In a footnote Jacob Wright says that an iron age crematorium has been found in that area. "David King of Israel" page 238. near Amman airport.
[160] See also 2Chronicles 16.14 which might also refer to a cremation.
[161] Catholics were allowed to be cremated from 1963

40

The Slain on Gilboa
2Samuel 1

It leads to a famous phrase, *"How are the mighty fallen?"* 2Sam 1.19. KJV

Here was the final defeat of Saul and Jonathan. It was here that they were unready to battle with the enemy. What caused their defeat? It could be that we as Christians have a battle to fight. We too can find ourselves unready for the problems of life. It is one of the saddest episodes in the life of any nation when their young men defending a nation are dead.

Let's learn a thing or two from King Saul. Where have some of those who seemed good Christians fallen, was it when they committed adultery? Was it when they ran off with the funds? Was it when they started teaching some unusual doctrines? No, it was because they had not been preparing for life's battles beforehand.

Was it the witch? Saul's prayers were unanswered, so he turned to a woman who was prepared to perform a séance for him. The man who, in a pious fit had mediums and witches killed, now turned in hopelessness to one himself. It was to a person who could tell him his future but was not able to change the future for him. No, Saul was not defeated because he turned to the witch of Endor, this was purely a final desperate cry.

Was it that Saul did not wait long enough for an answer to prayer? No, God was now out of his prayer range. The problem was further back. Sometimes we feel they can just go one step back. We have to go back to the cause of the problem. Why wasn't God listening?

Was it Saul's obsession with trying to remove David? No he had on several occasions tried to do that before. This was part of his personality that had diverted him from fulfilling his own life's purpose. We can become obsessed with things that we think are important, but God doesn't. It captures our mind and thoughts it turns us in certain directions. So we are not looking at the goal of life.

Was it when he killed the priests? 1Sam 22. What a thing to do? Henry II should have known better than to ask who will rid me of this turbulent priest? Thomas a Becket was hacked down in the Cathedral. Many leaders have killed ministers that would have brought sanity into the picture. It was then that Saul killed his conscience too. He lost the means to communicate with God. Have you done something that is against the Christian conscience and never sought the forgiveness and correction? Yet it was further back in his life that made him do such evil.

Was it Saul's depressions that caused it? 1 Sam 19. Some of us have a natural depression that is due to the chemicals in our body not being produced correctly. Sometimes it is due to a big problem in our life such as sickness, job loss, poverty, bereavement etc. But it can be due to the fact we have not put something right in our lives that is wrong. But it did not begin with his depression.

Was it Saul's jealousy? 1Sam 18. Who does not become jealous of others some time? Deal with it defeat it or it will defeat you! No, his jealousy might have caused his depression but was not the cause of the final defeat. It was step along the way. John the Baptist dealt with it, "He must increase and I must decrease." Peter was reprimanded by Jesus in John 21 when Jesus said about his interest in the future work of John. "Mind your own business." or "What is that to you, follow me!"

Was it his fear of people more than fear of God? 1Sam 15.25 etc. Now we are getting close, he was afraid of his friends as well as his enemies. Unfortunately, he was more afraid of them than God.

Saul thought he was unimportant but he was important to God. Not only in the sense that God loved him but also that he was part of God's leadership on earth. Part of his assessment of his own person was that he was not important. We are ambassadors for Jesus on this planet. We must be seen to act righteously and do what Jesus would do even at the cost of prosperity and friendship.

1 Samuel 15:17 *Samuel said, "Though you are little in your own eyes, are you not the head of the tribes of Israel? The LORD anointed you king over Israel.* NRSV

The moment you belong to God and are in the family of God and are a vital cog. You must do what He says. Saul considered that his fault was not important because he wasn't. If we look back over the failures of most Christians we can find it was their own lack of a personal daily walk with God. A failure of daily devotion in prayer and Bible reading, a failure to fellowship with other Christians, and a failure to obey his commands of the Lord Jesus. What would we think if the Army never kept themselves fit or if they never tested their weapons? They would fail in war time because they were unprepared in peace time.

41

Saul lost his life because he lost his way
1Chronicles 10.13

So Saul died for his unfaithfulness; he was unfaithful to the LORD in that he did not keep the command of the LORD; moreover, he had consulted a medium, seeking guidance. NRSV

The word used for unfaithfulness – MAAL could be translated treachery. This was the one-word analysis by the writer of Chronicles for the fall of Saul. We may never know how many people have been led astray because leaders have slowly drifted away.

Saul went to a clairvoyant instead of God. He went there because seeking God is a difficult thing and he needed to know some answers quickly. It costs you the price of a news-paper to know what the stars say for your life, it costs you nothing from God in financial terms, but there is a price, it means patience, it means concentration, and determination, it means zealous faith taken to the limit.

There are several different reasons to seek God.

- a] some want to know that he exists and that he cares.
- b] some want to know that Jesus is the Saviour.
- c] Some want to know direction for their life.
- d] Some want the fullness of God in their life.

For whatever reason you are seeking God there are principles that are the same.

- Only genuine seekers need to search. It is a waste of time for the unconcerned and half hearted. Jeremiah 29.13 *When you search for me, you will find me; if you seek me with all your heart.* NRSV
- You are Guaranteed a result. Matthew 7:7 *Ask, and it will be given you; search, and you will find; knock, and the door will be opened for you.* NRSV

The word translated "seek" means according to Strong: -

> to resort to, frequent (a place), (tread a place)
> to investigate, enquire
> to ask for, require, demand
> to practice, study, follow, seek with application
> to seek with care, care for

In days of instant packaged things, we find that God has not made it easy for us. You will frequent the place where God is worshipped, you will seek with care, and study and meditate on the Word of God to find him. There is no short cut. One Russian spaceman said we have been into outer space and not found God. But if he had not found him down here he would not have found him up there, unless as someone suggested he open the door.

1Peter 1.10,11 talks about the prophets searching, the word used was the word for the police seeking out a criminal and a dog having a good sniff around.[162]

The disciples were told by the ascending Jesus to stay in Jerusalem till the promise of the Father came. They were told what the promise was but not a description of it nor had they been told when it would happen. They were also in enemy territory, it was dangerous for them, but they waited till they received the Holy Spirit.

---

[162] "ereunao" See Kittel in location.

Compare 1Kings 19.12 Elijah had a problem, he had been zealous for God. His courage and steadfastness helped many people on the way to trust God. But it did not seem to help him. He felt that he had not changed a nation, nor had he converted the heathen queen.

Being zealous helped Phineas Numbers 25.10-13 *And the LORD spoke to Moses, saying, Phinehas, the son of Eleazar, the son of Aaron the priest, has turned my wrath away from the children of Israel, while he was zealous for my sake among them, that I consumed not the children of Israel in my jealousy. Wherefore say, Behold, I give to him my covenant of peace:* KJV

Perhaps you have done things that others have been rewarded for, but it hasn't turned out the same way for you. Other people have had their prayers answered but not you. Elijah wanted God to answer by fire and storm but to him he answered in the stillness the soft voice of heaven. There the answer came, Elijah found that God eventually spoke in the stillness.

42

An elegy or a eulogy?
2Samuel 1

The Tribute to Saul

An elegy for Saul, a song of lament, let ours be one of praise, a eulogy 2Sam.1.19-27. The battlefields of past generations have often become the cornfields of today. Hardly a sign anywhere to say what had happened on those blooded grounds of centuries ago. A few have become famous and people troop to see the memorials year after year to remember the dead. There are battles have changed the course of history, but this one was just an interlude along the way. Saul and Jonathan died fighting but they received an elegy not a eulogy.

Could it be that some matters we hold so dear to our hearts and fight for, are just trivia? They would not change the course of history whether we won or lost. Others have totally altered the direction of the civilised world. Saul's battle was not unnecessary. He was defending his country.

The Hand of God in our lives

Prior to this incident David was on the verge of fighting his own nation then God stepped in 1Sam.29.4 and made a way of escape for him. There will be a way of escape for us too when we make a mistake.

The Way out when things go wrong.

Get in the right frame of mind. David strengthened himself in God 1Sam.30.6 He could not ring up the local prayer line he had to overcome his natural feelings. Get guidance from God 1Sam.30.8. Go for it with the ones with the get up and go, v.10.

The fall of the mighty

The Northern half of Israel seems to have been captured by the Philistines. Saul was seeking to recover lost territory. Mighty men do fall sometimes. Some gloat, some ransack and pillage, some sorrow over their demise. David sorrowed, even though he was a beneficiary of Saul's death.

Solomon fell, led astray by his wives.

Judas fell, taken up by his love of money.

Samson fell, because of his lust.

Saul fell because of his obduracy, his unfaithful heart which he would not change. He did not fail over women or money, the medium of Endor was a symptom of his sin not the reason for it. His jealousy came as the result of earlier sin. His earlier sin was the result of fear of man more than the fear of God.

The battle fields of time are littered with the fall of the mighty.

The conies are but feeble folk yet they make their holes in the rocks. Where is your hiding place?

43

Don't lose your crown
2Samuel 2

There are things that are ours that we should never let go. Other things have to be forgotten and let go, they are no longer ours. This is a story of about some of those things.

The David Principle

The promise to David was now being fulfilled. The days of the desert living were over, peace had come. The fulfilment of the promise from God was near, the throne of Israel was in sight. *That which is yours, is that which has been promised to you by God.* Not that which you have commandeered, or obtained by ruthless means, nor that which has been obtained by deceit or subterfuge. That is the devil's way.

Timing is crucial in the fulfilment of the promises of God. David was a teenager when he received the promise, he was in his late thirties when it was fulfilled. He did not seek to engineer a situation, nor try to cause the downfall of Saul. He publicly disassociated himself from any actions against Saul and his supporters. If God has promised something he will cause it to happen in His time.

The Naboth Principle

It is something you have and must not lose. The vineyard that Naboth had was a family heirloom it was not for sale.

Naboth told Ahab, "The LORD has forbidden me to give you what I inherited from my ancestors."[163] Kings would like what you have in God. Don't lose it.

1Peter 1.4 *"We have an inheritance incorruptible and undefiled and won't fade in the sunlight."*

Hebrews 12.16 *"That there be no profane person like Esau who sold his birth-right for a mess of pottage."*

Hebrews 10.35 *"Cast not away your confidence."* KJV

Rev.3.11 *"Let no man take your crown."* It is better to die than to give up on faith, than to give up your work for God, than to throw away anything that you have that has come from God.

The Abraham Principle

Something you haven't but future generations will have. Abraham was promised by God a country and an heir. Romans 4.18. *In hope he believed against hope.... No distrust made him waver.* The time had to be right. Way back, many centuries earlier than David, Abraham had been promised the land of Israel because the inhabitants were evil living, this is what God said, *In the fourth generation your descendants will come back here, because the sin of the Amorites will not have run its course until then."* Gen.15.16. GW There are times when we live in anticipation of the hope we have in Christ – things that are yet to be. Zechariah spoke of the prisoners of hope, Zech.9.12. *Return to your stronghold, O prisoners of hope; today I declare that I will restore to you double.* NRSV The prodigal's father was a prisoner of hope; he was waiting for his son's return he could not move his home.

---

[163] see 1Kings 21.3 GW

The Michal Principle

Some things in the past are best left alone. This is one of the saddest stories of the Old Testament. Michal, David's first wife had re-married. That in itself was sad. Had she forgotten the sweet music of David? Had the vision of him grown dim over the years? Forgetting, perhaps though, had not forgotten him completely. Hope of a reunion had gone. Then David made a demand that in spite of her second marriage she was to return to him. *I will make a covenant with you. But one thing I require of you: you shall never appear in my presence unless you bring Saul's daughter Michal when you come to see me.*[164] No doubt Paltiel, her second husband risked his life by following after her. Perhaps she dearly loved him because she was soon seen despising David. (2Sam.6.16)

Deuteronomy 24 1-4 States the validity of a second marriage. Some things are non-returnable. The tradition of the age was that no person could have the king's wives or concubines. (2Sam.3.7 etc.) David would have been better sticking to the Scriptures. As we travel through life we seek sometimes to regain something lost in our earlier years. The past is past, go forward. Take only that which is yours by right now.

We often wish for things that are not ours by right.

Baruch sought great things, God said, "Don't." Jeremiah.45.5

Diotrephes loved a position which was not his. 3John 9.

When Howard Carter founded a Bible College in London, England, he went to a healing crusade where Stephen Jefferies was preaching. Howard saw remarkable healings and miracles and large numbers responding to the Gospel, he so wanted to have that ministry himself. God said to Him, "Sorry No." Afterwards he wrote, "**Let me never lose the all-important truth that to be in Your will is better than success and grant that I may ever love Yourself more than Your service.**" This became the motto of the British Assemblies of

---

[164] 2Samuel 3.13 NRSV

God Bible College. It is not wrong to want something that is in the shop window, (*covet earnestly the best gifts*) but it is wrong to desire what is in your neighbour's window!

NOTE The length of Ishbosheth's reign. (2Sam.2.10,11) The fact that David reigned over Hebron 7 years and Ishbosheth only 2 years may be explained that Ishbosheth was not crowned king until Abner had regained lost territory.

NOTE The wars of those days and for hundreds of centuries later were often played according to rules and equal fought equal. Or as in the case of Goliath a token fight decided the matter. As also in this case. (2Samuel 2.14-16 & 21)

44

Too Big for your Boots
2Samuel 2.22

Abner said again to Asahel, "Turn away from following me; why should I strike you to the ground? How then could I show my face to your brother Joab?" NRSV

Abner used the butt of the spear to kill Asahel. It seems strange to us but the IVP Bible Background Commentary says this: - "Spears often were made with a metal casing on the butt end that was not honed to a point but was tapered down to a sharp edge. This could be used as a goad or to stick the spear in the ground. Many of these metal ends have been found in excavations and are portrayed on wall paintings."

Asahel was taken with the moment. He was on the winning side. But he chose to fight someone too big for him. He knew the history of David and Goliath. Courage was not lacking. There were others that could take Abner on another day. He was not the only person to take on someone that was too big for him. Josiah did the same.

2Chronicles 35.20-23 *After all this, when Josiah had prepared the temple, Necho king of Egypt came up to fight against Carchemish by Euphrates: and Josiah went out against him. But he sent ambassadors to him, saying, What have I to do with thee, thou king of Judah? I come not against thee this day, but against the house wherewith I have war: for God commanded me to make haste: forbear thee from meddling with God, who is with me, that he destroy thee not. Nevertheless Josiah would not turn his face from him, but disguised himself, that he might fight with him, and hearkened not unto the words of Necho from the mouth of God, and came to fight in the valley of Megiddo. And the archers shot at king Josiah; and the king said to his servants, "Have me away; for I am sore wounded."* KJV So he died in an unnecessary fight.

Asahel died needlessly. The battle had been won. It was a waste of life. Just because David killed Goliath don't think that we will always succeed because he did. Brave lawyers have challenged corrupt governments and evil police forces. Often they have been disappeared or suffered even worse fates. Attempted coups against evil dictators have often lead to the massacre of those who attempted it. Can we suggest why Asahel's challenge failed? Abner no longer posed a threat to David and his people. He had lost the battle. Josiah was poking his nose into other people's business. Asahel was chasing a defeated man. Perhaps he was trying to make a name for himself, Joab and Abishai[165] were top notch soldiers. Asahel was in the thirty but not in the elite group of men at the top. His desire to be at the top lost him his life.

We can fall into the trap seeking to make a name for ourselves, rather than making a name for the Lord. God has no rivals. As Davy Crockett once said, "When a man gets too big for his breeches I say good bye." Paul put it like this, *I ask you not to think of yourselves more highly than you should. Instead, your thoughts should lead you to use good judgement based on what God has given each of you as believers,* GW Romans 12.3. Self-assessment means taking a close look at our weaknesses as well as our strong points. Isaiah, Paul and others saw their own weaknesses and were prepared to report on themselves. Personal examination must be a regular act. *"Therefore*

---

[165] 2Samuel.23.18 And Abishai, the brother of Joab, the son of Zeruiah, was chief among three. And he lifted up his spear against three hundred, and slew them, and had the name among three. KJV

let a person examine themselves ..." David was prepared to let God have a look at his inner thoughts and his motives for his actions. Psalm 139:23 *Examine me, O God, and know my mind. Test me, and know my thoughts* GW. Asahel had great qualities in athletics but not on the battle front. Where are your qualities best shown?

45

Dealing with People's Character defects
2Samuel 3

2Sam.3.39 *Today I am powerless, even though anointed king; these men, the sons of Zeruiah, are too violent for me. The LORD pay back the one who does wickedly in accordance with his wickedness!"* NRSV Zeruiah was David's sister so her son Joab was David's nephew as well as her other sons who were senior soldiers too, they were absolutely loyal to David. In years to come David arranged for Joab to be executed (1Kings 2.5). Yet it was the ruthlessness of Joab that helped David to the position of King. It was not David's place to forgive – nor could he deal with the matter because of his limited authority. It was put in the hands of God. He was not prepared to fight internal battles that would weaken him even though he could have been within his rights to do so. Sometimes we would destroy an organisation or a church if we sought a perfect system with perfect people. There comes a time when we have to turn a blind eye to some things leaving the matter in God's hands. Yet there is a line which must not allow people to cross.

People can change with the help of God. We have to leave others to their conscience but seek to limit the damage they do. David let others know that he did not want them to commit murder and never hesitated to show his disgust at assassinations by his family members.

In the parable that Jesus told of the tares, or as modern versions say weeds, the farmer gave this advice: - Mt 13:29 *"He replied, 'No. If you pull out the weeds, you may pull out the wheat with them.* GW So often people are flawed in character. It has been observed millions of times over by theologians and everyday Christians that not all the followers of Jesus are as Christ-like as they ought to be. Yet David too was ruthless at times and just as bad as Joab.

If David had tried to totally purify his loyal followers, who were a rough and ready bunch, he would have destroyed his band of followers. God has given us people to work with and we must work with them. When I came to the pastorate of my church some forty years and more ago, a man who I did not know knocked on the manse door. He had been a deacon some time before, but had left with others causing a major weakness in the church structure. He told me that one of the two deacons, there were only two remaining, was not any good and I should remove him. I said that God had given this deacon to the church, and I would not remove him. He turned out to be the very best of deacons. I remember walking back home in the snow with him one day, we wondered how God would provide for the heating of the building that winter, but his were words of hope and faith not doubt. God sends the right people; we just often feel they are the wrong ones. Don't plan their execution!

David realised the limitations of his personal power. King, but limited. So are we often found too weak to do all that we would like to do. A family living in the New Forest, England, were attacked in their house by a gang of burglars. The father fought back but was soon knocked to the floor and tied up. Later he said that he remembered thinking, this would not have happened to James Bond. We do not always have the strength to achieve all that would be ideal. Wisdom is often required to decide which battles must be fought and won and which must be left to another day.

Churches are often faced with the problem of power or authority. A minister may have been ordained but a faction on the church board can have the power to control decision making for the whole church. It can hamper the growth and success of the work of God.

Some years ago I was returning to the church office to prepare for the Sunday Evening service, outside the Nelson Public House on the way was a commotion. A police man and woman were trying to handcuff a man, all three were rolling on the ground and the police were not doing too well. The drinkers had stopped their drinking to enjoy the incident but certainly not to help, well not help the police anyway. The two police officers had the authority to arrest the young man but not the power. Not until other police cars came screaming up to help out. David was limited and so are many ministers God will deal with it in his time. Don't try to pre-empt God.

There are individuals that have not just a firm nature but also are cruel to others. Unfortunately, it can even be in a so called Christian. It is one thing to be tough it is another to be callous. The AV. Says that David complained that Joab and his brothers were, "too hard for me." It was the word used to describe Nabal, 1Samuel 25.3 *"he was harsh and mean."* It is a good thing to be strong and confident but another to be indifferent to the feeling of others.

46

A history lesson in character judging
2Samuel 4

Eshbaal[166] or Ishbosheth?

In 1Chronicles 8.33 He is called Eshbaal, named after a heathen god, (Man of Baal.) This then is another hint that Saul was two timing God. He is called here Ishbosheth, man of shame. Perhaps because his people were diminishing in numbers as they were deserting him and he was finally killed by his own people. Naming people is important, children become adults and adults can live up to their

---

[166] Archaeologists in Israel have pieced together a 3,000-year-old clay jar and found that it bears the same name as a biblical character from the time of King David. The large ceramic jar, which was broken into hundreds of pieces, was found to be inscribed with the name Eshbaal ben Beda. While Beda is not a biblical name, Eshbaal or Ishbaal was the son of Saul who fought against David for the throne and who was murdered by assassins (II Samuel 3,4). The researchers, Prof Yosef Garfinkel of the Institute of Archaeology of the Hebrew University and Saar Ganor of the Israel Antiquities Authority, say: "The correlation between the biblical tradition and the archaeological finds indicates this was a common name only during that period." The jar was found at Khirbet Qeiyafais, identified with the biblical city Sha'arayim. The city dates from the time of David, that is, the late 11th and early 10th centuries BC. In 2008 the world's earliest Hebrew inscription was uncovered there. Christian Today 28th July 2015

name. Yet it is not too vital, an Indian friend who came to Christ as an adult said one of his names was the name of a Hindu god. He kept his name. It was not going to affect his spiritual life, and it sure didn't. He went around the villages in England in his bubble car, stopping to preach the Gospel on the village greens to all who would listen. If the line of Saul had continued Israel could have become a heathen nation, the truth of one loving holy God who is spirit and the eternal creator would have been lost.

The men who assassinated Saul's son had not assessed the character of David before they acted. He asked them, "If I killed the one who brought news of Saul's death, can you work out what is about to happen to you?" David had assessed their character. They had changed sides, but had not changed their nature. David was not pragmatic in his approach to relationships. He was principled in his dealings with others, whenever he could be anyway.

Not everybody thinks like you! We are all different, assess the character of a person before you deal with them. Kind and loving people expect others to be like them. Rouges can never trust others because they think that the others too, think like them. A time comes in life when an individual will have grasped that we do not all think the same. As has been said, "Never smile at a crocodile." David realised that if they had turned on Saul's son, whom they were supposed to be guarding, one day down the line they could turn on him. Because their character had not changed. If a person gossips about another to you, they will gossip about you to them. Jeremiah asked the question: - Jeremiah 13:23 *Can Ethiopians change the colour of their skin or leopards change their spots? Can you do good when you're taught to do wrong?* GW

The Gospel of Jesus teaches that people can change. Yet there must be a clear cut conversion experience. Some Christians fail because they do not let the Holy Spirit deal with their weaknesses. There is a second point too, Christian ethics are often not clearly taught there is a tendency in preaching to encourage faith in God but not the morality of God. Throughout the four Gospels we can find not only the promises of Christ, but also the commands of Christ, mark them in the margin of your Bible, you will be surprised at how many there are.

47

Crowned the Shepherd King of all Israel
2Samuel 5

David did well caring for the tribe of Judah, when the rest of Israel, saw how he was achieving success, they were keen to join him. The psalmist put it like this: - Psalm 78.70 *He chose his servant David, and took him from the sheepfolds; from tending the nursing ewes he brought him to be the shepherd of his people Jacob, of Israel, his inheritance. With upright heart he tended them, and guided them with skillful hand.* NRSV

Jesus, in a parable, spoke of those who were wise in caring for little would be given much more to look after. How have we cared for those who are nearby and all around us? Yet the image of a shepherd is the one that captures our attention. The pastor, during my teenage years had a brother who had been a shepherd. I heard that he treated the city football team when they had non-fracture injuries. The natural talent he had, and the skills he had learned on the sheep, while he was a sheep farmer gave him his experience to treat people. David too worked his way up. Faithful in small things? *The king said to him, 'Good job! You're a good servant. You proved that you could be trusted with a little money. Take charge of ten cities.'*[167]

---

[167] Luke 19.17 GW

David never let Saul's personal animosity or hatred from others toward him become the focus of his attention. He constantly sought to strengthen himself, and his army and the followers. Then he set out to defeat any that would come against the settlements of Israel. This did not mean he was self-sacrificing and a model of morality. He married several women and certainly had a comfortable lifestyle compared to many. There is no doubt that David would have had many annoying habits and characteristics. Yet God called him and so that settled the matter.

Becoming deflected from the calling that God has given to us, is a common preacher's theme. Wealth, fame, and sex are all quoted as causes, as well as the mention famous cases of people who were not side-tracked and some who were. Becoming involved in personal squabbles and inter-Nicene wrangling is less often mentioned. Perhaps because we are all liable to become involved in it, and do not see it for the danger that it is. After New Testament times there were many councils, and conferences etc. The New Testament had its fair share too. Such as the Acts 15 conference. The post New Testament councils were often acrimonious and not a few dirty tricks were employed to keep some people away so the voting would go smoothly.[168] As for David, he kept his eye on the ball.

The third anointing of David was the coronation God had promised him. He could have felt the second was sufficient. He made it there because of faithful men and women, some who supported him, some who challenged him, but all were for him. Often when looking back on our lives we feel we have in comparison to many achieved so little. Face it, if we are older, most of us have not achieved a fraction of that which we wished to do. I have heard people who were made to retire saying that they had so much more to give. As well as people on their death beds feeling just the same. Perhaps we could compare ourselves to one of David's foot soldiers, rather than David himself, or than to the apostle Paul, Mother Teresa or Billy Graham. If we were to take away all the people who worked with

---

[168] Voting About God, Ramsey MacMullen, Yale University Press, 2006

these famous and successful people, they would have achieved a small fraction of the work done.

The Break-through. Here David had a realisation of the beginning of victory. He had many skirmishes with the enemy especially with the Philistines. Now he had a break through. He called it a break-out.[169] 1Chronicles 14.11 *So he went up to Baal-perazim, and David defeated them there. David said, "God has burst out against my enemies by my hand, like a bursting flood." Therefore, that place is called Baal-perazim.* NRSV. The word, PARAS (break out) was used to speak of the rapid expansion of Abraham's family in Genesis 28.14. We might have many difficulties to overcome in life but we can experience a break-though. It might not mean that the fighting has finished but it is more a mopping up operation rather than full scale war. Micah, who lived half a millennium later, gave a promise to the people of Israel. *The one who breaks out will go up before them; they will break through and pass the gate, going out by it. Their king will pass on before them, the LORD at their head.*[170]

Chronicles states that the idols captured were destroyed, the book of Samuel does not deal with the detail of what happened to them.

David was angry because God broke out when he was taking the Ark on a cart. See 2Samuel 6.8 We don't want God to break out against us, but to break out for us.

---

[169] PARATS "to break through," had something of a special meaning for the author seems apparent from its repeated occurrence in different contexts (cf. 13:2, 11; 14:11), although the nature of that importance has not been found. Word Biblical Commentary

[170] Micah 2.13 NRSV

48

Whose people?
2Samuel 5

The LORD said to you: It is you who shall be shepherd of my people Israel, you who shall be ruler over Israel." v.2 NRSV

There has often been a failure of pastors, prime ministers and presidents to realise whom they are captain over and whom they are shepherding. It is God's people they are looking after. Governments have sent thousands to war unnecessarily, church ministers have been prepared to discard members of the congregation rather than seek to build them up if they want to have a different style of worship or organisation. A young minister was considering taking over a church. He admitted that too many people would leave because of the style of "church" he would run. The deciding factor was not that many would leave but that the income would then be insufficient.

David made a covenant with Israel, then they anointed him. His covenant was with the people both to lead and to care for them. There was a sense of duty a calling this was not just a desire for power on the part of David, it was to fulfil a call from God. There will always be people that will not recognise a person with the call of God on their life. As there will be usurpers to claim a position that is not theirs by right or calling.

Jesus first called Peter to follow him with the promise of an apprenticeship that would make him a fisher of men. Two or three years later after the resurrection Jesus gave him instructions to shepherd, that was to care, and to provide for the lambs and sheep that belonged to the Lord himself. There was no apprenticeship and there was only one qualification, "Love for Jesus." It could be said that Peter fished more people for the Lord when he became a shepherd than when he was training to be a catcher of men and women for the Lord. It might be a good idea if a test were to be made for a prospective minister to be questioned on his love for the Lord, rather than his academic achievement and success in his or her previous positions.

David had the necessary qualification to be a shepherd of people, he loved God. So he therefore loved the people of God; and that extended far beyond his family and tribe. It was true also that David had fame and charisma which certainly does help. Finally, he had God's call upon his life, that is always a "Must."

Any failure to care for people whether spiritually, physically or materially must be down to a lack of love for the Lord. Because people belong to God and if you love God then you must love the family of God.

49

Jerusalem, hark how the anthems ring
2Samuel 5

The old city of Jerusalem had a large structure now known as the stepped-stones about 120 feet high. It was a curved structure like one side of a pyramid, plus there were additional fortifications of stones each weighing many tons. These could have been there for a century or two before David ever came to conquer.[171] The Jebusites were certain that they were safe and taunted David. There were various tunnels and Joab made use of one to enter and invade the city.

Archaeologists disagree as to the number of inhabitants in Jerusalem at this time, some say just two thousand others as many as five thousand. Nevertheless, the Jebusites felt that they could ridicule David saying that he would not be able to take their stronghold on the hill-side.

---

[171] The archaeologist Eilat Mazar and others have dated them to 12 Century BCE though some contend that they were more recent. It would seem this structure is known in the English Bible as "Millo."

The Egyptian Amarna letters suggest that Jerusalem of the fourteenth century BCE was an important city in the area.[172] For centuries the Jebu- sites lived successfully in Canaan, Israel had not been able to unseat them. Now a new day was dawning. A warrior king had come.

Saul's palace had been a few miles away from here. So David would have known the area well. He not only wished to make this his capital but also the centre for the worship of Yahweh. The latter desire was only to be partially fulfilled during his life-time. Some of the towns in Israel such as Bethel, Hebron or Shechem had meaning for the patriarchs, this was to be a new era. Jerusalem was to be the place to which the Israelites would look back, and consider it as the embodiment of all that they held dear, both for their nationhood and their spiritual centre. Psalm 137, the captives' despondent song, says, *By the rivers of Babylon, there we sat down, yea, we wept, when we remembered Zion.* And verse 5 follows with, *If I forget thee, O Jerusalem, let my right hand forget her cunning.* KJV It was to them the centre of their universe.

Jesus brought in the new era when he spoke to the Samaritan woman by the well. Pointing out that it was not going to be on mount Gerizim nor in Jerusalem he said to her, *Indeed, the time is coming, and it is now here, when the true worshipers will worship the Father in spirit and truth. The Father is looking for people like that to worship him. God is a spirit. Those who worship him must worship in spirit and truth."* GW. If only the Crusaders had realised the true centre for the worship of God, they would not have been on futile crusades, killing and destroying all that went before them. It could be that even today Christians are placing too much emphasis on places rather than people.

---

[172] Six of the letters from a pharaoh are addressed to Abdi-Heba, the ruler of Jerusalem (called Urusalim in the cuneiform text of the tablets). These letters refer to the "Land of Jerusalem" and to its "towns." The consensus of scholarly opinion is that during the Late Bronze Age, Jerusalem served as capital of an Egyptian vassal city-state the size and strength of which was comparable to other political entities in the region. "Jerusalem's Stepped-Stone Structure," by Jane C. West, Biblical Archaeological Society 2011.

50

Where could Israel meet with God?
2Samuel 6

2Sam. 6.3 *They took it from Abinadab's home on the hill and placed it on a new cart.* GW Now David was going to make a central meeting place for people to meet with God. The Ark of the Covenant had been left many for years at Kiriath-Jearim in Abinadab's house, it was never returned to Shiloh since Eli's sons had taken it into battle against the Philistines. Samuel was young when it was taken, the Ark was still there till after his death. In addition, there were priests at Nob near Anathoth, which was till Saul had massacred them and their families. While Samuel was alive he was mainly further north, for example, when Saul in his youth went to ask him for where the whereabouts of the donkeys he was in Ramah. Samuel often seemed to be moving around Israel. There were priests also still at Shiloh and Gibeon.

David wanted to take the Ark to Jerusalem. It is the preacher's delight to speak of the harm of using a new cart, instead of the time honoured way of the Ark being carried on poles by the priests. Yet it had not been moved for the best part of a hundred years, so they could have forgotten how to move it, had they read the Torah? Uzzah might have touched the ark many times before this time it was fatal. His brother Eleazar had been the consecrated person to look after it, he and his brother Ahio were charged with transporting it. There does not seem to be any record of the blessing on Abinadab's house unlike when it went to Obed's home. This time once again it seemed the Ark was alive with the presence of God, and the power of God was again there.

The Blessing is where God's presence is.

You would think that because David was bringing the Ark of the Covenant into Jerusalem that he would have received a blessing, but he didn't.

You would have thought that when the rich young ruler went to see Jesus he would have gone away blessed, but he didn't.

You would have thought that when they took the ark into battle they would have won, but they didn't.

You would have thought that taking communion would bless you, but it might not! 1Cor.11.29 *For all who eat and drink without discerning the body, eat and drink judgement against themselves.* NRSV

Our blessing today is not dependent upon us making demands upon God that he will fulfil, but upon us fulfilling his demands.

The ark was not being carried in the right way by the right people. So they did not get blessed. The rich young ruler asked Jesus for advice but he did not like the advice he received. The priests had not been living God's way when they took the Ark into battle. Jonah did God's bidding in the end but still picked a quarrel with God about a plant. We all tend to be obstreperous and self-willed.

Things go wrong when they should go right

Many had been invited from all the areas around. David was making a thing of it. 1Chron.13.1-9 *So David gathered all Israel from the Shihor River near Egypt to the border of Hamath in order to bring God's ark from Kiriath Jearim. David and all Israel went to Baalah in Kiriath Jearim, which is in Judah, to bring God's ark to Jerusalem.* GW

David's life was filled with tragedy as well as triumph. He made no bones about the fact that he was cross with God at what had happened. It marred his relationship with God and spoilt the people's blessing. But one family benefited!

There can be two sides to a coin. Some changes, to keep up with the times are necessary. It is said that teenage Isaac Watts told his father that the psalms they sang at church were lifeless. His father challenged him to write better ones, so he did.[173] And still we sing new songs today like David did. But some things must be done God's way through the power of the Holy Spirit and no other way. A para-church group were seeking to recruit workers. A prospective candidate was left in the office for a minute or two on his own while the interviewer slipped out. There on the recruiters desk he saw a book; it was about the psychology of influencing people. He turned the job down. You do not have to use worldly methods to achieve God's goal. They tried to do God's work man's way.

The Ark was left with a Philistine! The Gittites were known as a tall people. Many had come over to David's side and were his body-guards.

---

[173] Where would the church be today without: - "When I survey the wondrous cross." Etc. and all the modern worship songs.

51

Accepting our mistakes
2Samuel 6.8 Numbers 6

This much preached on story, the basic emphasis being that you not only have to have the right desires but also do things God's way. The Ark was to be carried by the poles by the Kohathites. After this tragedy Obed received a blessing. David so wanted the blessing of God that he was prepared to learn by his mistakes. He was learning to do things God's way. A radio programme had a discussion about airline pilots and surgeons owning up to their mistakes so that procedures could be improved.[174] A story was quoted of an aircraft-man who mislaid one of his tools on the flight deck of the aircraft carrier. The commander was told, he shut the whole operation that was ongoing down till it was found. Later in front of the crew the aircraft-man was commended for acknowledging his mistake. It could have had tragic consequences for a plane coming in to land. We make mistakes, that's life, a good leader will admit to them and then correct the procedures so there are no repeats. Are we big enough to take responsibility for our mistakes?

2Samuel 6.14 *The ark of the LORD remained in the house of Obed-edom the Gittite three months; and the LORD blessed Obed-edom and all his household.* KJV

---

[174] BBC Radio 4 19/6/2015

We take the Lord's supper to fulfil one of the requests of Jesus, *this do in remembrance of Me*. Also we gather together as the writer of Hebrews encouraged us to. That is a good start, there is more though. We have additionally given financially to help the work of God, so we are doing even better. In fact, we should be giving ourselves a pat on the back. But be careful there is something that we must check upon to get blessed!

People often keep watch to see if you are blessed. Mrs. Widdowson was healed in a service at our church. It was in the newspapers and on the television. Often people would ask her years later, "Are you still healed?" Yes, she kept her healing.

The local people saw that, instead of Obed-edom getting boils and tumours he was blessed. No family member had dropped dead. Great things were happening in his household. When we see others being blessed we like to know the reason why.

Let me ask a question, do you think you will receive the blessing today if you are holding a grudge? If you are intent on gossip, if you are cheating or lying? Or worse? If you considered that in spite of your unpleasant thoughts and desires you would get blessed, you are wrong, you won't.

There is a solution when we are needing a correction, first a warning has been given to us. *"Therefore, whoever eats the bread or drinks from the Lord's cup in an improper way will be held responsible for the Lord's body and blood."*[175] The next verse tells us what to do. *But let a man examine himself, and so let him eat of that bread, and drink of that cup.* Self-examination is better than leaving others to do it. I was reading this passage when taking communion to a housebound church member, it was in the days when you called them by their surname. I stopped at the verse before it said, *"For this cause many are weak and sickly among you."* Mrs. Hill said, "Read it all pastor, read it all." She was unwell through age, but she was prepared to answer the challenge of 1Cor.11.27.

---

[175] 1Corinthians 11.27 GW

We could be connected with the crime of the Cross, not with the blessing of the Cross if we do not look in God's mirror to examine ourselves. *Whoever, therefore, eats the bread or drinks the cup of the Lord in an unworthy manner will be answerable for the body and blood of the Lord.* The word "guilty" here "answerable" means that you have connection with the crime.[176] It is the word used in Matthew 5:21,22 *""You have heard that it was said to those of ancient times, 'You shall not murder'; and 'whoever murders shall be **liable** to judgement.' But I say to you that if you are angry with a brother or sister, you will be liable to judgement; and if you insult a brother or sister, you will be liable to the council; and if you say, 'You fool,' you will be **liable** to the hell of fire.* NRSV

Obed-edom was from Gath the city of Goliath, the city where the ark caused devastation. But he was prepared to have another go this time being on the right side of God. His family group had left Gath after David took refuge there for a while. They were among the loyal supporters of David and fled with him in times of trouble. They either had tunes or musical instruments that helped for the singing of Psalms 8, 81 & 84.

David wanted Obed-edom's blessing. This time he did it right, and got excited about it too! The Ark was carried in the right way it was the visible expression of the invisible presence of God. That is what I want, don't you?

Losing the plot - David and dignity. Michal lost the plot – David was not king because of his bearing but because of his calling.

You can be despised because of the things you do and the way you live. Hudson Taylor dressed as the Chinese people while evangelising in China. He was criticised by many of his fellow missionaries, but he reached the Chinese people, and don't forget Francis of Assisi and the way he lived and the Franciscan friars. Some admired their way of life others looked down on them. In his

---

[176] Enochos literally, "liable to," is used in the sense of being in "danger" of the penal effect of a misdeed, i.e. signifying the connection of a person with his crime

book, "Empire," Jeremy Paxman quotes Sir Harry Johnston the first colonial proconsul in the area of Nyasaland (Malawi) saying with contempt, "It was pathetic to see highly educated men from Oxford and Cambridge hollow-eyed and fever-stricken, crouching in little huts which no native chief would deign to occupy." But as Paxman commented, they practised what they preached.

Never be condescending to others, a national from the country where some missionaries were leaving commented, "You gave us schools and hospitals but you never looked us in the eye." The KJV is wrong in its translation of Romans 12.16 when it uses the word "condescend." The NRSV is better when it translates as: - *Live in harmony with one another; do not be haughty, but associate with the lowly.*[177]

We are followers of the one who as Isaiah prophesied was despised and rejected by people. Paul could say he was not ashamed of the Gospel of Christ even though it meant he was a follower of the "Crucified One." This does not give us the right to judge those who live extravagantly, nor should we criticise those who might not feel the same sense of belonging with everyday people it is their loss not ours. The young Harley Street doctor, Martin Lloyd-Jones was leaving a theatre in London with some friends. A Salvation Army band was marching past playing hymns. He said in his heart, "These are my people." So began the ministry of one of Britain's famous preachers of the twentieth century. As the people were worshipping the Lord David could say, "These are my people."

---

[177] Although the word empathy is overused and the Bible would seem to talk more of sympathy here it could almost be considered as attempting empathy with a person.

52

The Day of Rejoicing had come
1Chronicles 16

It was the culmination of David's hopes and dreams for the worship of God. If music had previously been occasional in the worship of God, it now became a major part of it. There was music and much of it, there was singing and what singing? The song he used to dedicate the tent that housed the ark was from three different psalms, not one of the three was designated as being written by David.[178] It would seem to me unlikely that David would have chosen songs by other authors so it could be that some of the unattributed psalms are his as well.

The Song of Moses in Deuteronomy 32 was to be recited for teaching and guidance purposes as well as worship. David wrote songs not only for worship but for prayer, for deeper insight, for teaching and for testimony. At the opening of the temporary Jerusalem temple[179] there was worship, testimony and teaching in one mighty triumph song. There were singers and musicians and the congregation must have made the skies resound.

---

[178] Psalm 105.1-15, Psalm 96.1-13, Psalm 105.1&47,48
[179] The original tabernacle was still at Gibeon, as was also the original altar during David's life time. See 1Chronicles 21.29

There were wind, string and percussion instruments. David would be at home in many modern church services. After centuries the Jewish synagogues quietened down their services. It is said that the early church followed that style of worship. One day organs began to be used in the churches. The story is told of a monstrous organ in Winchester, England, it had four hundred pipes two consoles and needed seventy monks to work the bellows. This was about 1000 AD and it was said the music could be heard all over the city.[180] Thomas Aquinas felt that alone among the musical instruments the organ elevated the soul. Yet there has been much opposition to musical instruments in church worship over the centuries. The Reformation as a rule discouraged musical instruments in the churches. Even the Methodists who loved their singing and are responsible for many hymns and songs were cautious about their use. A hundred or so years later the Salvation Army were sing the songs of Zion while marching through the streets of England's cities their brass bands playing at full throttle.

A cappella or cantata? John Wesley the founder of Methodism was asked what he thought to musical instruments in church. He said that he did not mind as long as they were neither seen or heard. The famous Methodist theologian Adam Clarke was strongly against their use in services commenting on John Wesley's statement he said, "I say the same, though better to spare the expense of their purchase."[181] A church I often attended as a teen never had an instrument and singing was "A cappella." What difference does it make, a cappella or cantata? Does God have a preference? Are the Eastern Orthodox Churches more scriptural singing a Gregorian Chant without instruments or a Charismatic Church singing songs with guitars, drums and keyboard?

---

[180] The organ in Winchester Cathedral today has 5,500 pipes.
[181] His comment on 1Chronicles 6.39 says, it does not appear that God had especially appointed these singers, much less any musical instruments, (the silver trumpets excepted), to be employed in his service. Musical instruments in the house of God are, at least under the Gospel, repugnant to the spirit of Christianity, and tend not a little to corrupt the worship of God. (Adam Clarke's Commentary.)

Firstly, there are no statements in the Scriptures banning the use of musical instruments in worship. God did not condemn David or Miriam while they were using them in his praise. The psalmist said, *Praise him with sounds from horns. Praise him with harps and lyres.* (Psalm 150:3 GW)[182] And that is in the imperative. Should the worship in the New Covenant be more sombre that the worship in the Old Covenant? I think not. Yet there is no doubt that some forms of present day services are working up disco fever rather that an experience of the genuine presence of God the Holy Spirit. Engaging their hormones rather than the holy.

There will often be clashes between the musicians and the minister. Johann Sebastian Bach had differences with his pastor regarding the music. His minister felt the music was too complex for the singers, he was probably right. Music should take us to the entrance of the holy, only our whole being in worship can take us to the throne room of God. As Jesus said to the woman of Samaria, *"But the hour is coming, and is now here, when the true worshippers will worship the Father in spirit and truth, for the Father seeks such as these to worship him. God is spirit, and those who worship him must worship in spirit and truth."* NRSV There is no song that is sufficient nor music profound enough to take us to that place. David knew the secret when he said: - *I will not set before my eyes anything that is base.* (Psalm 101.3 NRSV) Or Psalm 9.1 *I will praise you with all my heart.* GW It is the single eye, the one thing in focus, to meet with God. In Psalm 86.11 David said, *"Teach me your way, O LORD, that I may walk in your truth;* **give me an undivided heart** *to revere your name."* NRSV

It was not just music for praise or worship it was to open hearts to receive from God, prophesies to encourage, guide and enlighten the people. In 1Chonicles 25:1 it says, *David and the army commanders appointed the sons of Asaph, Heman, and Jeduthun to serve as prophets with lyres, harps, and cymbals.* GW David was always dependant on the power and presence of the Holy Spirit. This was not just to enact the law of the Lord to sacrifice for the forgiveness of

---

[182] Psalm 5 was written for the flute.

sins. This tent temple and the whole of the services was to meet and hear from God. He was a charismatic king, not only in the natural sense but in the spiritual. When Amos preached against the use of light-hearted music he said that David was a musical improviser.[183] He was not just jazzing things up he was seeking to lift his heart to the Lord. He wanted to be on a higher level. He was spontaneous in his worship.

---

[183] Amos 6.5 who sing idle songs to the sound of the harp, and like David improvise on instruments of music; NRSV.

53

God's refusal
2Samuel 7.1-29

There was a desperate longing in David's heart for a place for the Ark of the Covenant to stay permanently. In Psalm 132.1-5 He says this: - *O LORD, remember in David's favour all the hardships he endured; how he swore to the LORD and vowed to the Mighty One of Jacob, I will not enter my house or get into my bed; I will not give sleep to my eyes or slumber to my eyelids, until I find a place for the LORD, a dwelling place for the Mighty One of Jacob."* NRSV

David had the experience of doing that which was beyond the normal of everyday life. He, as a lad, killed a lion, a bear and a warrior. He escaped many a death threat. As a young son of a sheep farmer he was designated to be king. David was musical and handsome. He raised an army and became the king. Suddenly he and everyone thought he could do anything. Then God said no.

God has a boundary for the sea (Job 38.8) and for the nations (Acts 17.26). He has a boundary for us. *"My times are in your hands"*. God limited Moses to a look at the promised land. He restricted Simeon to a view of the baby Messiah. There is a limit to your life but it is not the limit of your natural strength but to the limit imposed by God. When God says no, don't try to do it!

When I was young we kept chickens. My father used to clip one wing so that they could not fly. Otherwise we would have to look all over the fields for the eggs. God clipped David's wing, so that he did a good job of what he was doing. God often redirects people.

John Wesley could not return to America because of a lawsuit against him. It meant that he was totally engaged in the ministry in Britain, and what a ministry?

Dr Barnardo wanted to go as a missionary to China, God said no, then gave him something closer to home, it was to look after thousands of homeless orphan children in Britain.

The Gadarene demoniac. *Now the man out of whom the devils were departed asked him that he might be with him: but Jesus sent him away, saying, "Return to your own house, and show how great things God has done for you." And he went his way, and published throughout the whole city how great things Jesus had done for him.*[184] He wanted an itinerant ministry God said it was a static one.

Proverbs 16.9 *The human mind plans the way, but the LORD directs the steps. NRSV*

Paul said, *I can do all things through Christ which strengtheneth me.*[185] There is a confidence that much more can be done than is naturally possible when we have the "Yes" of God.

When Paul's thorn was not taken away God said he would give him grace. *"My grace is sufficient for you."* 2Cor.12.9. KJV David was to have God's "No," to something he wished to do. If these chapters are in chronological order this was not late on in David's life. It would have been a major disappointment in mid-life. Yet he did have a promise of a firm foundation for his family. God limited him to building up the people. Stick with the work God has asked you to do. Continue to do the work you are good at. Building buildings can be exciting work, but eventually someone else will take them

---

[184] Luke 8.38 KJV
[185] Philippians 4.13 KJV

over. Many a church and chapel have been turned into warehouses or homes a century or so later. Building people is much more worthwhile.

David later elaborated, it was because of all the blood David had shed. *But the word of the LORD came to me, saying, 'You have shed much blood and have waged great wars; you shall not build a house to my name, because you have shed so much blood in my sight on the earth.*[186]

David's Acceptance

2Sam.7.18,19 *Then King David went into the Tent of the LORD's presence, sat down and prayed, "Sovereign LORD, I am not worthy of what you have already done for me, nor is my family. Yet now you are doing even more, Sovereign LORD; you have made promises about my descendants in the years to come.* GNB Some rebel against God's plans. Others accept them, and are the better for that. Yet, the negative answer must have hurt David intensely, he had sought to bring Israel to worship God alone. He also was seeking to centralise the worship of Yahweh rather than have the ark in one place the priests in another place and the remains of the tabernacle in another. This was a major disappointment to David.

For every Christian there is a promise of even more! God's business is an unlimited one! Are you content with all you have got, or are you looking for even more? Because there is more.

Great buildings are often the desire of ministers. God never seems as impressed with them as we are. The mega church buildings are often highly attractive, but the next minister might not have the same charisma and the work declines. A good number of the magnificent village churches of Britain have been closed as the villages have contracted in size, as have the congregations also. That work of previous generations is now wasted.

---

[186] 1Chronicles 22.8 NRSV

When King Amaziah made a mistake and lost much money paying for a hired army, the prophet said to him in 2 Chronicles 25:9 *Amaziah said to the man of God, "But what shall we do for the hundred talents which I have given to the army of Israel?" And the man of God answered, "The LORD is able to give you much more than this."* KJV Do not feel you have to go the way you planned. Be prepared to listen to God's alternative way. We all make mistakes, it just more difficult for us to acknowledge to ourselves that we are the ones that have made the mistakes. Would I, in the future, sacrifice wage increases to build our church extensions? I am not sure that I would. Though we must realise the aim of David was not wrong it was the timing that was out.

The important house

God said, *"I will build you a house."* 7.11 David wanted to build a house for God but God was going to build him one instead! Let us never forget that it is God who is building His house. Sometimes we carry on as though it was on our shoulders. Jesus said, *"I will build my Church"* Matt.16.16

People are always more important than buildings. David wanted to give to God but God was going to give to him. Someone said Mary washed the feet of Jesus but He washed her heart. You cannot do more for God than He will do for you. There are millions of people who would love the promise that God gave to David, that the blessing of God would be on their descendants too.

Yet later David stopped looking in God's storehouse and started looking in the devil's bargain basement. Things are always there to be looked at and that is the first step down the slippery slope, it was a look with the garden of Eden. In the Bible there is often a difference in the type of look a person gives, we use something similar. A glance, a look, or a stare, you cannot go window shopping in the Devil's arcade and come out smelling of Roses! The devil's bargain basement is a dead end drop out place.

The attitude of God to David.

2Samuel 7.18 says: - *Then King David went in and sat before the LORD, and said, "Who am I, O Lord GOD, and what is my house, that you have brought me thus far?* KJV Was David just sitting? Could he have been kneeling? Or does it just mean he stayed in the tent of God? He had a relaxed feeling towards the Lord and it is attractive to think he was just sitting in the presence of God. Although it is only used of the posture of Moses in prayer elsewhere.[187]

David spoke to the Lord like this. *"And even this was a small thing in your sight, O God; you have also spoken of your servant's house for a great while to come. You regard me as someone of high rank, O LORD God!"*[188] David said you treat me like a star. *"You are treating me like a great man."* GNB. This is the discovery of each person that God treats us with more than respect, with love and affection that we never dreamed was possible. Jesus spoke of the honour God gives: - *Whoever serves me must follow me, and where I am, there will my servant be also. Whoever serves me, the Father will honour.*[189] God is not in the "make do and mend" game. He blesses people and honours them. Hagar and Nathaniel were amazed to find that God knew about them. He not only knows about us but wants to honour us. That is in spite of all he knows about us.

NOTE! According to Josephus Hiram was king during the last seven years or so of David's reign this does not make sense with 2Samuel 5.11 unless it is not in chronological order. See on the desire to build the temple (Keil & Delitzsch)

---

[187] The Word Biblical Commentary suggests he might have been kneeling but also suggests as with Keil & Delitzstch that yashab might just mean "stayed" as it is used elsewhere. Moses sat in prayer Exodus 17.12
[188] 1Chronicles 17.17 NRSV
[189] John 12.26 NRSV

54

Ultimate honour
1Chron.17.16-19

Then King David went into the tent and sat in front of the LORD. "Who am I, LORD God," he asked, "and why is my house so important that you have brought me this far? And this you consider to be a small act, God. You've spoken about the distant future of my house. LORD God, you've shown me the generation of the great man. "What more can I do for you in light of the honour you have given to me and since you know me so well! LORD, you've done this great thing for my sake and your own desire. You made this great thing known to me. GW

CEV says in 2Samuel 7.18,19 *Lord All Powerful, my family and I don't deserve what you have already done for us, and yet You have promised even more.*

For every Christian there is a promise of even more! God's business is an unlimited one! Are you content with all you have got or are you looking for even more? Because there is more. Any act of giving is blessed with a greater return. Lu 6:38 *Give, and you will receive. A large quantity, pressed together, shaken down, and running over will be put into your pocket. The standards you use for others will be applied to you."* GW

In addition, God wants to honour you, he wants you to be higher than you are. The honour of men is often sought after. Some are invited to the Queen's Garden party. Others receive MBE's and knighthoods. God has his own honours list.

Mentioned in despatches Midwives Shiphrah & Puah received a mention for their courage. (Ex 1.) Mary was mentioned for anointing Jesus, he said in Mark 14:9 *I can guarantee this truth: Wherever the Good News is spoken in the world, what she has done will also be told in memory of her."* GW So many others were mentioned too.

Servant of God is a term of God's respect. as in Job & Moses. John 12:26 *Those who serve me must follow me. My servants will be with me wherever I will be. If people serve me, the Father will honour them.* GW.

Friend of God, as in the case of Abraham and also the disciples, Jesus said *I call you no longer servants but friends* John 15.15.

Where does Respect come from? John 5:44 *How can you believe when you accept glory from one another and do not seek the glory that comes from the one who alone is God?* NRSV

This is addressed to all those who want God's Okay and are not concerned about the acclaim of man but of God. You want the well-done of God? David got it then you can go for it too.

Another Startling fact. God wants to honour you even when he knows all about you! So David did not think too highly of himself. He did not say that he deserved the honour of God. Just the opposite. Now we know he was a bad lad at times. But God wanted to honour him.

Paul said... While we were yet sinners Christ died for us. David said: - Psalms 139:2 *You know when I sit down and when I rise up; you discern my thoughts from far away.* NRSV

Jacob said. Gen.32.10 *I am not worthy of the least of all the steadfast love and all the faithfulness that you have shown to your servant, for with only my staff I crossed this Jordan; and now I have become two companies.* NRSV

God's knowledge of us is complete not partial. Yet in spite of his knowledge of us He is after the best for us. He is after the best for you! He knows your problems, as well as the hairs on head, sparrow on ground.

Ephesians 3:8 *Although I am the very least of all the saints, this grace was given to me to bring to the Gentiles the news of the boundless riches of Christ,* NRSV Nathaniel, was known to Jesus, Jesus knew what Simon the Pharisee thought, what the disciples were talking about.

55

A Setback?
Psalm 60 2Samuel 8.1-18

Joab fought well but somewhere there was a setback. The title of the psalm refers to victory and leaves out the failure but the verses in the psalm suggest a setback somewhere.

While they were extending their territory they also had setbacks. David did not always record the negatives, and we often don't record them either. David Brainard died young, he was a missionary to the North American Indians, his diary is famous, but one thing he never recorded was his expulsion from a university. The Egyptian and Assyrian histories rarely include their defeats. The first church I pastored was a tin chapel in a stockbroker belt on the outskirts of North London. I was surprised to find that two well-known successful ministers had also begun their ministry there. They were not particularly successful while there, not that I was either! I guess if they wrote their life stories it would not have included much about pastoring at the tin chapel. Why should we emphasise our failures or lack of achievements anyway?

Psalm 60.2 puts the feeling that they had clearly, *"You have caused the land to quake; you have torn it open; repair the cracks in it, for it is tottering."* NRSV

A defeat or lack of success makes you think.

- Am I on the right track?
- Am I determined to carry on?
- Is it really worthwhile task?
- Is there something I am doing that is wrong?

It is always good to ask ourselves questions.

Job got thinking when he was ill, the defeat at Ai made Joshua examine the people. The fishing disciples had caught nothing all night and were ready for an alternative strategy from Jesus. (John 21.3)

Verse 3 sums it up. *"You have made your people suffer hard things; you have given us wine to drink that made us reel."* NRSV

Recovery from the setbacks v.4 *You have set up a banner for those who fear you, to rally to it out of bow-shot. NRSV.* God will give us a place to where we can retreat and regroup, Jeremiah had similar to say. Jeremiah 4.6 NRSV *Raise a standard toward Zion, flee for safety, do not delay.*

With God often the way forward is back. Back to where we started, back to the original message, to the original ambition for God. Get out of the range of the devil's darts. Moses, Paul and Elijah all went on retreats. Jesus said to the disciple, come away and have a time of rest. The British army have had major retreats such as Dunkirk, but have gone on to be victorious. Don't worry about a setback – God has it all under control.

They that wait upon the Lord will renew their strength. Isaiah 40.31 KJV

David feared being God's cast off. Psalm.60.1. John Trapp the seventeenth century Puritan preacher said, the Lord may let the world grow wild but not his garden.

The Mission – Often companies have mission statements: -

- To bring inspiration and innovation to every athlete in the world. Nike

- To refresh the world... To inspire moments of optimism and happiness... To create value and make a difference. Coca-Cola corporation
- Our mission: to inspire and nurture the human spirit one person, one cup and one neighbourhood at a time. Starbucks
- Our mission is to be our customers' favourite place and way to eat and drink. MacDonalds.

Israel with David at its head had an objective in mind. It was first local victory, Shechem v.6 Then it was national v.7 Gilead etc. Then international v.8 Finally the almost impregnable city of Edom. 3,700 feet above sea level. David was building a kingdom. A country that had the law of God and the revelation from God to guide them through a thousand years of turmoil and history. To prepare the world for the coming of the Messiah. He had to know who God is and what God wanted him to do.

Yet there was a greater mission that David had, it was to have a central place of worship for the Lord with songs, songsters and musicians where all could come to worship. It was not an afterthought it was part of his overall desire for Israel as a nation. If Moses brought the system of sacrifices David was to bring the music.

- David's mission statement was: - let's have a worshipping world.

When Jesus said to his disciples to go into all the world – and preach the Gospel he said to them, Jerusalem, Samaria, and the farthest parts of the world. Luke 24.47 *And that repentance and remission of sins should be preached in his name among all nations, beginning at Jerusalem.* KJV Acts 1:8 *But ye shall receive power, after that the Holy Ghost is come upon you: and ye shall be witnesses unto me both in Jerusalem, and in all Judaea, and in Samaria, and unto the uttermost part of the earth.* KJV

- The mission statement of Jesus: - Let's win the world

56

Expansionism
2Samuel 8

There can be few, if any, world empires that have been built without cruelty and barbarism, David's increasing domination of the countries around fledgling Israel is unfortunately no exception. There was the totally unacceptable murder of captives, and the gaining of considerable wealth by denuding the surrounding countries. Plus, the serious injury to animals to stop them from being used in warfare, though understandable but ruthless just the same. The IVP Bible Background Commentary just makes this comment about the choosing of Moabite victims for execution. "No known similar example is available in ancient history at this time." These were the people that offered asylum to David's family while he was on the run from Saul. Later the empires of the world had more revolting examples, yet there is one empire that is different.

Many Christian apologists quote what it is believed Napoleon Bonaparte said when he was on St Helena: - *I know men and I tell you that Jesus Christ is no mere man. Between Him and every other person in the world there is no possible term of comparison. Alexander, Caesar, Charlemagne, and I have founded empires. But on what did we rest the creation of our genius? Upon force. Jesus Christ founded His empire upon love; and at this hour millions of men would die for Him.* There is no definite proof he did say that, but it does seem to have been quoted not long after his death.[190] He also seems to have read some Christian books.[191] Yet it must be said that Napoleon was on the side of whoever he needed the most, Muslim, Catholic or Deist. It could be said that he was all things to all men. Yet the statement stands, Jesus' kingdom is based on love, no other in the world is comparable.

Now God had said David was to be a shepherd of his people Israel. It could be that he had gone beyond God's remit. If God had asked him to shepherd his people, then refused to let him build the temple because he was a man of blood waging a necessary war, that would have been unfair of God. But many of the wars he fought, and many battles won could have been unnecessary ones. There was no doubt some of the battles were defensive and others were to reclaim lost territory. But was David doing more than God asked. Could it be that today we seek to widen the mandate God has given us?

At this time, it was noticeable that people built monuments or steles[192] for the boundaries of their countries, or for themselves, as in the case of Absalom. Could it be that Christians have been building monuments rather than concentrating on people? From the saying of Peter, "Silver and gold have I none," many churches have become rich in goods and in property. It is said that Dominic who founded the order of preachers, otherwise known as the Dominicans, early in the thirteenth century, was shown the treasures of the Vatican. The pope said to him, "No longer can Peter say, 'Silver and gold have I none.'" To which Dominic is said to have replied, "Nor can the church say, 'Rise up and walk'"[193] Churches must be built of living stones with a living faith in a living Lord.

---

[190] The Divinity of Our Lord and Saviour Jesus Christ; Eight Lectures Preached Before the University of Oxford in the Year 1866. Fourth Edition. Rivingtons. London, Oxford and Cambridge, 1869. See also the Website History Stack Exchange.

[191] St Helena Memoirs, Thomas Robson, Pub. James Nesbit 1827 page 101

[192] 2Samuel 8.3 David also struck down King Hadadezer son of Rehob of Zobah, as he went to restore his monument at the river Euphrates. NRSV

[193] Aquinas and John Duns Scotus are supposed to have said it too. There does not seem to be any reference to original writings, but it is true often of Protestant as well as Catholic Churches.

57

Keeping Promises
2 Samuel 9

There are two main reactions we can have to this story. Firstly, the cynical thought that this was a Machiavellian ploy to keep a possible rival to the throne under observation. Secondly we can say praise the Lord David kept his promise to Jonathan. I feel sure it was the latter. There were others that were in line after Saul besides Jonathan's family. Nothing was done to them till later.

If the above understanding is the right one, then David was prepared to correct wrongs in his life and his nation. Often the story of Mephibosheth is used for the gospel illustration. Mephibosheth was in Lo Debar (meaning without pasture). He had his feet covered at the table when he was living with David so no one could see any fault with him. He ate like one of the king's sons. 9.11. The KJV has "I will show the kindness of God to him." What lovely words!

Who has had a rough time? Show the kindness of God to them. 9.3 Do you know someone who doesn't deserve what has happened to them? You are responsible for showing God's kindness. Putting right a wrong.

Some have been in prison and shouldn't have been.

Orphans are often put in with criminal young people.

Some have just had a raw deal in life in general.

Let us be in the restoration business. It may be there is something we did wrong that we can now put right. A miner gave his life to Christ at our church, he had taken valuable tools from the pit and decided to return the stolen property. The union man said, "Say you had a breakdown when you take them back," because theft meant dismissal. He said, "No I stole them it was no breakdown," The coal mine authorities did not sack him and he thrived at the pit. Some things are not returnable others have returnable value. Zacchaeus was able to make things good. We might hold on to something that is not ours by right. It may be that our country is to blame for damage to other countries in the colonial past, it could be possible still to show God's kindness through us to others.

Elizabeth Fry set about to improve the prisons in Britain, Wilberforce and friends sought to end the slave trade. Lord Shaftsbury transformed the working conditions of the poor of England. We are here to give back to the world that which God would want them to have.

I will act kindly to him like God. v.3 (Gesenius) *"Is there anyone remaining of the house of Saul to whom I may show the kindness of God?"*[194] NRSV Luke 6.36 *Be merciful as your Father is merciful.* GW

We deal not only with the forgiveness of a wrong but the correction of it too. It was normal practice to exterminate all claimants to the throne. This was different... Israelite kings became known for their mercy.

You are in the LIKENESS of God. don't lose the image!

---

[194] It is the superlative, it means the very best kindness, which is full measure pressed down shaken together and running over.

58

Misunderstood
2Samuel 10

When David sent official mourners to sympathise with Hanun over the death of his father it was mistakenly taken as a spying expedition, rather than what it was, a genuine show of friendship.

There could have been a good reason for the misunderstanding. David had been ruthless to the Moabites and they had looked after his family before. The Ammonites were neighbours to David while he was ruling from Hebron, they had obviously been supportive of him during that time. He was seeking to keep a similar relationship continuing. But they had seen another side of David.

It is important how we approach others. Sometimes when we are from different cultures misunderstandings can occur. A bank illustrated it in a television advertisement. An Englishman was entertained by his Chinese hosts to a meal. Although it was not to his taste he ate all. They promptly brought out more and more which felt he had to eat. In England it is polite to eat the whole plate of food to show you enjoyed it, in China you always leave a little on the plate to show that they provided you with more than enough. He was being polite as far as his culture was concerned but not as Chinese culture.

The relationship between the Jewish and Gentile Christians became a problem to the early church. The difficulty was solved by the Gentiles providing meat killed in kosher fashion, with one or two additional matters also dealt with as well. From the north to the south of Britain there are many sayings that the non-locals do not understand. It is the same with people on the continent and our Atlantic cousins. It has caused serious communication problems when allies have been fighting wars alongside one another.

Could David have dealt with it in a more delicate way? All of us have asked that question when there has been a communication break down between friends.

- A seeming friendly approach by another must always be taken as such, even if we have reservations about their true intentions.
- We can be wrong at times in keeping our guard up when a person that has previously let us down makes an attempt to heal the breach.
- Any approach we make to others must be made with consideration how they are likely to receive it.
- When individuals have been bereaved there can be considerable differences in how they cope with grief. Some wish to be alone, others desire company. A gentle phone call can often solve the problem; do they want to talk or are they a little brusque?

No blame can be attached to David; it would seem he was genuine though it might have been good to send one or more of his sons. The behaviour of the Ammonites was over the top; diplomacy was obviously not their strong point. Paul put it plainly to the Roman Church *If it is possible, so far as it depends on you, live peaceably with all.* NRSV Romans 12.18. Sooner be misunderstood than misunderstand.

59

Bathing Bathsheba
2Samuel 11

David's immorality is not lessened by the immodesty of Bathsheba, nor by her willingness to come to him. We can take it that her action was deliberate and she sought to entice. Voyeurism is sin. He should have immediately looked away. While working in engineering we were constantly subject to all sorts of pictures of naked females on the walls and locker doors. As a Christian man, a firm decision had to be made that you would never let your eyes linger on them. It is regrettable that a high percentage of ministers are said to enter pornographic sites on the internet, while many men in their congregation working in factories and on building sites have to constantly watch their heart and mind every moment at when at work. Job could say, *"I have made a solemn promise never to look with lust at a woman."*[195] Jesus put it this way: - *everyone who looks at a woman with lust has already committed adultery with her in his heart.*[196] There is a saying, "It takes two to tango." Bathsheba was part of the double act.

---

[195] Job 31.1 GNB
[196] Matthew 5.28 NRSV

David committed "virtual" adultery first and then in real life, besides his later act of murder. There are no mitigating circumstances. There is the **observation** that a person is attractive, the **admiring** of that person, then the **desiring**. Stop at the observation. There is a further point to be made. How do we look at another individual? Are they an object, a chattel? Or are they a person like us? A person with emotions, thoughts and needs like us. Some years ago now the Diary of Anna Frank was shown on German television. The nation's attitude changed from an abstract almost, unfeeling knowledge of the Holocaust to it being a heartfelt national grief, because it was personalised in a teenager's diary as she was approaching her death.

When David should have been out fighting he stayed at home. It was aggravated by idleness. Keep in work even if it is less profitable than the unemployment benefits. It is at the weakest point, at the vulnerable time that temptation comes. Being busy takes your mind of hurts, disappointments and a thousand other things.

Sin causes hurt to other people, God's people. The pet ewe lamb was killed without pity. The picture that Nathan painted expressed the emotion that the sin caused. The animal charities would have done well in David's day too!

David was the prime mover in this case but Bathsheba was no innocent party. Someone said about the mourning of her husband: - *The whole of her conduct indicates that she observed the form, without feeling the power of sorrow. She lost a captain, and got a king for her husband, and therefore, "She shed reluctant tears; and forced out groans from a joyful breast!"*[197]

Beware of benefiting from the evil actions of others. Bathsheba surely was complicit in the murder of her husband. No jury would be able to convict her though. Her future was assured of luxury and she would have the influence of a queen of the realm and later as the queen mother. Yet she too could not have had clean hands

---

[197] Treasury of Scripture knowledge 2Samuel 11.27

or a pure heart in this matter. Matthew in his genealogy of Jesus never hesitated to call Rahab the prostitute by name, but referred to Bathsheba as, "the wife of Uriah." The book of Kings speaks of David's failure this way, *"David did what the LORD considered right: David never failed to do anything the LORD commanded him to do his entire life (except in the matter concerning Uriah the Hittite).*[198] The Apostle Paul put it this way: - 1Timothy 5:22 *Don't participate in the sins of others. Keep yourself morally pure.* GW.

---

[198] 1Kings 15.5 GW

60

Voyeurism[199]
Job 31.1

The Problem. A young wife was horrified to find the pornographic Internet sites her Christian husband had been looking at on the computer. When sharing her anxiety over this discovery with friends from Church she soon realised it was far from just her husband who had been delving into them. Not only do many "Christians" use the Internet for such purposes, but also considerable numbers are looking at "adult films" too. When a prominent church minister was found to be searching pornographic sites on the internet a tabloid newspaper heading was, "***Porn again Christian.***"

Accident or an incident? Many have claimed that they entered the adult pornographic sites accidentally. Three methods of entering by mistake are often mentioned, pop-ups, rogue emails and sites that are referenced when they are looking for "spiritual" information on "angels or goddesses" etc. It is generally considered by Internet

---

[199] Voyeur, one who obtains sexual gratification from seeing sexual organs and sexual acts; broadly one who habitually seeks sexual stimulation by visual means. (Longman's Dictionary)

experts that people using the Internet sensibly would not mistakenly go into these sites. Certainly, *if once bitten, we should be twice shy.*

Unfortunately, this use of the Internet seems to include older as well as younger "Christian" men as perhaps also women, but even worse some who have positions within the Christian Church such as worship leaders, children's workers and perhaps even the occasional minister. In fact, American surveys have suggested it could be up to fifty percent of ministers, which we sure hope is not correct.

An epidemic or endemic? Even if we allow for the once or twice in a lifetime accidental entering of a pornographic site, it would seem that voyeurism is endemic among a considerable proportion of Christians.

Voyeurism cannot be a Christian practice. Although adult pornography is legal in in most countries, as far as the Christian Church is concerned it is immoral and unacceptable. Jesus stated that the thought, never mind the viewing, was as bad as the deed. Matthew 5:*28 But I say to you that everyone who looks at a woman with lust has already committed adultery with her in his heart.* NRSV The law of many western countries comes down severely on those who enter child pornographic sites on the Internet just as much as on those who actually are guilty of child abuse. Therefore, stating by implication that the viewing of something unacceptable is as bad as the deed.

Nothing New under the Sun. Voyeurism is as old as the hills. When Job began to cross-examine himself (Job 31) it was the first sin he mentioned, but he had already dealt with it at source, having made a covenant with his eyes. He was a man that did not take a second glance. The AV states, "think upon a maid," the NRSV says, "look[200] upon a virgin." The "Message Bible" translates, *I made a solemn pact with myself never to undress a girl with my eyes.*

---

[200] *It is a hithpolel, Delitzsch translates it, "fix my gaze upon." The covenant with his eyes is one made by a superior to a vassal state. Delitzsch translates, "as Lord of my senses I prescribe this law for my eyes." He was in control.*

Help don't hinder. The difficulty that some Christians have in seeking to overcome their deviant or excessive sexual feelings must be helped not ignored. People who have become Christians in mid-life often have sexual practices that have become addictive to them. Origen took rather drastic steps to overcome the strength of his sexual feelings we don't encourage that. Yet, as Churches, must seek to avoid anything that would titillate or provoke feelings toward sexual thoughts, we should not predispose a person to sin. Paul and Peter in the New Testament were concerned that women should not seek to draw attention to themselves, neither by extravagant or immodest dress.

Tertullian some years later was preaching against the North African women seeking to dress and dye their hair to look like the Gauls. The Puritans were much concerned with such things. Yet it would seem that no less a man than Britain's leading theologian of the time, John Owen was criticised for being dressed in figure hugging clothes to show off his physique.

We must also make sure that we clearly practise and teach that voyeurism is unacceptable for a Christian person. This can be helped by seeking to make church a sex free zone.

It is serious. Evangelicals do not classify sin in terms of venial and mortal sin. But we do hold that different sins can have graver consequences upon our spiritual life and the effectiveness of our ministry than others. In the Old Testament fornication was categorised in a different way to adultery. The latter was the same act but by a person or persons who were married, therefore having an effect upon a family. It may be that we should view voyeurism the same way as we view fornication, even if the person viewing is married, (because there is no immediate involvement of a family), which is still, totally unacceptable. Certainly it is a degrading habit it makes people feel bad about themselves. It must not be swept under the carpet but rather dealt with and overcome.

Continual acts of sin produce a sickness, or as Jesus put it, *"Very truly, I tell you, everyone who commits sin is a slave to sin."* (John

8:34). NRSV This sickness of voyeurism is becoming or has become endemic within the Christian Church.

The Solution. One of the problems of modern Western life is the increase in leisure time and as the old proverb says, *"The devil finds work for idle hands."*

- A fulfilling job and a busy life helps people to sublimate their feelings.
- Paul encouraged Timothy to treat young women as he would his own sister, so personalising the situation. (1 Timothy 5:2 *to younger women as sisters—with absolute purity.* NRSV This way of thinking gives people a lovely attitude towards others; it could also help to stop the desire to see an unacceptable image on a screen. We should never view anyone as an object.
- There are practical methods we can adopt to stop unsolicited and accidental incursions into pornographic sites, (if they could happen), such as always having the parental lock on the Internet search facility and keeping the Spam filter on at all times. This would ensure those with difficulty resisting temptation would have less trouble in overcoming their weaknesses.
- Finally, the fruit of the Holy Spirit includes self-control[201] Gal.5.23, Peter makes it plain that God has given to us sufficient divine power to overcome all such temptations in life, 1Peter 1.3-7. We must be the masters of ourselves. Proverbs 25:28. **Like a city breached, without walls, is one who lacks self-control.** NRSV.

Guilty? When Luther was writing his 95 Thesis he quoted an old German proverb, *"Not to do it again is the highest form of penitence."* You can put it right today with Job's covenant.

---

[201] The NIDNTT states: - egkrateia, (self-control) *the possibility of fashioning one's life in the way God desires, is never something firmly at one's disposal. It must always be received afresh as the gift of the Spirit in one's commitment to the gospel.*

61

When the bad guy owned up
Psalm 51

The background 2Samuel 11 & 12

Often David was saying in the Psalms how good he had been compared to others – not so here. He was the bad guy. And he was bad. Adultery, murder and cover-up.

"When Nathan came," says the introduction to the psalm, it would have been better if we could have said, after Bathsheba, or after Uriah but it was after Nathan who had challenged him. He thought he was getting away with it. He was guilty of adultery, intrigue and murder. The initial attempt was a cover up. **Some want a white wash others want washing white.**

Some years ago a well-known American television evangelist misbehaved. Prior to the discovery of his sin he had engaged, at a high salary, an Assemblies of God minister to work for him, who's job previously was to help ministers who had misbehaved morally. For years he had dealt with sin of people by exposure and correction. Now knowing the evangelist had committed adultery he sought to cover it up and so became part of the sin rather than the solution to the wrong doing. There are times when we can be on the good side and if we are not watchful we can transfer to the wrong side.

David first attempted to cover up was no good either for himself or for God. There is another thing guilty people do, which is to blame someone else, as in the case of Adam.

A sign of lack of repentance can be the indifference to the consequences for others. The solution is genuine sorrow.

David was not in a spiritual position, though he was a spiritual man. The status quo could remain. There were temporal consequences to David's sin and that was the rebellion of Absalom. It would seem that so often our sins are excused; we come to deal with them not to cover them over.

Man's part is finished when the confession is made and there is repentance. God takes over with His loving-kindness. In recent years some have sought to emphasise a covenant relationship in the translation of the Hebrew "hessed", but it is more the mercy of God and not just a contract between man and God.

He knew the possibility of blotting out it could be translated obliterate! In some Psalms David was saying that he had been more righteous than some, here the boot was on the other foot. It was not just to seek the removal of God's anger; it was to have the charge against him removed. Although the answer never came in the Old Testament it came in the New Testament.

Bildad asked the question. Job 25:4 *How then can man be justified with God? or how can he be clean that is born of a woman?* KJV Isaiah saw the promise in the future Isa 53:11 *He shall see of the travail of his soul, and shall be satisfied: by his knowledge shall my righteous servant justify many; for he shall bear their iniquities.* KJV

The shortcoming of the old law was solved when Jesus came. Acts 13:39 *And by him all that believe are justified from all things, from which you could not be justified by the law of Moses.* Paul lays it on the line God does not just forgive but declares a person right living when they have been wrong living. Romans 4:5 *But to him that works not, but believes on him that justifies the ungodly, his faith is counted for righteousness.* KJV

The statement that sin was against God. Uriah was a child of God. God's name was blasphemed. 2Sam.12.14 see AV. "Scorned the Lord" NRSV. Psalm 51.4 *I have sinned against you, especially you. I have done what you consider evil. So you hand down justice when you speak, and you are blameless when you judge.* GW. Every evil act against another person is an act against God. Jesus put it in the positive saying that whoever gives so much as a cup of cold water to another will be blessed.[202]

The cleansing.

Blot out v.1

Wash me v.2

Purge me v.7 Whiter than snow v.7

Then he states "Create in me a clean heart re-new a right spirit within me." See the use of the hyssop for cleansing of the leper. Leviticus 14

v.8 *Let me hear the sounds of joy and gladness; and though you have crushed me and broken me, I will be happy once again.*

He was concerned because he knew what happened to Saul.

v.11 *cast me not from your presence Take not your Holy Spirit from me.* (The first use of the Holy Spirit in Psalms)

v.12 *The joy of Salvation Uphold me.* See other versions. Then he could help others – see: - Luke 22.32 *but I have prayed for you that your own faith may not fail; and you, when once you have turned back, strengthen your brothers."* There was no need for it to be permanent.

What is original sin? Sin is lawlessness 1John 3.4 Original sin is that disposition to sin and its guilt that has been passed on from Adam.

---

[202] Mt 10:42 I can guarantee this truth: Whoever gives any of my humble followers a cup of cold water because that person is my disciple will certainly never lose his reward." GW

Guilt or condemnation Romans 5.12,15 *Sin came into the world through one person, and death came through sin. So death spread to everyone, because everyone sinned.* 1Cor.15.21,22 *Since a man brought death, a man also brought life back from death.* Pollution *"The human mind is the most deceitful of all things. It is incurable. No one can understand how deceitful it is."* Jeremiah 17.9

In Victor Hugo's Ninety-Three, his novel about the French Revolutionary War, a ship is caught in a terrible storm. The crew's plight is further compounded by the realisation that a cannon is loose below deck. Every wave turns the unchained cannon into an internal battering ram. Two brave sailors risk their lives to go below and secure the loose cannon. On their descent into the ship, they discuss the fact that the cannon within is more dangerous than the storm without. Although there is much to fear in life, our greatest danger is the sinful nature within us. We state that the inner desire to sin, is sin. Compare Pelagius and Augustine. The flesh is us, not an outside source. *"O wretched man that I am."* Romans 7.24.

This is one of the most well-known Psalms some say it is the most important because it deals with guilt and pardon peace and purity, repentance and cleansing. Yet we know from history that there were consequences to the sin. The rebellion of Absalom for one. We can be forgiven but live with the consequences.

62

The unfairness of life.

Think of the time good men seemed to lose out in life and in the Bible. Many of the prophets were killed culminating in the death of John the Baptist. Naboth lost to a wicked king and innocent Uriah here lost to a good man behaving badly. He walked about carrying his own death warrant with him. If only he had the fault of curiosity, he would have lived longer. In real life the bad guy often wins!

Could it be that Uriah had heard the gossip? and so acted in the way he did with no further desire to live? The Psalmist said "Why do the wicked prosper?" Success and prosperity are no proof of God's blessing. Though not an Israelite by birth Uriah was a worshipper of the Lord. He also behaved as one too.

- a) **Evil is often a random thing.** As the accident at Siloam (Luke 13.04) We look for a cause for evil. *"Who has sinned we say, this man or his parents?"* **Jesus does not point usually to a cause but to a purpose**. God will work it out for good. Romans 8.28. Now the "Ale House Philosophy" says, "Why should it have happened to Uriah he was a good man?" But the sun shines on the righteous and the unrighteous.
- b) **Many of life's anomalies can be overcome by faith and prayer.** *"This poor man cried and the Lord heard him"* said the Psalmist. God will only allow evil so much rope, then he

will step in. As with Israel in Egypt (Ex.2.23) *"Will not the Lord avenge those who call unto Him day and night?"* Luke 18.7 There is a point at which God steps in.

c) **Thirdly and most importantly it will finally be put right.** "We all have to give an account of ourselves before God." Worldly philosophy does not take that into account.

The true measure of a man or woman.

a) It was not Uriah's poor fighting that got him killed, it was his righteousness. David was not king because he was good. Therefore, fame and success of individual are to be questioned, it is not to be taken for granted that the person is good. During the latter part of the twentieth century Robert Maxwell built a newspaper empire in Britain, he was the toast of prime ministers yet took a fortune from his workers' pension fund. Others too are to be remembered causing heart ache and poverty to millions.

b) It was not Uriah's failure as a husband that his wife was unfaithful. It was that he did that which was right and had self-control in his life.

c) Don't start looking to be a failure though, many righteous people have done well!

The correction of sin

Psalm.32.3 Speaks of his feelings then. *When I kept silent about my sins, my bones began to weaken because of my groaning all day long.* GW It was a while afterwards that Nathan challenged him. What powerful words, *"You are that man."* David had just pronounced the death sentence on himself.

The Consequences of his Sin.

a) he missed extra blessings 1Samuel 12.8
b) He would have family troubles 12.11
c) The child would die. 12.14

63

I will go to him

2Samuel 12.16-23

A wife who loses a husband is called a widow. A husband who loses a wife is called a widower. A child who loses his parents is called an orphan. But...there is no word for a parent who loses a child, that's how awful the loss is![203]

The servants with David thought if he refuses food while the baby is sick how will he respond to his death? He was totally different, David washed and changed he was recovering from his grief because his attitude to death gave him hope. "I shall go to him, but he shall not return to me,"

Daniel, my sister's handsome, blond twenty-one-year-old son died by drowning while on a canoeing holiday in France. We were all devastated. Some months later my parents, who were of course Daniel's grandparents, were talking with Sylvia one of the Gypsy women at their village church. A son of hers had died some years before. She said to them something that helped. She told them that every morning as she awoke she felt was one day nearer to seeing him again. David felt that too, heaven was not just a place name,

---

[203] Neugeboren

it was home to his child. To all bereaved people that love the Lord there is that great anticipation too.

"There is no relationship like that of parent and child. It is unique and special...The bond between parent and child is so powerful that its strength endures time, distance, and strife. No loss is as significant as the loss of a child...On the death of a child, a parent feels less than whole."[204]

John and Lisa had just seen off their eighteen-year-old daughter who was returning to New York from England to her year out job as a nanny. Over Lockerbie in Scotland the plane exploded, there were no survivors. Like all grieving parents John and Lisa have sought over the years to come to terms with their lovely daughter's tragic death. One-day John said something to me that put the death of a child in context, he said, "The death of your child is not like a sickness you will recover from. It is like the amputation of a limb that you will forever have to live without."

Every person's grief is felt to them in a unique way. We all feel the pain of bereavement, but it comes to each one of us in a variety of ways. Yet there is this one thing that we can say, "We will meet again." There was a chorus of years ago, it went something like this: - "Each day tramping, nightly camping, one day nearer home."

How did David view death?

The woman that Joab sent to David to plead for Absalom's return said, *"For we must needs die, and are as water spilt on the ground, which cannot be gathered up again;"*[205] She was talking as if there was no life after death. Years earlier Samuel's mother Hannah had a positive view, especially after her prayer for a child was answered. *"The LORD kills, and he gives life. He makes people go down to the grave, (sheol) and he raises them up again."*[206] What did David have to say about it?

---

[204] Arnold and Gemma 1994, 25-27
[205] 2Samuel 14.14 KJV
[206] 1Samuel 2.6 GW

David saw death as the end of life on earth not as *the* end. When speaking of the considered necessary execution of Solomon's enemy he used "sheol" a place or a state, not an end in itself, (1Kings 2.6,9). Though some may not hold the titles of the psalms as authentic, we must also quote Psalm 16.10 *For you will not leave my soul in hell (sheol)*. KJV Though he did not see the departed dead as being in a state of joyful worship of God. It was not to him a none existent state, nor it would seem that he regarded it as a final state. He considered it a place where loved ones will meet again. Nathan the prophet too said as much, 1Chronicles 17.11 "you will go to your fathers." As the song says, "Loved ones will be waiting there." He could have possibly seen it as a place of rest.

64

An Inadequate response towards evil
2Samuel 13

The failure of Eli and of Samuel was the failure of David too. They all had let their children do what they wanted to do. There was insufficient discipline and correction. Nor was there any advice or guidance in sexual matters. Some things are difficult to deal with but we have to bite the bullet. One of the workings of the Holy Spirit in our lives is self-control.[207] If we allow our emotions to control our minds as our minds control our bodies we will be weak people. We become powerless to deal with inner thoughts. The power of God's peace must be the umpire of the raging in our hearts. Colossians 3.15 *Also, let Christ's peace control you. God has called you into this peace by bringing you into one body. Be thankful.* GW Amnon never sought to control his lust and it controlled him.

Having failed to guide and help his children David then compounded the problem. He never sanctioned Amnon for his evil deed. Though Tamar suggested the possibility of marriage, the law of God forbade it, but it would seem that it was acceptable to the society of the day.

---

[207] Galatians 5.23

Temptation increases the value we place on ourselves and decreases the harm it will do to others. Jezebel said to Ahab, *"You are the king you can have the vineyard."*[208] Jonadab, Amnon's cousin said, *"You are the king's son don't let anything keep you back from getting what you want."* Power and position does not give us the right to do something. It would seem that these cousins were used to having their way with women. Here was one young woman that seemed out of their reach.

There were two things that destroyed Amnon. One, his lack of self-control, and two, his choice of companion. After the rape his self-seeking became self-loathing, he destroyed not only Tamar but himself too. Paul gave advice on thought control to the Philippians.[209] Get looking at the good things and the good folks in your life. We must not let our passions be they sex, greed, jealousy, anger or bitterness captivate our thoughts. In David's life his companions and friends helped make him what he was, in Amnon's life his relationships destroyed him.

It is often suggested that rape is an act to prove that one person has power over another. This may certainly be so in some cases but I feel that rape is, in most situations, the lust of a person that has gone wild and uncontrollable, some men have far stronger sexual desires than others. So there was no deeper or ulterior motive to Amnon's evil deed other than he was out of control and desperate to have his own way with Tamar.[210]

Deal with your difficulties. In the Greek version of the Old Testament it adds more to 2Samuel 13.21 this is what it says: - (*When*

---

[208] 1Kings 21.7

[209] Philippians 4.8 Finally, beloved, whatever is true, whatever is honourable, whatever is just, whatever is pure, whatever is pleasing, whatever is commendable, if there is any excellence and if there is anything worthy of praise, think about these things. NRSV

[210] For an alternative suggestion see the Word Biblical Commentary, "Hence it is plausible that Amnon's love for Tamar was, largely, part of his plan to put Absalom and his family in their place!" Suggesting that Absalom would be next in line for the throne if another son of David had died.

David heard what had happened to Tamar, he was very angry.) But Amnon was his oldest son and also his favourite, and David would not do anything to make Amnon unhappy. The NRSV seems to be happy to follow it.

David did not deal with the situation. We are often guilty of the same practice, if we can avoid a matter we often will, and it is true that some problems will fade away with time. If there is something clearly wrong, and can be seen to be wrong, we must deal with it, if it is in our power to do so. Time is rarely on our side, we do not need the second law of thermodynamics to tell us we, and situations tend to decay over time.

65

Don't beat up David.

David was not the idea father. But we must be cautious, not all children are born angels. There is a story told of a theologian, he was an Oxford don who went to teach at a Pentecostal Bible College that later became the Assemblies of God College in England. He had a sympathetic belief with the early British monk Pelagius, who did not believe in original sin. When his first child reached two years of age he was something of a rascal. So he felt he needed to cast the demon out. Needless to say it did not work, there was no demon to cast out. Some children are more of a problem than others.

On July 12th in 2010 the "New York Times" quoted at length an article by Dr Richard Friedman a professor of psychiatry at Weill Cornell Medical College in Manhattan. It resulted in a large number of emails in response. He pointed out that good parents can have bad children. Not that that is anything new. Our life observations let us know that to be true. Friedman stated: - For better or worse, parents have limited power to influence their children. That is why they should not be so fast to take all the blame — or credit — for everything that their children become.

At my first church a new lady started to attend, her name was Charmayne. She and her husband had a very bright child. At two or three years of age he suddenly went within himself and was diagnosed as autistic. Charmayne used to take him to the psychiatrist. She told me she felt as if they were really attempting to analyse her more than her son. So often parents are scrutinised when there are problems with their children.

There is the possibility of deep darkness in the heart of mankind. The mighty power of the Gospel is life changing, we anticipate that a bad person will become good and an already good person will be even better through the power of Jesus Christ. The hope that all children will become good because their parents are good is sadly wrong. Allister McGrath quotes Terry Eagleton, a cultural theorist, who describes the dream of untrammelled human progress as a bright-eyed superstition.[211]

Teachers, parents, preachers and others all have input into the lives of young people, hopefully for good. Not only to inform their consciences but also to seek to activate their consciences to deal with everyday situations in a moral and caring way. David could be charged with failing to do all that he could do for his sons. The trouble is so many of us accuse ourselves of the same, and when our children fail we are haunted every day with our failures. Perhaps we should not condemn ourselves so much.

Often when discussing the bringing up of children the Bible proverb is quoted: - *Train children in the right way, and when old, they will not stray.*[212] This is a proverb and proverbs are not promises and must not be mistaken for such. It is a principle that is generally true but we cannot hold God to account when we have done our level best at the instruction part and unfortunately the child does not measure up to our satisfaction. Nor can we accuse parents of failing in their duty because of a wayward youth. We are left to cry to God for mercy and help. He is always on our side and will pursue them to the ends of the earth, they cannot escape his love.

---

[211] Alister McGrath, Inventing the universe, 2016 page 131
[212] Proverbs 22.6 NRSV

66

The sea-change Jesus brought
Mark 9.42

We have not let David completely off the hook when we admit that not all children are born good. There is a matter to consider. The Old Testament was very strong on the importance of respect for parents. As the commandment says, "Honour your father and mother." Without a doubt Jesus also clearly spoke of the importance of that command. Especially when some were failing to care for their elderly parents.[213] Yet Jesus taught with a different emphasis, he said be careful you do not destroy the faith of one of these young ones. Paul furthered the theme saying, *"And, fathers, do not provoke your children to anger, but bring them up in the discipline and instruction of the Lord."*[214] Jesus sought to change the way people considered who their neighbours were, and how they should treat their enemies as well as the way men should respect women. He almost alone of the rabbis took women around with him as well as men. Then there was this additional change of emphasis on the importance of children's relationship with God and with adults. It was a sea-change in sexual equality, in personal relationships, as well as raising the profile of children.

---

[213] Matthew 7.10-13
[214] Ephesians 6.4 NRSV

Perhaps David changed for the better as he grew older. He challenged Solomon to be faithful to the Lord and he also prayed for him as well.

David's Charge: - 1Chronicles 28:9 *"And you, my son Solomon, learn to know your father's God. Serve the LORD wholeheartedly and willingly because he searches every heart and understands every thought we have. If you dedicate your life to serving him, he will accept you. But if you abandon him, he will reject you from then on.* GW

David's prayer: - 1Chronicles 29:19 *"Make my son Solomon completely committed to you so that he will obey your commands, requests, and laws and do everything to build the palace I have planned."* GW The palace, being of course, the temple of God.

Could it be that we are missing out as Christians by failing to give a challenge to young people? Paul gave a charge to Timothy, in fact more than one. Though Timothy was not Paul's literal son and this was a charge to care for the people of God and the Gospel of God. Yet there could be a case as young people leave home for the parents to challenge their children to follow Jesus, making it a special occasion in the life of young people.

67

Knowing which way the wind is blowing
2Samuel 14

Joab always seems to have had his ear to the ground. He knew David's longings and knew the feeling in the nation. Absalom had been exiled long enough. His use of a female actor was subtle, and perhaps necessary. David might not have listened to him. Had he taken a leaf out of Nathan's book, or was this a practice among the people?[215] Little Thomas Bilney from Norfolk practised something similar. Early in the sixteenth century he found salvation by faith in Christ alone. He asked the strongly Catholic Hugh Latimer to hear his confession. In that confession he spoke of the peace he found through believing, and his being adopted into the family of God. Latimer later said that he leaned more in that confession than in much reading for many years before.[216] Anyway Latimer found peace in believing that day too. Bilney was later burnt at the stake in Norwich and Latimer some years later at Oxford.

Joab was aware of the political climate, people talked and he listened. When Nathan took his rebuke to the king, he was opposing the action of David, here it was different, Joab knew the king just

---

[215] See comment in BBCIVP It was not an unknown strategy but would require a woman of skill to carry it out.

[216] History of the Reformation of the Sixteenth Century, Volume 5 Jean Henri Merle d'Aubigné

needed a push in what he thought was the right direction. He never anticipated the damage Absalom would later cause. He felt it was right at the time to invite Absalom back. Who could say otherwise? The law of God said life for a life. Mercy said otherwise. The pain parents feel because of sibling murder cannot be over-estimated. A family connected to our church had a son put in prison, he stamped to death his brother in a drunken rage. The murdered man never lived to see his first and only child. The young widow was left to fend for herself. The mother of the sons had the pain of prison visiting and was mother of the victim too. She would know how David felt.

As Christians our code of ethics is found from the Word of God. Although some would consider this arbitrary,[217] we consider differently. God is not only good and just but also loving and merciful. There was an obvious lack of repentance by Absalom. Someone who takes vengeance into their own hands can sometimes be ruthless in other areas too. God's ways are the best ways. They are not always the easy ways though. There can be a wind of opinion that is blowing throughout a society but it is not always the right way. Leaders must not always give in to the prevailing wind that is blowing in a church or country. It must be "What does the scripture say?" Absalom exiled himself it was good that he did and better if he had been left there too. David was guilty of sinful mercy.

In saying Christian ethics are based upon the Word of God, we can perhaps define what is meant. Hebrews 12.2,3 speaks to the downcast and despondent Christians saying: - verse 2 "Turn your eyes away from other things and look to Jesus"[218] and verse 3 "Think about Jesus." Although Aquinas and others talk about our natural feelings and our inner conscience the simple formula, "What would Jesus do?" is a better way to decide the rights and wrongs of a situation. The Gospels give us a sufficient view of Jesus and the New Testament letters give us clear guidance on the way to go. Our natural consciences can be damaged at times.[219]

---

[217] See Ethics Matter by P & C Vardy, SCM Press 2012. for ethical considerations.
[218] Aphorao – see Thayer etc,
[219] 1Timothy 4.2 kauteriazo

68

You must choose right or wrong?

For thousands of years, people have sought a viable philosophy for ethical answers to moral questions. If we override justice because of our emotions as David did, we can be in trouble. Jesus never spoke of justice in the beatitudes but he did of mercy. Often Christians have absorbed philosophies that are of non-Christian origin to guide them on that which they believe is a moral course. Were they right or were they wrong? Aquinas had no qualms about taking hold of the thoughts of Aristotle and intermingling them with his theology. He was a Dominican, the Franciscans had no time for Greek philosophy. The Anglican, Bishop Berkeley of Cloyne, in more recent times took to Utilitarianism. Should we follow their example or lean a little more to the Scripture alone?

Is it naïve of us to say, "Scripture alone," as the guide, not only for our means of salvation, but also for our way of life? And that the basis of our morality is the example of Jesus and the outworking of that in the lives of the apostles? My answer to that is no it is not naïve. Peter clearly thought how we were to act in times of persecution was to follow Jesus. It may be simple but it is not simplistic.

1Peter 2:21 *God called you to endure suffering because Christ suffered for you. He left you an example so that you could follow in his footsteps.* GW.

The question, "What would Jesus do?" has been used in comedy sketches and often made fun of. Yet Peter taught that we could trace over the life of Jesus, copying his manner of life. Spurgeon preached it, Thomas a Kempis wrote about it, as also Sheldon in his novel entitled, "In His Steps," Let us consider it.

Jesus taught the equality of all, young or old, rich or poor, male or female. He never suggested, "The greatest happiness for the greatest number," was the way forward. Nor that the natural law was the sum total of our decision making for morality. But would this work for modern ethical dilemmas? Saviour siblings, gene manipulation, in vitro fertilisation as well as abortion, euthanasia, same sex marriage which are just a few of the problems we have to deal with today. Yet when we think about it, Jesus is a saviour sibling, he was always healing too. We do not always need things spelt out, they can be dealt with by comparisons of the attitudes and actions taken by Jesus and the disciples. The more we read of the life of Jesus the more we can be in tune with God's attitude to what is right and wrong. I have sometimes been surprised at devious and unpleasant practices of those who claim to be followers of Jesus. They have caused hurt and harm to others and have been unchallenged without anyone saying, "Is this how Jesus would have done it?" How could a Christian be acting like a sociopath? They will not if they make the decision to always ask, "What would Jesus do?" And then do it the Jesus way.

A Charismatic Bishop in the Church of England was being made the Archbishop of Canterbury. He was fitted out in all the regalia of an archbishop for his ordination, a friend came to him and asked the question, "I wonder what the man with sandals would have to say?" How would the man that had no lodgings for the night react to the news of ministers having multiple houses and executive jets?

Abigail Disney produced a film in 2015 called "The Armor of Light." It focused on an American pro-life minister coming to the realisation that being pro-gun is inconsistent with his pro-life stance. Could we ever even think of Jesus carrying a weapon? He who would sooner be killed than kill, no way!

***It is not so much our doing, it is our
becoming, becoming like Jesus.***

If we can have a Christian ethic for an individual person, is it possible to have one for a nation? Although Jesus spoke in terms of Jew and Gentile he never spoke in terms of nationhood. Though there may be a Muslim nation adhering to the Sharia law, there is not, in the same sense the possibility of a "Christian nation." Yet of course people will refer to some countries as being Christian. Though Jesus spoke of respect for the government, even when it treated its people unjustly, as did Paul, Jesus never gave advice for running a country. There are principles a nation can take from Jesus, such as mercy overshadows justice, and many others in a similar vein. In fact, Jesus did not make a big thing of different nations. Are we today making too much of boundaries and land that Jesus would not have done?

69

When the chickens come home to roost
2Samuel 15

Nathan had prophesied to David 2Sam.12.11 *Someone from your own family will cause you a lot of trouble, and I will take your wives and give them to another man before your very eyes.* NRSV

Don't let Anger turn to Malice. (Malice – to hold on to vengeful feelings) We can only have a little understanding of Absalom's feelings toward his half-brother Amnon for raping his sister if we have never been through the experience ourselves. Something should have been done by David there and then but it wasn't. **Yet the sin of Amnon caused Absalom to sin.** Don't let the sin of others cause a build-up of resentment and bitterness in your life. Ephesians 4.26 *Be ye angry, and sin not: let not the sun go down upon your wrath:* KJV There is no way that Tamar's rape could be forgotten overnight. Anger must be there or righteousness wouldn't be. Yet the principle holds good, don't let it turn to malice. God is not talking about a literal twenty-four hours, He is asking you to do your best to deal with it as soon as is possible and with some things it will take years.

Observing an Absalom

Absalom was David's own son. An Absalom in our life is any person who wishes to take what is rightfully ours. He was prepared to wait for a long period of time 2Samuel 13.22 – he would pretend friendship – he would steal affections 15.4 – no act was too bad for him to do – he involved others in his evil – he was ambitious for himself. We have a phrase, "Two Faced," it fitted Absalom.

Dealing with an Absalom

Don't let them get under your skin. They are people that would run off with your friends, husband or wife or your daughters or sons or life savings and if you are a pastor, your church. It made it appear that David condoned Absalom's acts by allowing him back in Jerusalem. If you have reason not to trust someone keep them at arm's length. Do not endanger your family or friends. Absalom would not have been such a danger to David if he had been left in exile. There are many people who regret making friends with some people!

A friend in need is a friend in deed.

This surely must have been an occasion when David wrote one of his psalms. Psalm 55.12-14 *For it was not an enemy that reproached me; then I could have borne it: neither was it he that hated me that did magnify himself against me; then I would have hid myself from him: But it was thou, a man mine equal, my guide, and mine acquaintance. We took sweet counsel together, and walked unto the house of God in company.* KJV

He was let down by Ahithophel (whom he mentions here in the psalm), as well as his own son. He further mentions betrayal in Psalm 41:9 *Even my bosom friend in whom I trusted, who ate of my bread, has lifted the heel against me.* NRSV Because betrayal is the ultimate hurt. He then discovered his true friends. People who had only been with him for a short time but risked all with him such as the Giittites from Gath. Other people who might have been looking for a quiet life, old men who in weakness stood for righteousness (2Samuel 19.34). Have you heard the saying, "They don't know who their true friends are"?

This is one of the greatest stories in the Bible – intrigue, strategy, counter intelligence, disinformation, confidence boosting tactics are all here, and there was a winner.

70

A time to run?
2Samuel 15

Ecc.3.1 *To everything there is a season, and a time to every purpose under the heaven:* KJV David did not have a famous last stand – he was too wise for that. Sometimes there is need to retreat and gather yourself together. There are times of evangelism and times of prayer. Times to shout out loud and times to be quiet before God. David's actions saved a country and no doubt many people's lives as well, even though some would later die in battle. We must be prepared to make wise choices as well as brave ones. Jesus would sometimes rest a while as well as being in the forefront of the battle for souls. Be careful of a retreat it must be essential. When Billy Graham was due to hold a crusade in one city some suggested he cancel and spend more time praying, he refused, and there was one mighty crusade that set the USA talking.

Hushai's reasoning seems very sensible to us, though of course he was giving bad advice deliberately. Ahithophel's advice seems chancier. Yet Ahithophel knew he was so right and took his life knowing the final outcome before it happened. He had taken into account some factors that Absalom had not reckoned with. One was the surprise factor. David had not expected a rebellion by one of his own sons and a personal colleague. Trouble had come from an unexpected quarter. The discovery that his own flesh and blood, one whom he loved, was prepared to take his life was an emotional shock.

Traitors have various reasons for their acts of betrayal, whether in marriage, friendship, or the betrayal of a country. It could be that they are caught in a trap, or they see a chance of self-aggrandisement or even because they feel it is the right way to go. Often the remorse is great for what they have done. Judas had given a kiss he could not forget and so took his own life. It was said, "Ahithophel was with Absalom," but Absalom was not with Ahithophel. He knew the writing was on the wall for him, there would be no place like second in the kingdom for him. Absalom could be influenced by anyone who flattered him.

Our church was composed mainly of people who had come to Christ locally through the church and our ministry. I remember a personal setback when some of our own converts left and went to another church. One could accept people who had been previously Christians and had not originated from our fellowship moving on. But these were people who had been saved and changed through our ministry. We have to get up as quickly as possible when we are knocked for six. Yet we need time to readjust and build ourselves up again. Ahithophel knew that, and took into account the psychological effect on David and his stalwart soldiers who would be faithful to the end. When I was young I considered a Christian going on a retreat an unnecessary act. Now I know differently.

There was a second factor. David had passed his prime. His agility and energy levels were on the decline. Ahithophel must have considered it, Absalom had dismissed it. Age reduces our physical output, but there is no need for us to be overcome by the weakening of our bodily ability when our experience and expertise can point us in other directions to achieve the same results. Caleb was the exception, at eighty-five he said he was as strong as when he was forty-five.[220] Mind you that was his assessment of himself. The preachers might challenge all the old age pensioners with such

---

[220] Joshua 14.11

texts but the truth is the older we are the slower we become. If you are thinking of doing something that requires physical strength do it now! When John was writing to the church he spoke of the knowledge of the "fathers" but the strength of the young.[221]

The courage of Hushai can never be over-estimated, nor of the others that formed the network of spies for David. To remain calm and convincing while amongst the enemy is no mean feat. Jesus said to the disciples, "I send you out as sheep among wolves." Wars have been won through the courage of people such as those in the SOE and French Resistance during the second world war. Can we compare the courage of the disciples after the death of Jesus to those such as Hushai? Yes, we can, although they were known for being Christians, as opposed to those who had infiltrated the enemy ranks, they knew they could be arrested and imprisoned and executed at any time. There are millions of Christians in such a situation today.

---

[221] 1John 2.13

71

Post-mortem of the Rebellion
Psalm 3 & 2Samuel 15.1-31

How did David feel while this was happening? The introduction to Psalm Three mentions that David wrote it while they were running from Absalom.

Hymns have often been written during times of crisis. Charlotte Elliot was an invalid, one night when others had gone out to raise funds for a school to be built she could not help and felt very down. Out of that experience she wrote, "Just as I am." So we could continue with "What a friend," "There were ninety and nine," and many others. David gives the occasion of his writing in about fourteen psalms they help us to get to know a little of his life story and his personal feelings.

It was a clash between the cultures of youth and of age. It was a breakdown in family relationships. It was based in part on genuine grievances, it could have been true that there were insufficient judges.

David might have liked the bowing and scraping. He was now king of a small empire! Absalom found a weak spot. His rebellion was popular! It would seem that Absalom couldn't lose. There was perhaps a silent majority for David but not enough to fight, Shimei felt free to stone him.

The Rumour Psalm 3.2 ... God had parted company with David. The people said God had left David. He would remember the time God and Saul parted company and no doubt that would scare him. What others say to you affects you far more than you might think. He seemed to be on a one-way ticket from Jerusalem, but God had the return ticket waiting for him.

David's attitude: - he called out to God. He said you are My Glory and the lifter of my head. He left Jerusalem with his head bowed but he would return with his head lifted high!

The Problem is Solved: - when you can sleep again. Some said don't count the sheep, talk to the shepherd. How long should you pray? Until you receive an answer. It is not wrong if you cannot sleep because of a problem it is wrong if you do not pray it through so you can sleep. I remember praying much for a family member for a long period time. Then one day an assurance came in my heart that all would be well. Peace came into my heart. And all was well.

After Assurance What? The second part of his prayer was, "I know it is all going to be all right but O God do it now, Arise O Lord." Let others see it. "Smack them in the mouth!"

David came into Jerusalem with: -

- Saul has killed his thousands David tens of thousands.
- Out in the dead of night let down the wall by knotted sheets.
- In with the tribes asking for him
- Now out a hunted man only to return again another day.

An aspiring young minister came down from the pulpit deflated after preaching a rubbish sermon, "If thou wentest up as thou camest down." Said the good Yorkshire Deacon, "Thou wouldst have comest down as thou wentest up!"

The Butler in Genesis 40 had the same experience as David. It was palace to prison then back again. Joseph also could have written a book on the ups and downs entitled, "From pit, to position, to prison, to palace then to prominence."

David's attitude is not the brazen look of a defiant sinner, nor the courageous last stand of a Jezebel, nor is it the smirk of a man who has escaped conviction. It is the joyful smile of a man in love with God, magnanimous in victory, weeping for the wayward. God will lift up your head too!

72

Allegiances
2Samuel 15.14

There comes a time when we must choose to whom we give our allegiance. It happens in democratic countries, when a choice is made for a government to run the country. When families split up and children have to decide on which parent to live with. Then when there are altercations between individuals, such as between Paul and Barnabas. Yet the vital one comes when a decision has to be made for or against the Lord Jesus. Life is full of choice making. David's friends and acquaintances had to come to a decision. Were they for or against Absalom?

Ittai from Gath had to make a decision, he had only recently joined David in Jerusalem. He could have stayed and served Absalom, but he chose David. Although he served with Joab and Abishai at the beginning of the battle with Absalom no mention is made of him at the end. It might have cost him his life. Why did he make that decision to be with David? He was no fair weather friend. It was the character of David that he loved. He was happy to leave his children and relatives in David's care. Did he too have a love for God? It may be that he knew of Obed-edom[222] who was blessed when the ark of

---

[222] 2Samuel 6.11

God was in his house because he too was from the Philistine city of Gath.[223] Allegiance can be costly but there comes a time when we have to make choices.

David was again soon to find his true friends from his time-serving friends. One shock for him was that Ahithophel had been conspiring against him. Ahithophel was a one-man think-tank. Like Herman Kahn of the Hudson Institute in the USA during the "Cold War," Ahithopel's IQ was off the scale. He could work out the best strategy and would know the end result before the battle had been fought. But he was a step behind God and so he lost out.

Faithful Friends. The priests, Abiathar and Zadok (though their names are usually in the reverse order), and Hushai whose IQ was nearly as good as Ahithophel's were risking their lives and the lives of their families for God. The sons of the priests were about to have the adventure of a life time. Who knows their age? They may still have been teenagers. Like many youngsters who risked their lives working for the French and Dutch Resistance during the second world war, and others who kept silent about Jewish people their parents were hiding. Allegiance should be a family affair. Joshua could say, "As for me and my house we will serve the Lord."[224]

In any allegiance or alliance there is the possibility of betrayal. These that retuned to Jerusalem had to trust one another. In addition to those joining David along came Ziba the servant of king Saul and more latterly the servant of Mephibosheth, but more of him later. He too was prepared to risk his life with David, had he judged that he stood a better chance with David than Absalom or was it a genuine heart felt choice he made?

What makes us decide on our friendships? Could it be personal ambition? Or what seems the safest option? Then how do our family fit in to the direction we are taking? Now what about loyalty and trust as well as affection? We can love a leader but many "pastors"

---

[223] They were called Gittites.
[224] Joshua 24.15

have lead people "up the garden path." Jonestown[225] and Waco[226] are but examples. The decisions must be what is right and what is wrong, not on who will win. It has been noted that the "West" think in terms of innocence or guilt but the "East" in terms of shame and honour. We might feel for someone but if they are in the wrong then we must correct the matter before we proceed with any union. Just because an individual has made a mistake, as David did, it does not mean we should write them off. Choose with prayer, choose with the Word of God, choose to be with godly people at your side. David did not try to force any to follow him. A true leader will not coerce, force or in any way put pressure on you. To whom or what you give your allegiance must be your choice and yours alone.

Pragmatic relationships work on a simple, but dangerous basis, such as my enemy's enemy is my friend. Which can have drastic consequences for the future.

---

[225] In 1978 over nine hundred people committed suicide either by force or willingly. They originated from the People's Temple, Indiana under the leadership of Jim Jones.

[226] In 1993 over seventy people were killed in a siege by the FBI

73

Keeping life in perspective
2Samuel 16.5 - 23

Shimei the mud-slinger. He was throwing stones, David had weapons of war. Abishai wanted to remove Shimei's head from his neck. David put it in perspective. This was one of King Saul's followers. Many were against them and if David's own son was, then why should Shimei be killed when other were far more dangerous? There will always be people that are against us, or let's say people that are not on our side. Shimei was not wrong in what he called David, God called David a man of blood too!

David made a statement that was true for him but might not always be right in every situation. He stated that if God was with him he would return victorious and could deal with the situation of Shimei then. But there is a sense if something is in the plan of God it will come to fruition. Gamaliel also gave the same sentiments to the Sanhedrin.[227] Perhaps we can make a distinction between two situations. If it is part of God's eternal plan, then it will be dealt with. But if it is a case of justice and right or wrong it may be left to the judgement day before it is put right. There are multiplied times in the Scriptures when the people in the right were wronged, and

---
[227] Acts 5.34-39

never saw justice on this earth and Revelation speaks of them by the thousand.

If we feel because we are in the right then justice will be done and we will be vindicated, it might not be in this life, but one day it will be put right. Don't be side-lined from your purpose in life. David was soon to have the battle of battles for him and his followers, out gunned and outnumbered fighting with loyal but tired out troops.

We, like Abishai, can seek to crack a nut with a sledge hammer. When we are in trouble we tend to lose perspective on the situation. Small matters can become magnified and take our eyes off the real problem. Let side-issues remain side-issues. So if your Shimei comes out cursing don't seek to defend yourself. Mud does stick, but maybe you can wipe some of it off at a later date, wait till it dries it is easier.

Life's perhaps. 2Samuel 17.12 *Perhaps the LORD will notice my misery and give me some blessings to take the place of his curse." GNB* David not only spoke of the need for reasonableness in dealing with Shimei but he also had a hope. God was still going to give him something good. It was the psalm of Moses that turned this "perhaps" into a prayer. *Psalm 90.15 Give us now as much happiness as the sadness you gave us during all our years of misery. GNB.* My wife has often prayed this prayer for people who have had rough time. I never thought much about till I saw that it was David's prayer too. Have you had a tough time? Then make your prayer, "Lord can I have some blessings as well as the problems."

74

Ahithophel's not so sweet counsel
2Samuel 17

If Psalm 55.12-14 is a reference to Ahithophel then David describes him as a man with the same interests and of the same mind, rather than rank.[228] The GNB says, *"But it is you, my companion, my colleague and close friend."* Betrayal can be the ultimate hurt. His close friend might have been the originator of the coup d'état rather than Absalom. There was no doubt of Ahithophel's early involvement, see 2Samuel.15.12.

Once, when a young woman left her husband for his friend, I suddenly felt the pain of betrayal myself. She had stood before me and God saying that she would be faithful to her husband only letting death part them. It was not the first marriage break up I had faced in Church but it somehow hit me deeper in my being. It was then I realised that Judas' betrayal of Jesus was also a betrayal of the disciples. They would feel the pain of it too. God speaks of his pain when being deserted by those he loves.

---

[228] See Word Biblical Commentary lit. "a man according to my value (or rank)." The idea of rank is likely to be secondary to that of similarity of mind and interests. NIV has "like myself." NAB has "my other self," and NEB has "a man of my own sort."

Ahithophel advocated a quick short sharp surgical strike, so Hushai knowing this would be the most satisfactory way of destroying David offered the alternative of shock and awe tactics with overwhelming force. It gave David time to escape and gave Joab the opportunity to select the battleground so that a mass of troops would not have the advantage.

Shimei's neighbours.[229] The courage and bravery of everyday people must have put the treacherous actions of Ahithophel into context for David. This story makes most spy novels look tame. A young servant girl, a woman at home, and other everyday people were changing the course of history. So often we feel we have to be doing something for God every day of our lives. It is not so. It may just be one action for which God wants us,[230] and that one act can change the world around us.

Philip Haille wrote of the little village of Le Chambon in France, a town whose people, unlike others in France, hid their Jews from the Nazis. Haille went there, wondering what sort of courageous, ethical heroes could risk all to do such extraordinary good. He interviewed people in the village and was overwhelmed by the ordinariness. They weren't heroes or smart, discerning people. Haille decided that the one factor that united them was their attendance, Sunday after Sunday, at their little church, where they heard the sermons of Pastor Trochme. Over time, they became by habit people who just knew what to do and did it. When it came time for them to be courageous, the day the Nazis came to town, they quietly did what was right. One old woman, who faked a heart attack when the Nazis came to search her house, later said, 'Pastor always taught us that there comes a time in every life when a person is asked to do something for Jesus. When our time came, we knew what to do.' Between three and five thousand Jews were saved by this one village!

---

[229] The woman that hid the messengers down the well was in the same village as Shimei. Her family were in considerable danger.

[230] Ephesians 5:16 Redeeming the time, because the days are evil. (Time here is kairos – an opportunity, rather than chronos – time in general. Not forgetting Esther coming to the kingdom for "such a times as this."

"The responsibility of Christians," their pastor, André Trocmé, had reminded them the day after France surrendered to Nazi Germany, "Is to resist the violence that will be brought to bear on their consciences through the weapons of the spirit." It is said that the villagers never considered the things they did as heroic, it was several decades before their actions became well known.[231]

It was not only the young but also the old who rallied around David. Now others were coming with provisions. Notably one was eighty-year-old Barzillai, he could feed the troops even if he could not fight the enemy. Some have suggested that this could have been tribute from some but they seem to have willingly given the supplies and were well rewarded after the event.

World War II was considerably won by the provision of weaponry for the war, not just won by the fighting men. The British aircraft production[232] and the American ship building[233] industries made a major impact. And I must mention my mother who left the library in her youth to work in a factory making shells and other armaments for the war effort as well as hundreds of thousands of other women. Every person can play a part in the divine scheme of God. For every David there is a Ziba and Barzillai, just as there was a donkey waiting for Jesus on Palm Sunday. There is excitement at the battle front, but there is a sense of belonging and achievement behind the scenes too. Every soldier on the front line appreciates the medics and cooks and all the others checking the kit for the next sortie.

The leaders that came with Barzillai, (who was most likely of the tribe of Manasseh,) are of interest to us. One was Machir from

---

[231] Bible.com and Wikipedia See also the film on the village.
[232] a *Time Magazine* cover story declared, "Even if Britain goes down this fall [1940], it will not be Lord Beaverbrook's fault. If she holds out, it will be his triumph. This war is a war of machines. It will be won on the assembly line."(Wikipedia)
[233] Henry Kaiser's shipyards once built a 10,500-ton ship in less than five days. The average was a ship every forty-five days. (Wikipedia)

Lo-debar who was the protector of Jonathan's son Mephibosheth.[234] He, seeing how David had cared for him, would be sympathetic to him. He would also be from Manasseh's tribe. This leaves us with Nahash, who could be the King of Ammon at this time. (His father's name was the same as the king who fought against Saul.) He might have thought it wise to give to David but it could be that old enemies had become friends, and was genuine in his giving.

Paul spoke of Phoebe a deaconess in Romans 16.1,2 *I commend to you our sister Phoebe, a deacon of the church at Cenchreae, so that you may welcome her in the Lord as is fitting for the saints, and help her in whatever she may require from you, for she has been a benefactor of many and of myself as well.* NRSV. He uses the feminine word "prostatis" (benefactor) which means a helper of those without citizenship, a patron. Let us be "patron saints"!

---

[234] 2Samuel 9.4,5

75

O Absalom, Absalom my son
2Samuel 18

David's love for Absalom was not in question. The army generals were all threatened to save him alive. The end of this chapter is one of the most touching heart cries in the Old Testament. A king weeping for the death of a wayward son. The fact that hundreds of sons and husbands had died on both sides of the conflict had not burned into his soul. It was one of his sons that had died, the fact that Absalom would have killed him never registered with him.

We too can be callously indifferent to the death of other people's sons yet sorrow for our own as if no one else mattered. In 1982 Margaret Thatcher the British prime minister ordered the armed forces to retake the Falkland Islands from the Argentinians, nearly one thousand troops in total from both sides died. Just earlier in the year her son, in his late twenties, went missing in the Sahara Desert in a car race. At least one of the newspapers wrote that she was seen to have wept in public when her son was temporally lost in the desert. Just a month or two later the British and Argentinian troops were fighting and dying around the Falklands. One of the queen's sons was also among the British forces. The Iron Lady as she was known was affected just the same as David. She coped with the death of hundreds of young men but went to pieces when her own son was missing.

The difference can be felt when we are personally affected by grief. A civil war can be the most devastating of wars, three quarters of a million people died in the American Civil War,[235] far more than in any other war in which Americans were involved. This was a civil war that set brother against brother, well at least cousin against cousin and father against son. The effect is not only on the loss of life but also on the long term legacy of hatred to others who caused unnecessary suffering, grief and death.

Though David wept for his son yet there is a question that comes to mind. When he knew that Absalom was on his way to Jerusalem with the rebel troops he could have left on his own and handed power to his son by default. There was a greater reason why he could not have surrendered to his son, simply this: Absalom had shown little regard for people and was prepared to worm his way by flattery into the position of king. David saw beyond the easy way out, because there was a fatal flaw in the character of Absalom. We must never take the easy way out for ourselves if it leaves others in danger. Many years ago I knew a teenage girl. She had left home to escape the abuse of her own father. More than that she told the police of his abuse, not for justice alone, but to keep her younger sisters from the same fate. It was at considerable personal cost, but it saved others. There are times when we cannot ignore a wrong because it would harm individuals too. It cost David, and many others, but it had to be done, to strengthen the morality of their fledgling nation.

Defeating an Absalom.

Joab took no notice of David's request for the life of Absalom to be spared. It was Joab who was instrumental in previously bringing back Absalom to Jerusalem after he murdered his brother, so he must have felt responsible himself. He chose the battleground, and made short work of him. It was necessary for the kingdom to

---

[235] New York Times 2 April 2012 twenty percent more than the original figures.

be secured for the future – don't let sympathy for a wrong person cloud your judgement. Joab let the Sudanese man take the message because he knew that Ahimaaz (2Samuel 18.19) would represent good news, but for David it was good and bad news, for Absalom was his son. There are times when we have to give bad news. I once had to tell some friends of my nephew Daniel that he had died tragically by drowning. I was still in shock, but seeing the look of horror and utter grief on their faces to what I was saying hit home to me. When we have good news we must share it, bad news is horrible to share.

Magnanimity in victory. (Magnanimity – above petty feelings)

Joab did not continue to chase the defeated enemy (18.16) – they were of the same race. David did not allow Joab to kill some of the people who gave David a hard time. It has been suggested there would not have been a second world war if Germany had been treated better in their defeat after the first world. After the second war the defeated were treated much better. If you are ever right in your discussions with another never rub it in! If you are to deal with great things you are to rise above the petty small things in life.

76

Acting defeated in the day of Victory
2Samuel 19

He had seen the loss but not the gain. Things had got out of proportion Joab said I think you would have preferred all of us dead to your son.

The Rebuke of a leader. V5 *"Today you have covered with shame the faces of all your officers who have saved your life today, and the lives of your sons and your daughters, and the lives of your wives and your concubines, for love of those who hate you and for hatred of those who love you. You have made it clear today that commanders and officers are nothing to you; for I perceive that if Absalom were alive and all of us were dead today, then you would be pleased.* NRSV

David needed a friend to tell him he was wrong. He did not know his friends from his enemies. People have willed their entire possessions to people who have never cared for them and given nothing more than a token to friends and relatives who have looked after them for years. One lady I buried left in her will that she knew her friend who had helped her was not money conscious so she gave it to others!

Many Christian live in defeat when they could be enjoying the victory. (A Japanese soldier lived for years in the Indonesian jungle not knowing the 2nd world war was over.) They grasp all the negatives but do appreciate the positives. It was because of this that Paul prayed for the Ephesians this prayer: - Ephesians 1.16-19

I do not cease to give thanks for you as I remember you in my prayers I pray that the God of our Lord Jesus Christ, the Father of glory, may give you a spirit of wisdom and revelation as you come to know him so that, with the eyes of your heart enlightened, you may know what is the hope to which he has called you, what are the riches of his glorious inheritance among the saints, and what is the immeasurable greatness of his power for us who believe, according to the working of his great power. NRSV

David put on a show but still did not enjoy the moment. We can feel for him. His loss was great, yet his son would not have failed to kill him if the tables had been turned. Are we living in the negatives and not the positives? Non-Christians are all too aware of the supposed negatives in the Christian life. Some forty years ago two young sisters came to Sunday School, they must have asked if we had a television because many did not. When we answered in the positive they said to Beth, my wife. "Ah, but you can't watch the dancing girls." They needed to know all the positives of Christian living. Christians are living as though there is no resurrection either for them or for the Christ. They are living as though there is no joy in the Holy Spirit, as though there is no consolation in Christ. Living on the wrong side of Easter.

Get looking with the heart. What are you seeing at the moment? Our natural eyes see the temporal and our spiritual eyes see the eternal. Perhaps one reason we close our eyes to pray is because we need to get our heart in focus. Some have dreams and visions this is not that experience it is reading God's word with the eyes but looking with the heart. It is taking it to a greater depth than before.

1. Get a glimpse of heaven,

William Booth suggested that his officers took a look at hell, Paul went one better, he wanted people to have a gaze at heaven. Some explorers have told of better lands either truthfully or otherwise.[236] When you have someone you love there in heaven you think more about it. The only way that the Bible describes it is by saying what and who are not there and that who is there. Weeping isn't there, dying isn't there. Immorality and hatred isn't there. But Jesus is there.

2. Discover God counts you as His riches,

Robinson said, "Our riches are in God, God's riches are in us!" God is anticipating a profit from each one of us. He considers us a worthwhile investment. So often we have sung, "It will be worth it all when we see Jesus," Yet God considers us worthwhile The Cross and the Grave were worth it. In the words of Isaiah "He shall see the travail of his soul and be satisfied." It does not take an auction in a saleroom to put a value on you! You're worth many sparrows. 1Corinthians 6:20 *For you were bought with a price; therefore, glorify God in your body.* NRSV That is the value God has placed on you and considers you were worth it!

3. That we might see what power is available for us.

That we might know this is the resurrection power of God that is available. v.20 That we might know the position that Jesus holds, far above all! All things have been made subject unto Him, the church is His body to do the work of heaven on earth.

Romans 8:11 *If the Spirit of him who raised Jesus from the dead dwells in you, he who raised Christ from the dead will give life to your mortal bodies also through his Spirit that dwells in you. Romans 1:16 For I am not ashamed of the gospel; it is the power of God for salvation to everyone who has faith, to the Jew first and also to the Greek. 1 Corinthians 1:18 For the message about the cross is foolishness to those who are perishing, but to us who are being saved it is the power of God. Philippians 3:10 I want to know Christ and the power of his*

---

[236] Erik the Red was said to have named Greenland, Greenland so people would be attracted to it.

resurrection. NRSV When we by faith grasp the eternal hand and see what is available to us we have a greater power than the atom bomb! It was the power that made Elijah able to overcome a king with an army. It was the power that knocked back the soldiers who came to arrest Jesus. Hallelujah!

Overcoming Emotion.

Joab was wise in many respects – though he was often in tune with the feeling of people and made his decisions accordingly. For example, he knew that David was missing Absalom and arranged for the woman to act up for him (2Samuel 14.1). This was another case (2Samuel 19.7) David was selfishly considering himself when hundreds of other were also in mourning for friends and relatives and Absalom was the cause of it all. ***To let our emotion control our lives, is a recipe for disaster.***

77

Love's Excess
2Samuel 19.6

What is this--loving those who hate you and hating those who love you? (Message Bible)

David did not sufficiently appreciate those who were his friends. He sought the love of those who did not love him and ignored the love of those who loved him. He was not the first person nor the last either to squander his love. Joab could say you have announced your love by your behaviour. In times of crisis we tend to declared what we really are and what makes us tick by our actions. He would not have been a normal father if he had no grief for Absalom. The cry of David, "O my son Absalom, O Absalom, my son, my son!" can be felt by every parent of a wayward child.

A leader must at times disguise the personal feelings they have for the good of those they lead. Yet if they are shown to be without emotion they can be as scary as an automaton.

An excess of love is when a blood relationship has a value placed on it greater than the faithfulness of friends. David often failed to support his loyal supporters. Mrs. Hall was a lovely elderly Christian lady. For years each Sunday a hard working niece would take her home for dinner. One day she stopped picking her up. Perhaps because Mrs Hall constantly extolled the success of her only son who did little for her. Eventually it must have got on the niece's nerves constantly hearing about someone doing nothing when she was exhausting herself. So she called it a day.

Jesus was approached by his family who were not in full support of him at the time. Luke put it this way: - Luke 8:19 *Jesus' mother and brothers came to him, but were unable to join him because of the crowd. Someone said to Jesus, "Your mother and brothers are standing outside and want to see you." Jesus said to them all, "My mother and brothers are those who hear the word of God and obey it."* GNB Jesus was in no way advocating a cultist behaviour, God forbid that any Christian organisation should ever be accused of such. He was pointing out that there was time and place for everything.

Paul had a disagreement with Barnabas over his blood relative, John Mark. James' and John's mother wanted preferential treatment for them she was related to Jesus' family. There is a saying, "blood is thicker than water."

So often ministers have regretted failing in the care of their children when young. Unfortunately, like David's experience, it cannot always be made good when they have reached adulthood. David's grief for Absalom was accentuated by the death of his son while in rebellion. A reporter cornered a woman going to visit her son in prison. The journalist asked what she thought of her son's horrendous crimes. The mother acknowledged the wickedness of the murders but then stated he was still her son so she was visiting him. Millions of parents know the pain of having a rebellious offspring. Only God can fully alleviate the suffering, after all he has had many such straying children.

78

Bring Back the King
2Samuel 19.9 – 40

2Sam 19.10 *All over the country they started quarrelling among themselves. "King David saved us from our enemies," they said to one another. "He rescued us from the Philistines, but now he has fled from Absalom and left the country. We anointed Absalom as our king, but he has been killed in battle. So why doesn't somebody try to bring King David back?"* GNB

There may be times when in our personal lives we have failed to glorify God as we ought. In church we might have depended on things and people rather than the Holy Spirit of God. There may, at times, be a place for us to put the matter right and bring the King back! It was a repeat of 2 Samuel 3.17,18 which ends with, *"Now then do it!"* Have we left God the Holy Spirit on the side-lines instead of in the centre of our worship?

Many people have turned to alternatives to Jesus. Jesus who said, "I am the way, truth and life." Jesus who died for them, Jesus who healed the sick, Jesus who would prefer to be killed than to kill. Jesus who offers peace joy and hope in a fear charged world. It is a good job there is more than a twenty-eight day cooling off period to turn back to Jesus. This is the story about a country that decided to ask their king back after they had rejected him.

David's story is a great story. It is the triumph of the weak against the strong. It is a story of betrayal, intrigue, lust, murder, love and hatred. It is about vengeance and jealousy. Of secret agents, double agents, courage and cowardice, deceit and honesty, sacrifice and greed, and a hundred other things and is the story of the world's greatest song writer, and the story of a small time shepherd boy becoming king.

How had this happened? How had David nearly lost his throne? Absalom had seduced the world around him. Good looking and pretending to be a man of the people, he gave promises he would be unable to fulfil. He flattered and sympathised, and in the words of the bible he stole the hearts of the people.

- **Some can be bought A** New Zealand cricketer, Lou Vincent, admitted attempting to fix matches. His apology came in stark style. In the confession video he exhales loudly. Then he said, "My name is Lou Vincent and I am a cheat." He had been bought and fixed matches. Judas settled for thirty pieces of silver, but as someone said it was his own soul he sold.
- **Some can be tricked;** two hundred men went with Absalom not knowing be was trying to overthrow his father's government. Tens of thousands have lost their savings to fraudsters. You can be cheated too. What shall it profit a man if he gains the whole world and lose his own soul? Asked Jesus.
- **Some can be seduced**. Absalom was a person who stole hearts by his personality and by his promises – promises that he could not fulfil. *O foolish Galatians! Who has bewitched you?* Was the question Paul asked the Church in Galatia. Adulterers steal hearts, Absalom like Hitler groomed and stole a nation. Sin is always sugar coated. When looking at snake venom under a microscope it looks beautiful but it is deadly poison. "Enticing words," is the phrase Paul uses for the Colossians being conned by another person. James puts another suggestion to us, we can suffer from self-deception, (Galatians 3.1 & James 1.22).

Manfred, Freiherr von Richthofen was a famous German First World War fighter pilot, better known as the Red Baron because he flew a distinctive red Fokker aircraft. He shot down more combat planes than anyone else on either side in the first World war. His known kill tally was 80. On 21st April 1918, he began chasing a Canadian plane that was trying to escape the battle over the Morlan-court Ridge, near the river Somme. As the Red Baron pursued his prey, he strayed behind Allied lines. He dived too low past the enemy lines, and he also he missed a Canadian pilot (Arthur) "Roy" Brown coming up on his tail to help his comrade. We do not know whether it was a shot from the ground - or a shot from Brown that killed Richthofen. But what we do know is that the "Red Baron" came to his end because he made the mistake of pursuing that Allied 'plane "too long, too far, and too low into enemy territory" And many committed Christians have been shot down because they have followed temptation too far, and too low into enemy territory.

They came to their senses when they said *"David delivered us from our enemies."* In fact, Absalom had done nothing for them except made promises. *Let us bring back the king.* So they asked for him to come back. It is a lovely thing that he came even when they did not back him in the first place, when they would have left him to die at the hand of his own son. Jesus is like that, even if someone turns away from him when they had a chance to receive him, and they change their mind, they only have to invite him in. He will return!

You can bring back the king of kings.

In life there are always some people that you don't know which side they are on. When I worked in a factory they all spoke as if they were voting Labour party – but the Conservatives used to get in by a wide margin. They said one thing and in the secret of the poll booth voted another. Some people you never know whether they are for or against Jesus. It depends who they are with. They run with the foxes and hunt with the hounds.

Such were some here, who reluctantly had him back.

Shimei was one. He had stoned David as he left the city. 2Samuel 16:13 *As David and his men went along the road, Shimei was walking along the hillside parallel to him. Shimei cursed, hurled stones, and threw dirt at David.* GW Now he was having to face the king coming back!

2Sa 19:21 *But Abishai, replied, "Shouldn't Shimei be put to death for cursing the LORD's anointed king?"* David spared him. But Shimei was a reluctant subject. GW

You know some seem to be reluctantly following Jesus, instead of enjoying Jesus and all that he offers. It cannot really be done. We used to sing a chorus, "I'm enjoying being loved by Jesus." If Shimei had been fighting alongside David, if he had seen Goliath being beaten, if he had enjoyed singing the psalms then he would have been pleased to have David back as king.

Mephibosheth was another case. It was a case of was he, wasn't he? He had the hospitality of David for years. Lame and unable to saddle his mule he said he had waited without washing for David to return because he could not travel with David. His servant said otherwise. Who was right? David was not sure. Some folks you are not sure about their Christian commitment. One thing is certain, God knows. He might have been hedging his bets.

Have you left King Jesus out of the main part of your life? It might have been because Jesus was unpopular with the crowd you were with. It might have been because you thought the cost was too high and now you have discovered it was nowhere near as high as the cost of unforgiven wrong doing. Invite Him in. Make it plain, make it certain. Get enjoying Jesus.

John 1.12 *Some, however, did receive him and believed in him; so he gave them the right to become God's children.* GNB

79

A War of Words
2Samuel 19.41- 43

2Samuel 19.43 But the people of Israel answered the people of Judah, "We have ten shares in the king, and in David also we have more than you. Why then did you despise us? Were we not the first to speak of bringing back our king?" But the words of the people of Judah were fiercer than the words of the people of Israel. NRSV

This was a discourse that lead to discord. Sometimes words are best left unsaid. Words can so often hurt, as in the case of Paul and Barnabas: - Acts 15.37 *Barnabas wanted to take with them John called Mark. But Paul decided not to take with them one who had deserted them in Pamphylia and had not accompanied them in the work. The disagreement became so sharp that they parted company; Barnabas took Mark with him and sailed away to Cyprus.* NRSV

Words can rupture relationships like nothing else can. Sometimes it is caused by cultural misunderstanding. During the Korean war a British captain understated the difficulty he was in to the American commander at the base. As the Americans tell it like it is he thought the captain was doing the same so he did not send reinforcements. Blunt speakers can offend polite people. Even in the United Kingdom not only are regional accents sometimes difficult to understand but often sayings can be hard to interpret.

The problem that Paul and Barnabas had (mentioned above) might have been amicably resolved if the words were less violent. The history of the early Christian Church by Luke is authentic to the point of being a little too truthful. Two apostles used non-Christian words to one another. Elsewhere Paul wrote to the Corinthians, speaking of love he sates this: - *Love doesn't force itself on others, Isn't always "Me first," Doesn't fly off the handle.*[237] The same word used by Luke to describe the cutting words used between the two Apostles is here translated by Peterson as "doesn't fly off the handle." I guess all preachers are sometimes preaching against themselves and their failures, except you and me of course.

Ecclesiastes 3.7 says, *there is a time to keep silence, and a time to speak.* KJV The first part is most difficult but can be rewarding in the long run. Judah had let David down. They were slow to respond to ask the king back. All the other tribes had invited David to return. It was a matter of pride for Judah and they wanted people to know that David was one of theirs, they were seeking to capitalise on his return. If someone wants the acclaim for what you have done it is often best to let them have the praise. One day all of us will be getting medals in the meantime enjoy life and the scenery all around.

---

[237] 1Corrinthians 13.5 Message Bible

80

Conciliation or Compromise?
2Samuel 20

v.13 David sent a message ... *"Tell Amasa you are taking over leadership of the army from your cousin Joab."* A day earlier Amasa would have been killing David as well as Joab if he had won, and he and his army had killed many of their troops. Was David "sucking up" to the people? Or was it because Joab had killed his son who incidentally was Joab's own nephew? It could have been both. Some courses of action seem wise on paper but taking into account people's personalities cannot always be accommodated on a piece of paper. Amasa had not seen the importance of immediate action about a matter.

Some problems need immediate attention, and a further revolt by the tribe of Benjamin under the leadership of Sheba needed an instant response. When we think about it David asked a losing commander to replace a successful one. But Amasa was also a hesitant slow leader that had not the wisdom or warfare experience of a ruthless soldier like Joab. We cannot condone the actions of Joab, killing a rival in cold blood, but we can admire his achievements in keeping the throne for David. Don't leave difficult decisions and actions till later. There are things that can be left and they will fade away of their own accord. There have been times when folks have set up house groups without asking the Church leadership for permission. It was often better to let them die a natural death than to seek to close them down. But there had been occasions when matters in church needed dealing with as quickly as possible before they were out of control. Our church was in an area where windows were often broken. We replaced them straight away or it would look as though we did not care.

Joab was all for David, Amasa did not have the same desire for the king. It was a job for Amasa, it was a calling for Joab. Are you in a "calling" or is what you are doing for God a just something to do?

Sheba made a stand in the north of Israel at Abel. It was a city that was to face more wars to come but an old lady stopped the destruction of their city this time by getting the people together and agreeing to execute Sheba. The matter was over and done with without too much loss of life. It is always worth listening to old ladies. They seem to be able to assess what others cannot. Many a youth has been saved from major mistakes by taking notice of granny, and millions more could have done better if they had taken note.

81

Natural disasters
2Samuel 21.1 - 14

These last few chapters of 2Samuel have often been considered as being out of place chronologically. Nevertheless, we can examine them in situ because to try to reposition them could cause further problems.

Saul's massacre of the Gibeonites is unrecorded elsewhere. They were promised security from attack many years previously by Joshua, when they convinced him they came from a distance away.[238] So often when things go wrong religious people like to put it down to a reason, either they or someone has done something wrong and this is the judgement of God. Many sick people have been accused of hidden sins that have added to their anxieties and often caused animosity toward Christians. When my church was going through a tough time I received a letter telling me I should repent, and all would go well. They failed to specify my particular wrong doing though. Church like people and families have both good and bad times. Fortunately, God sends times of refreshing and all the negatives and false allegations are forgotten in the time of blessing.

---

[238] Joshua 9.3-27

Jesus clearly states there are life accidents, they just happen it is not because anyone is guilty.[239] Often theologians will call these incidents as "natural evils," such as hurricanes, earthquakes, famines and tsunamis. The word "evil" might not be the best word here because there has not been a deliberate attempt to cause suffering.

David did not listen to the other alternative of financial compensation for the Gibeonites. When they bargained with David they left two suggestions. It would seem that their preference was for vengeance on Saul's family. Now in ancient times they would start off by saying they did not want anything then they would work upwards[240] whereas in the West we ask for more than the item is worth from the prospective purchaser then work downwards. David could have refused the slaughter of Saul's sons. Then made them accept financial compensation but he was happy to eliminate any rival to his throne. It was very convenient for David to do this. If there is a comment we can make it is this: - He asked God for the cause of the three-year famine but people for the cure, he could have asked God for the cure as well as the cause.

We are far too happy at times to make excuses for some of the great men and women of God. But they have often made major errors of judgement in their lives, they may be our examples but we must observe and cautiously question the rights and the wrongs of their actions and their behaviour. This action of slaughter for recompense was not unknown in the lands around at the time. David had no need to copy the surrounding nations.

It tells us that the rains came after this, God had answered them. God would have ended the famine without the bloodshed. What broken hearts those two mothers must have had. David had been so used to killing that his heart seems unmoved by executing young men who were related to him through his marriage to Michal. He

---

[239] Luke 13.4 see also Joh 9:3 Jesus answered, "Neither has this man sinned, nor his parents: but that the works of God should be made manifest in him." KJV

[240] See Abraham dealing for a plot of land to bury Sarah Genesis 23.1-20 Also David asking for the threshing floor.

had become a man of blood. Down through history ruthless people have eliminated their rivals. God had promised David a throne. God secured it for him, he had no need to do this.

Is it possible that we have hard and unfeeling hearts? That we too have become ruthless in our actions, when there are kinder ways to achieve our goals? Companies will at times make workers redundant to obtain greater profits for their shareholders. Church boards and ministers can be unfeeling to their workers and volunteers in the decisions they take. As a youngster I remember a man coming to our house to see my father. His hair had turned white almost over-night because they voted him off a church board. Let us put ourselves in the shoes of the person with whom we are dealing.

A lady on our church oversight commented about me one day after over forty years at the church. She had noted that I had become kinder over time. The discovery that I had been less than perfect in dealing with people should not have been a surprise to me. It was better that I was improving rather than deteriorating in my care of people. Perhaps coming from an engineering background and dealing with machinery and mainly men made me less thoughtful to the feelings of others. How are we doing? Are we abrasive, curt, and inconsiderate, or have we sought to have the mind of Christ?[241]

---

[241] Phil.2.5 The effect of humbleness is consideration for others, Romans 12:10 Be kindly affectionate one to another with brotherly love; in honour preferring one another; KJV

82

Ritual Killing
2Samuel 21

Throughout history we have been aware that many societies have ritually sacrificed people. Even in this twenty first century there have been rumours of such happening in secret. The scriptures speak of the challenge to Abraham to sacrifice Isaac, and of Jephthah promising the first to come out of his house door to be sacrificed.[242] Though many consider that his daughter was just forced to remain unmarried.

This story of the famine is a story of ritual killing for the supposed purpose of appeasing God. It must be remembered at no time has the Bible ever said that there should be human sacrifices, animals yes, people no. I have previously stated that this did not need to happen and seemed a device by David to limit any attempt to challenge him or his progeny to the throne. These men who were killed were related to his wife Michal and to Mephibosheth as well, it would not have helped with family relationships!

There are so many acts in the life of David that we have to question, "What was his understanding of God's love towards people?" David complained of Joab's hardness but it would seem David was

---

[242] Judges 11

considerably insensitive to any feelings of the pains of others. Can we excuse him on the grounds of "A life for a life?" It is a possibility they all may have been part of the attempt to destroy the Gibeonites. This might mitigate our feelings toward David providing men of Saul's family to the Gibeonites for slaughter. We will leave the verdict to the final judgement day, we were not there at the time.

The question can be in the mind of a Christian, "Is the death of Jesus in any sense a ritual slaying?" Firstly, in no way was Jesus unwilling in his determination to go to the cross. Jesus is quoted as saying: - *No one takes my life away from me. I give it up of my own free will. I have the right to give it up, and I have the right to take it back. This is what my Father has commanded me to do."* John 10.18 GNB

The Scriptures state that Jesus died in our stead and on our behalf.[243] We can say his death was a ransom for the many, the great difference was the willingness and the desire of Jesus to go this way for us. Yet there is in the term, propitiation,[244] a sense of appeasement. Again there is a further difference, there was not in the minds of the crucifiers any suggestion that it was for ritualistic purposes. Though afterwards the words of the High Priest were quoted that the death of one was better than many deaths. The association of the prophecy of Isaiah 53 was noted after the event and not before. "In my place condemned he stood, Sealed my pardon with his blood, Hallelujah what a Saviour." It was news to all except Jesus what he was about to do by his death.

---

[243] Matthew 20.28 & 2Corinthians 5.15
[244] Romans 3.25 & 1John 2.2 etc.

83

Goliath's Relatives
2Samuel 21.15

David was nearly defeated by Goliath's brother. What a headline! This has been another favourite stomping ground for preachers for many generations. When David overcame Goliath in his youth he was later nearly defeated in maturity by a relative of the giant. So often people have started well but ended badly. This enemy was perhaps Goliath's son but no matter, Abishai had to come to the rescue. David could not win alone. A time had come when he was weaker physically. There are also things we have overcome in the past that have almost knocked us off our feet in later years.

David's defeats: -

- Some people consider the sexual conquest of another person a win. God considers it a defeat, David lost.
- Some mark-up battle scores, God called David a man of blood.
- Some take pride in their life success, but God did not want David to number the people, so taking the credit for the increase on himself. He did and lost out.

These are some of the bigger things but there are others, such as his failure to humanely treat prisoners and to take more care in bringing up his children. Come to think of it he could have had more failures than successes!

Psalm 91.6 says, when talking about destroying powers of the night and day: - *the destruction that wastes at noonday.* KJV A biographical author asked permission of a famous preacher to write about his life. "Wait till I'm dead," the preacher said. "Far too many fall at the last hurdle." We can fail at the noonday of our life. Complacency and over confidence can be the ruin of many. It nearly happened to David. The inner feeling that we have achieved this before, so it will be a doddle, is a recipe for disaster. At different times of our life we can find that there are temptations that match our weaknesses at that time of life. Jesus spoke to Peter telling him that he might be all right now but there was to be a difficulty to face at the end of his life. We can never be complacent.

If we are constantly on the edge of seats worrying about the possibility of failure, the tension becomes too much. We must choose what to be relaxed about and what must be taken seriously and dealt with thoroughly. Jesus told Martha that she was far too anxious about the cooking. She was losing out because of a desire for perfection in an area that a thousand years later would not matter, in fact in less time than that! David had become complacent about his fighting skills, that sure did matter. We must choose the vital things to hone to perfection and not worry if the remainder is mediocre.

84

Song of Victory
2Samuel 22.1-51 Psalm 18

A choir boy at the thanksgiving service at the end of the second world war noticed that tears were streaming down Winston Churchill's cheeks. There is a time when all the pent up emotions can flow. This was such a time when David could say God had delivered him from all his enemies.

How do we see the psalms, just as praise or just prayer? They are far deeper they are complaints, disappointments, sharing of sorrow as well as talk of the greatness of God and the universe. They are talks about holiness, see Psalm 24 and 139, they are speaking about the rejection of God such as psalm 14. They are talking about what God is like. Here is a song after victory. But it is not a victory song.

Margaret Thatcher, the British prime minister, wanted a victory service for the Falklands war but the bishop of London rejected that type of service. Thanksgiving is okay, rejoicing is out for these things. Jesus would not have wanted anyone to rejoice over the death of others.

Out of his depth – David gives the impression of being in deep waters without a life belt. Such as v.5 *The danger of death was all around me; the waves of destruction rolled over me.* GNB Then comes deliverance – v.16 *The LORD reached down from above and took hold of me; he pulled me out of the deep waters.* GNB

When victory finally comes. This was after the death of Saul in battle, after a period of years when David was on the run. When it uses the word for "hand" of Saul it is the same word David used for the "paw" of the lion and the bear (1Sam 17.37). When finally, Saul had been defeated in battle. Then could David relax and know that all was safe for him.

Someone divided the psalm as follows: -

The Refuge 1-7

The refuge God gives is not outside of our troubles. He is a refuge within the storm. The troubles and temptations we face will not disappear overnight. David felt at the bottom sometimes. v.4&5. Let us see God as our refuge. He saw God as the high mountain refuge. "Hiding in thee …. thou blessed rock of ages I'm hiding in thee." David saw himself tangled up with death and the devil. It could not be much worse!

The Rescue 8-19

The rescue is final and complete, he expected God to do something, it was not just a blog to be read, it was a prayer to be acted on. Mary Queen of Scots said she was more afraid of John Knox's prayers than an army. David's playing made him a court musician, but his prayers made him king. After we have sought refuge we then seek rescue.

The Reward 20-21

The reward was "a large place." When you have been confined in a cave, cooped up in a small area, a large space is great to be in! God knows the opposite to the fear you have. He will give you that. We give up too easily sometimes our fear is that we will not break out from the things that constrain us.

The Reason 22-28

The reason was because he had kept his hands clean. Far more than just his hands, it meant his whole being. Yet they often saw it as a figure of righteousness. (Think of psalm 24 [245]) We want to give God a reason to bless us. It's often good to do a check list Job did it in Job 31. Charles Finney the evangelist did it.[246] Because we are a forgiven people, that does not stop us from seeking to live right. (v.26 "pure" is a niphal, which suggests an action, to purify yourself.) God will answer man on his own terms, with the crooked he will respond in similar fashion.

The Rules 29-39

The Rule that God works by: v 36 *Thy gentleness has made me great.* KJV *"By my God I have ..."* that is the secret he did not do it on his own. Are you giving him the glory? He got his strength from God in a remarkable way. It was when he needed it.

The Recovery 40-46

It was not that David had only escaped but that he was the conqueror of his enemies they were subject to him. We have not just escaped but we are conquerors through him that loved us.

The Rejoicing 47-51

After recovery came rejoicing. He was enjoying what God had done for him. It is often at this time we begin to think that we have achieved it ourselves.

It has been pointed out that this Psalm fits the Lord Jesus. (Calvin etc.) So some commentators apply it to Jesus all the way through

---

[245] Ps 24:3 Who may go up the LORD'S mountain? Who may stand in his holy place? 4 The one who has clean hands and a pure heart and does not long for what is false or lie when he is under oath. 5 This person will receive a blessing from the LORD and righteousness from God, his saviour.. GW

[246] See the book "Power from on High" by Charles Finney

because it fits Him even more than David. He is great David's greater Son.

Some one-liners: -

You save those who are humble, but you humble those who are proud. Psalm 18.27 GNB

It is you who light my lamp; the LORD, my God, lights up my darkness. Psalm 18.28 NRSV (2Samuel 22.29 You are my Lamp ...)

Here we have a description of a fighting man being helped by the Lord. To many Christians warfare is unacceptable, to all of us it must be avoided if at all possible, especially with the words of Jesus, *"Love your enemies, do good to those who hate you."* Many, many wars could have been avoided, one wonders if some prime ministers and presidents would so readily go to war if their sons and daughters were going to be on the front line?

Some of David's battles were unavoidable, the defence of people is essential. When I was in my first pastorate a young woman came to see me, she had been beaten by her partner. Amazingly it transpired that the violent young man's own father was present when his son attacked her. I asked the father why he did not intervene, he replied that he was a pacifist. I have a feeling his failure to protect her was more to do with cowardice than pacifism. We are often faced with violence in parts of Western society. To seek to avoid violence is essential, but could our country have stood aloof and avoided fighting Nazism and starting another world war? David showed considerable restraint in seeking to avoid fighting at times. Though not as many times as God would have liked.

The kings of Israel were known to be more merciful than other kings around them. 1Ki 20:31 *His officers told him, "We have heard that the kings of Israel are merciful. Allow us to dress in sackcloth, put ropes around our necks, and go to the king of Israel. Maybe he'll let you live."* GW

85

When mighty men make a man mighty
2Samuel 23

1Chronicles 12.16-18 *Some Benjaminites and Judahites came to the stronghold to David. David went out to meet them and said to them, "If you have come to me in friendship, to help me, then my heart will be knit to you; but if you have come to betray me to my adversaries, though my hands have done no wrong, then may the God of our ancestors see and give judgement." Then the spirit came upon Amasai, chief of the Thirty, and he said, "We are yours, O David; and with you, O son of Jesse! Peace, peace to you, and peace to the one who helps you! For your God is the one who helps you." Then David received them, and made them officers of his troops.* NRSV

Of these that originally came to David in the early days were some who would have been normally natural enemies. Besides people from Saul's tribe there were perhaps Anatolian Hittites and other nationalities. Some were the fighters (1Chron.12.2) others the intellectuals (1Chron.12.32) Similarly the disciples of Jesus were different types, one a collaborator with the Roman conquerors and another an independence fighter for example.

Thomas Carlyle suggested that history was the story of "Great Men." David was a great man, but he would have achieved little if it had not been for the people alongside him. Was he the product of his society? Or was he the shaper of his world? He was God's man at the moment when God said it was Israel's time.[247] He was just part of the story but a big part. God was shaping the world through them. God is after people that can change the situation. Ezekiel 22:30 *"I looked for someone among you who could build walls or stand in front of me by the gaps in the walls to defend the land and keep it from being destroyed. But I couldn't find anyone."* GW

Togetherness - No man can achieve much on his own. He must have a team. Some to give advice, some to carry out the commands and some just to support. Twice a year the government of Britain gives honour to individuals, from Knighthoods to Companions of Honour. The military also give when the occasion demands medals, from Victoria Crosses to being mentioned in dispatches, David's men were honoured too. These men were essential to making David king. We will never be anyone without anyone.

We can have different types of relationships, working ones, blood ones, friendship ones, loving ones. Then there are those relationships that are not too definable, they have both affection and friendship combined. They are usually composed of the same sex. David had that relationship with his men it was not a subservient, controlling relationship but a sort of unspoken understanding of one another. It went far beyond having the same objectives and the same goals. These were men of equal courage and of similar abilities as David, he, unlike Saul, was prepared to let them be who they were meant to be and never saw them as a threat to his leadership. Saul wished for superiority among the others around him perhaps suffering from "illusory supremacy." Saul had not grasped what it was to be the first among equals (primus inter pares).[248] David's men knew he was the rightful king and were happy to fight with, not just for, him.

---

[247] See Jacob Wright's rejection of Carlyle's thesis. "David king of Israel," page 230.

[248] It is typically used as an honorary title for those who are formally equal to other members of their group but are accorded unofficial respect, traditionally owing to their seniority in office. (Hutchinson Encyclopaedia)

The Christian relationship is based on saved sinners knowing that Jesus should be crowned king over the lives of all peoples. But also having a love for one another that will face any trial and come out strong and victorious. *"Hereby shall people know that you are my disciples that you love one another."* (John 13.35 KJV)

It is said that the huge redwood trees in California are the largest things on earth and the tallest trees in the world. Some of them are a hundred metres high and several thousand years old. Yet the trees have a shallow system of roots, but they all intertwine. They are locked to each other. When the storms come or the winds blow, the redwoods stand. They are locked to each other, and they don't stand alone, for all the trees support and protect each other.

Someone has said light-heartedly. "When the church began on earth, the Pastor was being executed as a criminal; the chairman of the board was out cursing and swearing that he had never even been a part it. The treasurer was committing suicide. Most of the rest of the board members had run away. And about the only ones who showed any signs of faithfulness were a few ladies from the woman's auxiliary." It is most remarkable that the Holy Spirit was able to weld together people that would turn the world the right way up. The weak became mighty because they were prepared to stay together and wait for the blessing of God to fall.

- Unity brings the presence of Jesus, "Where two or three are gathered in my name," said Jesus, "I am present with them." Matthew 18.20
- Unity produces witness, "People will know you are my disciples because you love one another." John 13.35
- Unity cultivates caring, "God's purpose was that the body should not be divided but rather that all of its parts should feel the same concern for each other." 1Corinthians 12.25 GW

When the Christians began in Jerusalem there was a comment made by the writer of Acts in chapter two: - Ac 2:1 *And when the day of Pentecost was fully come, they were all with one accord in one place.* KJV

"Accord" is translated from a compound Greek word meaning with passion in unison.[249] God cannot do anything with apathetic and disjointed believers. Let us make it our prayer and our action to be one with Christians and to be on fire for Jesus.

---

[249] Homothumadon homo, the same: thumos, to breath hard.

86

Obsession with numbers.
2Samuel 24.1 - 25

He assessed his success in life and paid the price.

When we seek to encourage ourselves in our own success we fail. We must encourage ourselves in the Lord, in his goodness to us, in our relationship with Him, and what He has made us. David never took the advice of Joab – which on this occasion was good, he insisted on counting the men of war.

We can guess he was going to say "I started with two hundred and ended with one million three hundred thousand.[250] Toward the end of his life David was seeking to gain solace by his achievements, Jacob said, *"Few and evil have been the years of my life."* He did not feel satisfied with his life's work nor will we. As one writer said, "I wish I had given him more."

Exodus 30.12 Warned that a token gift by each person was to be given to God as a ransom if there was to be a census. Which does not seem to have been obeyed. For whatever reason taking the census was not a good thing to do.

---

[250] It could be that the numbers are not in our thousands, but who knows?

The incitement – God gets the blame. When the New Testament so strongly says that God does not tempt, we are left pondering how to explain this wording. The "Message Bible" translates it, with tongue in cheek as, "God tested David". Then we note 1Chronicles 21.1 says that Satan put David up to it. It must be remembered that in the final analysis God is responsible for allowing things to happen and the Hebrews had no hang-ups for saying it as they saw it.

I remember being incited to do something that was unwise. It became like a dare, or a challenge to say you are weak if you do not carry out your threats, unfortunately I succumbed. Watch out for the inciters who encourage your weaknesses. Evil people are often incited to do the evil that they do. As in the case of Ahab.[251] See also the case of David's son raping his half-sister.[252] Choose your friends wisely.

The objection – For once Joab seemed to be on the right side. He advised against the count. When our emotions are involved common sense flies out of the window. David brushed aside Joab's objections. If only we could consider all situations unflappably, but we cannot. When family members or personal problems are involved we can "lose it." There must be an attempt on our part to seek solutions and actions that are sensible when we can deal with things in the cold light of day. Vengeance, sexual desires, pride and self-will can become uncontrollable passions once we spend our time contemplating them. That is why Paul wrote to the Philippians saying: -

Finally, beloved, whatever is true, whatever is honourable, whatever is just, whatever is pure, whatever is pleasing, whatever is commendable, if there is any excellence and if there is anything worthy of praise, think about these things. Philippians 4.8 NRSV. It is vital that we control the thoughts of our own minds otherwise our whims and fancies will control us.

---

[251] 1Ki 21:25 There was no one else like Ahab. At the urging of his wife, he sold himself to do what the LORD considered evil. GW

[252] 2Samuel 13.1-14

The desire - James 1:15 *when that desire has conceived, it gives birth to sin, and that sin, when it is fully grown, gives birth to death. Do not be deceived, my beloved.* (NRSV) We can have good and bad motivations. Look at it from David's point of view. We know from David's census that he had moulded and made Israel a nation of reasonable strength. It has only been in recent years that archaeology has discovered one or two references to David's existence.[253] Before this even David's existence was questioned by some. There is always a desire to prove our worth, perhaps this was the wrong motive in asking for a census.

The regret – The KJV says that David's heart smote him. Today we might say to a person, "Don't beat yourself up," when they are feeling bad about themselves. I remember seeing on a television news bulletin a former British Prime Minister sitting in a Cathedral congregation. He had, some years before, sent the army to fight what many regarded as an unnecessary war. This was a memorial service. Hundreds of soldiers had died and more had been maimed. One look was enough to see he felt awkward and uncomfortable, he left by a rear entrance to avoid the bereaved relatives. So many adulterers, murderers and others feel the regret of the sin they have committed, and once an arrow has left the bow it cannot be recalled. The consequences of sin so often will cause pain to others. Think

---

[253] The Tel Dan inscription, or "House of David" inscription, was discovered in 1993 at the site of Tel Dan in northern Israel in an excavation directed by Israeli archaeologist Avraham Biran.

The broken and fragmentary inscription commemorates the victory of an Aramean king over his two southern neighbours: the "king of Israel" and the "king of the House of David." In the carefully incised text written in neat Aramaic characters, the Aramean king boasts that he, under the divine guidance of the god Hadad, vanquished several thousand Israelite and Judahite horsemen and charioteers before personally dispatching both of his royal opponents. Unfortunately, the recovered fragments of the "House of David" inscription do not preserve the names of the specific kings involved in this brutal encounter, but most scholars believe the stela recounts a campaign of Hazael of Damascus in which he defeated both Jehoram of Israel and Ahaziah of Judah. (BAR, 2011)

The Mesha Stella (Moabite Stone) also could have a reference to David.

carefully about any action you will take, is it really necessary? How will it affect others?

Suffering of the innocent. Again we must ask the question why this suffering by people uninvolved in the sin? And again the answer is that we have to leave this with God. If this life on earth were the only life, then we would not easily be satisfied to put the matter on file. But we believe that all will be put right one great day.

Never give to God that which has cost you nothing. 2Sam.24.24

A good principle to live by. The sacrifice of a broken and contrite heart God will not despise. Our old tutor Howard Carter, when talking about sermon preparation said, "Never give to God that which cost you nothing," don't copy other people's messages, Get yours from God. Nor will God despise that which is given to Him from our best. When Paul spoke of our sacrifice he said in Romans 12.1 *I beseech you therefore, brethren, by the mercies of God, that ye present your bodies a living sacrifice, holy, acceptable unto God, which is your reasonable service.* KJV

87

Extraordinary Means
1Kings 1.1-4

The hot water bottle.

It could be that David recovered a little later on, because 1Chron.29 suggests that he was able to go to the tent temple towards the end of his life when Solomon had been crowned for the second time.[254] Solomon might have shared the throne with his father as co-regent when David declined in health. We must feel sorry for Abishag being so misused as a hot water bottle. We cannot excuse the advisers for what they did. The attempt to keep David alive was important for the stability of the country but they had to bow to the inevitable. In the late twentieth century the Yugoslavian leaders seemed to attempt to keep Marshall Tito alive as long as they could. Their country was an amalgam of states at enmity with one another. It was not many years after his death that Yugoslavia disintegrated which resulted in a blood bath. It could have been for similar reasons they tried to keep David alive to save a fledgling country from falling apart.

Death causes different attitudes and differing emotions in the people observing from the side-line. Those who love the person

---

[254] 1Chronicles 29.22

that is in extremis often cannot concentrate on other things their every thought is tied up in the emotion of the moment. Others are planning a takeover or wondering what is in the will while weeping crocodile tears. It was Charles II of England who apologised to those gathered around his death bed because he was taking so long to die. Like George V the doctors seemed to hasten him on his way, though in his case it was by accident.

David did not take full advantage of the extraordinary means given to keep him alive. The Catholic Dictionary comments on extraordinary means to prolong life as follows: -

Such means of preserving human life as cannot be obtained or used without extreme difficulty in terms of pain, expense, or other burdening factors. The burden applies either to the person whose life is at stake or to those on whom his or her welfare depends. In addition, means should be considered extraordinary if, when used, they do not offer a reasonable hope of benefit to the one for whom they are intended.

There is no general obligation to use extraordinary means to keep alive, on the premise that God does not exact what is beyond the ordinary power of humans in general. At times, however, one may be bound to employ extraordinary means to preserve life. The two conditions under which such an obligation becomes binding are that a person is necessary to one's family, to the Church, or to society, and the success of the extraordinary means is very probable.

Extraordinary measures will differ in time and in space. Far more techniques and interventions are available now to sustain life than there were fifty years ago. And in differing areas of the world an intravenous drip with nutriments and vitamins will be an extraordinary measure while an organ transplant could count for the same in a more advanced country.

Protestants are far less likely to voice their value system regarding such matters than the Roman Catholic Church. It could be because of diverse views within the Protestant Church. Sometimes this is good, and stops people from shooting from the hip and asking questions afterwards. I think Jesus might put it this way, "If our receiving extraordinary measures to keep us alive when we are in declining years means a greater need for another cannot be met, then we should decline those extra means even if they are available to us." Usually in a nation with a National Health Service this is automatic. Though to be at the bedside of a friend and church member where they have been told no further intervention will be given is not the easiest of situations to be in. Nor is it an enviable position for a government body to have to decide which drugs are too expensive to use because of limited resources, even though they are efficacious.

No one would ever question the decision if it was a choice between a grandmother and a young mother caring for children who should have the life lengthening intervention. Unless of course the grandmother holds to ethical egoism then she would disagree! But what if that grandmother was the leader of a vast nation and holding the power to stop a civil war taking place, it does make life a little more complicated, doesn't it? What would Jesus do? If we took the story of Jairus' daughter, then Jesus would heal both of them.

88

The Snake Rock Conspiracy
1Kings 1.5-53

When good people behave badly.

The choice of the next king divided priest from priest, soldier from soldier and advisor from advisor. Abithar the priest had been with David through thick and thin yet this time had gone against David's wishes. Joab, David's general had fought all the battles with him, also took the side of Adonijah. David had often failed his children. It was said of Adonijah that he was utterly spoilt.[255] There may be times when one person seems as good as another for a position. Yet God has an ideal person for his work. Sometimes it is not who we think is best.

Dissension is difficult to deal with, but they knew it had to be immediately combated, otherwise it would have led to civil war. Paul and Barnabas had a strong disagreement.[256] They went their own ways and God was with them both, but it does not make for easy

---

[255] 1Kings 1.6 *His father had never at any time displeased him by asking, "Why have you done thus and so?"* NRSV He was also a very handsome man, and he was born next after Absalom.

[256] Acts 15.39

reading. Here with the replacement for David there could only be a right and a wrong. There could be only one king.

Throughout the history of the Church there have been major disagreements. Doctrine, styles of worship, then also personality come into play. Nor can we ignore the mistakes, the immorality and sometimes fraud that ministers have failed in. Congregations have been too strict or too lenient. Jesus said the poor you always have with you and we can add that there will be from time to time dissension too. Each one of the rebels was dealt with separately. Forgiveness for the priest but loss of status. The pretender[257] to the throne was to have an eye kept on him and on the first act of indiscretion he was executed. But no mercy for the General Joab. He was still plotting it would seem with Adonijah, there was a subtle attempt to steal the crown.

It is difficult to have a smooth transition from one leader to another. The importance of Bathsheba cannot be under estimated in this battle for the crown. When Solomon became king he gave her a throne next to his. David did not show a preference for his own mother like many of the nations around. Yet Bathsheba as a wife obviously had a considerable influence on his decision making. We can be as guilty as Joab and friends. They took the stance that the eldest should be next in line. The fact that Adonijah was utterly spoilt was not considered by them. God gives us the power of choice. He often leaves us to it to make decisions. We are not always thoughtful enough in taking every aspect of a person's character into account.

---

[257] Adonijah was older than Solomon. David took a decision that mean the king was chosen by royal prerogative.

89

Passing on the baton
1Kings 2.1-12

The Christian life is not a sprint or even a marathon it is a relay race. Much of our work will be unfinished. There are unfinished symphonies, unfinished buildings and books that are incomplete due to death, we are unfinished too. *I'm convinced that God, who began this good work in you, will carry it through to completion on the day of Christ Jesus.*[258] The work of God is a continuous work, and will remain so until the Lord returns. It is for us to pass the baton on, you hand it on when you are slowing down and the next runner is gaining speed.

1. David, though forbidden to build the temple was preparing it for the next generation 1Chron.22.2. It was known as Solomon's not David's Temple! That was the spiritual side.
2. He was strengthening his kingship so that others taking over would have little opposition. 2Sam.20 etc. That was the external side.
3. He was removing overpowering influences for the future king to have freedom in decision making. That was the internal side.

---

[258] Philippians 1.6 (GW)

Jacob said, *"Few and evil have been the years of my life."* He did not feel satisfied with his life's work nor will we. William Grimshaw was an eighteenth century Church of England minister in Yorkshire where the Bronte sisters later lived said, *"When I die I will have the greatest sorrow and the greatest joy, sorrow in that I have done so little for Him, joy in that I am about to see His face."* Thomas Aquinas was one of the greatest theologian of the middle ages, he wrote about ninety volumes. Toward the end of his life he seemed to have an experience with God, though some have tried to call it a breakdown. After this experience he said all his life's work was straw. John Owen was perhaps England's greatest theologian. He said he would exchange his knowledge and intellect for John Bunyan's wit.[259] We need different qualities for the work of God. Do all you can, then pass the baton on; we are not running a marathon we are in a relay race, the baton must be passed on.

Paul could say, *"I have fought a good fight, I have kept the Faith, henceforth there is laid up for me a crown ..."* He left his achievements for history and for God.

An Assessment of David's right-hand man.

David would not have achieved what he did without the help of some of the people around him. He had counsellors and generals, bodyguards and priests as well as wives! These were supportive of him. Without doubt the strongest character was Joab, he was with him in the tough times and in the successful times, increasing the power of David. Yet he was ruthless, he never hesitated to kill in cold blood[260] when he thought it necessary. David finally had Joab killed which was not much of a repayment for his faithfulness to him. Joab was David's barometer, he was able to assess the mood of the nation and acted accordingly. Yet ultimately he misjudged the situation and the time of proclaiming a king in seeking to be a king maker he

---

[259] John Owen was able to have Bunyan released from prison with a government grant. Owen had a fine physique, and wore tight fitting clothes that was not altogether to the liking of his fellow Puritans.

[260] The KJV says, "he shed the blood of war in a time of peace."

failed. We must always be supporters and not controllers of people and Churches, control is God's job, and he will do it better.

David could see that Joab was wanting still to be controlling. A new day was dawning a new generation coming. Winston Churchill saw Britain through to a remarkable victory in the Second World War. Yet when the vote came after the war the people voted for another party they needed a time of peace. David had fought and battled he knew his people needed peace too.

Those who had given their support to David unconditionally were to be encouraged. Just as he had cared for Jonathan's son, so Solomon was to look after Barzillai's children.

Often we have to hand the baton on, to our children, to our work colleagues, to our Church elders we have to leave them with a prayer for their godliness and as few problems as possible that would tie them down.

Perhaps we could say one thing more about Joab. David wished to build a place of worship for the Lord. That was his ultimate aim. Joab did not seem to share that part of the vision. He was more concerned for the success of the nation of Israel which was not the complete goal of David.

The Final words of David 2Sam.23.1-7

2Sam.23.1 *Now these be the last words of David. David the son of Jesse said, and the man who was raised up on high, the anointed of the God of Jacob, and* **the sweet psalmist of Israel,** *said, "The Spirit of the Lord spoke through me..."* KJV

The final prayer of David 1Chronicles 29.1-30

David seems to have had as many "finals," as a long-winded preacher. Yet that which blesses me is not the final words but more **the last prayer** found in 1Chron.29.10-13. *Yours Lord is the greatness and the power and the glory and the majesty and the splendour, for everything is yours.* KJV He acknowledged that all he had come from God, all he achieved came through God, and that he had become.

It was not only the material things but the spiritual gifts he had received for which he gave God glory.

Jesus said the servant's words were Lu 17:10. *So likewise ye, when ye shall have done all those things which are commanded you, say, "We are unprofitable servants: we have done that which was our duty to do."* KJV

90

Whose eyes are you looking through?
Psalm 36

The success or failure of a person's life is left to the final judgement of God. Until that day it depends on whose eyes we are looking out of, that the judgement comes. David spoke of this in Psalm 36.2. *For they flatter themselves in their own eyes that their iniquity cannot be found out and hated.* NRSV

Some succeed in their own eyes, some in the eyes of others and some in God's eyes. We are constantly warned of making judgements of our own. Jesus said the measure we use for others is the measure by which we will be judged.[261]

In your own eyes? This man, David spoke of, flattered himself. You cannot get much worse than that can you? Samson was happy with his decisions in life. Judges 14.3 *She pleases me well* (right in my eyes.) One young person said they thought God was a "let down". When I knew about their life I thought that God might think that they were a little bit of a "let down", and that was to put it mildly.

---

[261] Matthew 7.1,2 "Stop judging so that you will not be judged. Otherwise, you will be judged by the same standard you use to judge others. The standards you use for others will be applied to you.

Proverbs 3:7 *Do not be wise in your own eyes; fear the LORD, and turn away from evil.* NRSV

Proverbs 21:2 ¶ *All deeds are right in the sight of the doer, but the LORD weighs the heart.* NRSV

Proverbs 30:12 *There are those who are pure in their own eyes yet are not cleansed of their filthiness.* NRSV

Some were unhappy with themselves. Job 42.6 Job could say, "*I despise myself and repent.*"

Gen. 45.5 Don't be angry with yourselves said Joseph to his brothers who sold him for twenty pieces of silver. Peter went out and wept after denying the Lord. More seem to be unhappy with themselves than pleased with their achievements.

How about you? Job despised himself, Jacob's sons were angry with themselves. Peter was disappointed with himself. It's not a bad place to start because a broken heart is not despised by God. You might despise yourself but God doesn't. Psalm 51.17 *The sacrifice acceptable to God is a broken spirit; a broken and contrite heart, O God, you will not despise.* NRSV

In other people's eyes? A missionary had a problem with one of the Amazon Tribes. When he told them the story of the cross they thought that Judas was the hero of the hour. They practised deceit on their enemies seeking to gain their confidence over months, then kill them. The eyes of others cannot always be the wise judgement of our actions.

Pilate signed for the crucifixion of Jesus in order to please the people, Mark 15.15. Saul, like most of us, set out to please people rather than God. He wanted others to like him.

1Sam.15.17 *When you were little in your own eyes... 24 I did it for the people ...* Saul changed, once he was the "little tall man." Then all that changed he became the big tall man! You need not be worried what others think of you. It matters what God thinks of you!

In God's eyes? In the book of Kings, it often describes the king whether he did it right in the eyes of God or not. e.g. 2Kings 10.30. Who were failures in God's eyes? Some were churches such as Laodicea, or people who were great in other's eyes, such as the Herod of Acts 12.20. Who were successes in God's eyes? The widow woman with two mites, the centurion who believed God, as well as Zacchaeus who was hated by all, and Lazarus at the rich man's gate begging.

Whose eyes are you looking out of? God says have my eye ointment Rev.3.17 Look through God's glasses. How are you doing? It is difficult for us to act beyond our natural strength. We often have emotional, moral and intellectual decisions to make, ones that could give us heart attacks, breakdowns, insomnia etc. There comes a time when we must overcome our natural weaknesses and act with valour, through faith in God alone.

Job thought little of himself, and his friends thought even less of him. God had a different opinion, "Have you seen my servant Job?" was God's speech about him. It was not his failure that God saw it was his reaction to the things that happened to him.

Jesus warned us about the yard stick we make for others. Matt.7.7 God has a yard stick[262] and it has different units to the ones we work in. Use God's yard stick, and measure your life alone.

Jesus said to Nicodemus, *"But those who do what is true come to the light, so that it may be clearly seen that their deeds have been done in God."*[263] We always need to look at the work we do in the cold light of day. Bright lights are essential, are we taking a day by day examination of ourselves?

---

[262] You could call it a benchmark.
[263] John.3.21 NRSV

91

The Song of the slandered saint (CH Spurgeon) Psalm 7

It is difficult to know the exact part of David's life when this was written. So it is left as a separate note.

Slander: - is a false and defamatory oral statement against another person. It is often said that when mud is thrown some always sticks. Once your name has been blackened it is difficult to wash it clean. The Italians say that reputation is like a cypress tree once cut it never grows again. But with God things are different. He can do a good clean up job.

In some modern translations the title misses out that it was the words of Cush that were the problem. Leaving it that Cush was the whole problem. The Septuagint translation includes "the word of Cush" so we will leave it the same as the KJV and some modern translations.

Jewish commentators often said that it was King Saul himself that slandered David, (Saul's fathers name was Kish.) Or it could have been another Benjaminite who made allegations against him.

When was David slandered?

There were many occasions when people were willing to side with Saul against David[264] and no doubt they were ready to fire up Saul against David. Some commentators suggest it was later in his life; when David was accused of being involved in the death of Abner, 2Sam.3, and remember Shimei the mud-slinger, 2Sam 16.5.

The accusation in verse 4 of the psalm was that he had rewarded evil for good, further that he had attacked others without good cause. Some people enjoy trouble. That is when they are not in the middle of it! Someone was enjoying this.

Hebrew poetry is composed in a different way to Western poetry, there is a form of rhythm but it is different to ours. There is a further matter. A line of Hebrew poetry is made up of two colas. Each cola generally has three words. The way it works is generally in three different ways.

- There are two similar statements, when the second echoes the first See Psalm 103.10 *He does not deal with us according to our sins, nor repay us according to our iniquities.* NRSV
- When one statement compliments or amplifies another. See Psalm 63.8 *My soul clings to you; your right hand upholds me.* & Psalm 145.18 *The LORD is near to all who call on him, to all who call on him in truth.* NRSV
- When we are looking at it from the other side of the coin. Such as: Psalm 37.21 *The wicked borrow, and do not pay back, but the righteous are generous and keep giving;* NRSV

Two close friends fell out, one believed a false allegation made about the other. Many years later the man who had believed the untruth went to apologise and ask for forgiveness as his former friend was dying. The sick man asked him to take his pillow outside and scatter the feathers around. Though considering it foolish he did as he was asked. When he returned to the bedside, the dying man then said now go and collect all the feathers again. For years the slander had

---

[264] 1Sam.19.19 22.9 23.7 23.19 24.1 26.1 etc.

been passed around and had travelled far and wide. Like the feathers they could not all be collected where the wind had blown them.

How to be victorious in slander allegations.

1. **An affirmation of faith.** v.1 *O LORD my God, in you I take refuge;* NRSV It can seem like a backward step. It can appear that you are doing nothing. Trusting God can be the most difficult thing to do when we wish to justify ourselves. It can mean no further action to be taken until we get the go ahead. We are leaving the ball in God's court.
2. **An Affirmation of innocence.** v.3 *"If I have done this," then God is off the hook.* He is not responsible for our sins of which we are guilty. Both the guilty and the innocent proclaim their innocence. For the observer it is often difficult to tell who is truthful. Often time sorts the matter out.
3. **A call for action.** v.6 *Rise up, O LORD, in your anger."* NRSV One thing that is noticeable in the Psalms is that there is a cry for God to act. It is not the passive acceptance when nothing is to be done. It is first to sort the matter out with God then ask God to sort the others out! We can feel hard done by. It is good to ask when something will be done, as when you are asking someone to repair an object that is broken. So he was asking God to do something now. not in the indefinite future.

   Anslem said: -

   My God You hide Your treasure to kindle my desire!
   You hide Your pearl to inflame the seeker;
   You delay to give, that You may teach me to importune,
   Seem not to hear to make me persevere.

As one man said a week in prison is longer than a month at liberty. Our strong wish for God to act quickly is rarely answered. Hold on and wait for God's timing.

4. **Vindication not vindictiveness.** v9 *O let the evil of the wicked come to an end,"* NRSV It is not wrong to ask for right to be seen to be right.
5. **Way of escape for the wicked.** v12 *"If one does not repent,"* NRSV he realised that there was a way for the wicked to change as he himself had previously done. It was open to his enemies as well as his friends. See Rev. 2.16.

Christopher Jefferies, a retired Christian school teacher was wrongly arrested for the murder of a young woman in Bristol, England, near Christmas 2010. The Newspapers and most of the media took it that he was guilty. They vilified him mercilessly without proof. When finally, the real murderer was caught and convicted eight newspapers had to write apologies and paid him hundreds of thousands in damages. At the time it was friends who implicitly trusted him who took him into their home when he was bailed, and saw him through. We all need friends like that and we all need to be those friends.[265]

---

[265] Christopher Jefferies was falsely accused of the Murder of Joanna Yeates in Bath, England, see Wikipedia. A former pupil directed a film called the Lost Honour of Christopher Jefferies, He was invited to observe its production. About one scene he said, "It didn't seem to me to be necessarily the most sensitive thing to invite me to go and see." However, despite his ordeal, Jefferies said he had never been bitter. "I think I've been incredibly fortunate. Partly in the legal representation I had, which couldn't have been better. And in the support I had – because I'm quite certain that I wouldn't have been able to cope if – on being released from custody – I'd had to stay in a bail hostel, or something like that. (Guardian 29.11.2014)

92

David in the desert place
Psalm 63

Although Delitzsch says it was written during Absalom's rebellion. David did not go to the wilderness of Judah to escape him. As there is no other clue as to the occasion we will take it as then.

David was in the desert yet king. When we are in success there can be setbacks, failure can stare you in the face. When the coup d'état came with Absalom leading the troops the non-aligned people of Israel might be saying well Absalom is David's son does it matter? - There was one difference. David was the chosen of God, imperfect as all people, yet chosen that was the difference. Still king but in the desert of Judah.

This Psalm has been used by many song writers.

1. **David's concern was not just for the kingdom** or for himself it was for his relationship with the Lord. He must have asked is God with me or not? What have I done? If we suffer we often ask ourselves while in the desert experience, are we in the wrong? Have I hurt others, Have I offended God?

There are many other questions, am I thirsty for God? Have I lost the first love I had? Very often people that have left the Lord are not even aware of it, Samson is an example. Or they are busy blaming others for their problems. Neither are they prepared to correct the matter anyway.

2. **David had a personal relationship with God.** We can see that he is love with God.

    v.2 that he felt the presence of God.
    v.4 that he sang praises to God
    v.3 that he saw God as a giving God.
    v.6 that he constantly thought about the Lord. I think it was E. Peterson who said the word meditate here can be used as, "a dog chewing the bone."

This is a man who does not just acknowledge God but one who loves God. There should be evidence of this in every Christian. They will want not only to know more about God but also to know God more than they do. There will be spontaneous joy. Every revival movement has been accompanied with song, the Methodists, Salvation Army, the Pentecostals etc. They showed a thankfulness and joy with God. If people do not exhibit some of these characteristics, then there is something wrong with their personal experience with the Lord.

3. **Emptiness or thirst?** Many will say that they feel empty but not thirsty – are you missing something or seeking more of God? Once David spoke of his thirst for the waters of Bethlehem. The world is full of empty people – empty of purpose or satisfaction – we can continue to rattle, see 1Cor.13. Or we can get filled. See the woman at the well in John 4. Jesus gave her a thirst for the living water. She soon started drinking at the well.

4. **What he wanted to see.** v.2 The works and wonders the power and the glory – of God. As in the sanctuary. Some things are only achieved in the sanctuary, Jesus put others out when he raised Jairus' daughter, Peter when praying for Dorcas put the other widows out. But we cannot always go to

a quiet place. David must have experienced the power of God in the sanctuary or he would not have mentioned it.

David loved the house of God - *"I love the house where you live, O LORD, the place where your glory dwells."* Psalm 26.8 *"I have asked the LORD for one thing; one thing only do I want: to live in the LORD's house all my life, to marvel there at his goodness, and to ask for his guidance."* Psalm 27.4. GNB Remember he wanted to build the temple. It was there he went for getting direction from God. It was there he saw the beauty of the Lord.

5. **Two sides to God's keeping power.** There have always been people that have fallen away from serving God. Jesus told the parable of the sower in Mark 4 and how some quickly fell away and others after a longer period of time. Yet many have remained faithful even after many set-backs.

We have our own personal desire to go on with God and we also have the keeping power of God. It is seen in the Old Testament as well as the New Testament. Lev.20.7,8 ***Sanctify yourselves therefore****, and be ye holy: for I am the LORD your God. And ye shall keep my statutes, and do them:* **I am the LORD which sanctify you**. KJV. In the New Testament we have similar Phil.2.12,13 *In the same way continue to work out your salvation with fear and trembling. It is God who produces in you the desires and actions that please him.* (GW)

6. **From Thirsting to feasting.** v.5 *My soul shall be satisfied.* When the disciples returned from shopping in Samaria and they saw Jesus talking to the Samaritan woman Jesus said, *"I have meat to eat that you know not of."* (John 4).
7. **Something better than life** v.3. The presence and company of the Lord was better to David than life itself. Paul could say, 2Cor. 5:8,9 *We are confident and prefer to live away from this body and to live with the Lord. Whether we live in the body or move out of it, our goal is to be pleasing to him.* GW David put it this way: - *Because your steadfast love is better than life, my lips will praise you.*

So very often our hopes and ambitions are for things we wish to achieve in this life on earth. Yet our lives are not long here, we should not only have a hope but also an ambition that looks beyond the grave. Whether it is just a, "Well done my good and faithful servant," or a desire to have our loved ones with us in heaven, often illustrated by a mother asking, "Are all the children in?" There is more that points to us having eternal ambitions. Jesus spoke of putting our treasure where no thief could break in and steal.[266]

The hope and future enjoyment of heaven was part of David's psyche, he finished psalm 23 with his certainty, "I shall dwell in the house of the Lord forever." He had heaven in his soul. If you feel that this was just his wish while on this earth,[267] David said at the death of Bathsheba's child, "I will go to be with him." David believed in an eternal day and in the meantime wanted a continual relationship with the Lord. He feared that the Spirit of God would leave him. When separated from a place of worship he longed to be able to go there again.

---

[266] Matthew 6.20 store up treasures for yourselves in heaven, where moths and rust don't destroy and thieves don't break in and steal. Your heart will be where your treasure is. GW

[267] Most commentators suggest that it was about his life on earth he was talking about.

93

God has a long nose
Psalm 86 and others.

Verse 15 is translated in the NRSV "God is slow to anger," in the KJV it is "long suffering." In the Hebrew it is "long nose" a short nose is a short temper! When David was speaking of the qualities of God they were in total contrast to the qualities of the heathen gods. The "Message Bible" translates this verse as: - *But you, O God, are both tender and kind, not easily angered, immense in love, and you never, never quit.*

David talks of God's relationship to people and the forgiveness available, how the Lord will remove our sins from us as far away as the east is from the west. There is not only the sense of cleansing of sin but also empowering him and others to achieve great things. He could say, *"By my God I have leapt over a wall, run through a troop,"* and etc., David sees that God was not just forgiving us but also helping us to achieve great things. The Lord is not only in the correcting but also in the improving and enhancing of people. David also talks of his relationship with God saying that he is steadfast in his faithfulness to God as God is faithful to him. He would often ask the lord to defend him. Although many times he would have been in physical danger, very often he would complain about slander as much as any other problem. The GNB translates Psalm 140.3 as,

"*Their tongues are like deadly snakes; their words are like a cobra's poison.*" Yet in the same song he also speaks of being in danger. Vicious words often lead to physical violence. He is often ready to ask God to deal with the people. There was no hesitation asking God to curse them and bless him. It could be that he had one or two things to learn from Jesus, just as James and John the sons of thunder did too.

The psalms of David are full of theology, He speaks of the omnipresence of God, and again of God being all powerful and all knowing. Psalm 139.2-7 says: - *Even before a word is on my tongue, O LORD, you know it completely. You hem me in, behind and before, and lay your hand upon me. Such knowledge is too wonderful for me; it is so high that I cannot attain it. Where can I go from your spirit? Or where can I flee from your presence?*

NRSV The major part of this song is filled with David marvelling at the immenseness of the Almighty. Though he does not hesitate to talk about his, and God's enemies as well. At the end of the psalm David asks the Lord to search his heart. He knew God had done it already. During the New Zealand revivals of 1936, Edwin Orr overheard some Maori girls singing a beautiful song, the "Song of Farewell." The melody of that song stayed with him until after a stirring Easter morning service he put words to it, using Psalm 139:23-24 as his inspiration, on the back of an envelope as his script paper. The hymn, "Search Me, O God," was written and is considered one of the most beautiful and challenging of all hymns.

David wanted God to teach him his ways,[268] he gave the Lord access to his own heart, "Search me," he said, knowing that the Lord would interact with him. Realising he still had lessons to learn, quite a few actually! But who would dare to point so much as their little finger at him. He was after God's own heart. We must be prepared only to ask God to search our hearts and not another's not even David's.

---

[268] Psalm 86.11

In psalm 8.4 and also in Psalm 144.3 David is entranced by the fact that the Almighty God would communicate with human-kind, he asks the question: - Ps 8:4 *what is a mortal that you remember him or the Son of Man that you take care of him? (GW)* The modern song writer asked the question, "Who am I that a king should bleed and die for?" Charles Wesley put it, "Amazing love! How can it be that Thou my God should die for me?" When David wondered at the interest God showed in him and his family we too can wonder at the loveliness of God who takes interest in all our ways and our doings and our family. May we never lose that wonder.

94

I'm the Good Guy Lord
Psalm 17 and others.

Betty, like many Christians read the New Testament a lot, when I visited her once she told me about the difficulty she was having with some passages of the Old Testament. The execration Psalms or Cursing Psalms have always been a problem to Christians, whether new believers or mature ones. David saw forgiveness as a God thing, not so much as a people thing. It was vertical rather than horizontal with him. There is a question we must ask, "Is this peculiar to David or is it part of the Old Testament psyche? The Law of Moses was eye for eye and tooth for tooth.[269] It was Jesus who put the matter straight in Matthew 5 he said, "*38,39 "You have heard that it was said, 'An eye for an eye and a tooth for a tooth.' But I tell you not to oppose an evil person. If someone slaps you on your right cheek, turn your other cheek to him as well.* GW Although the law of Moses was to cover the running of a country as well as moral and ethical considerations for the Jewish faith, it still left them with an overriding view of judgement rather than grace.

David seemed to have considered his own way and lifestyle as somewhat better than the behaviour of many of his contemporaries

---

[269] Exodus 21.24

as in Psalm 17.1 he felt he came through with flying colours. In Psalm 26.4 he states: - *I do not sit with the worthless, nor do I consort with hypocrites,* NRSV he is so sure of himself and his morality. Yet there comes a time when he realises that he too is a failure, and not before time. In psalm 40.12 he says, *"For evils have encompassed me without number; my iniquities have overtaken me, until I cannot see; they are more than the hairs of my head, and my heart fails me."* NRSV

David seemed to have it in for his enemies, their wives and their children too. He might have reluctantly put vengeance in God's hands but he sure was certain to remind the Lord about the problems he was having with people. Not that he was going to leave it always to God.[270] This is David talking, is God talking as well? Can we take the theology of David and ignore him cursing his opponents? Yes, we can. His understanding of who God is and what he will and can do must not mean we reject all the teaching of the Psalms because of David railing against his foes. Like all of us David was an incomplete person. We refer to some people as having a personality defect yet often with all of us there are shortcomings that need overcoming. He was an imperfect saint and has at times been painted in colours that are too glowing.

David found great happiness in God in Psalm 4.7 he could say: - *You have put gladness in my heart more than when their grain and wine abound.* NRSV See also Psalm 18.28 *It is you who light my lamp; the LORD, my God, lights up my darkness.* NRSV He had a mighty strong emotional attachment to the Lord. He was no-fly-by night. When talking to the Lord he could genuinely say, O LORD, I love the house in which you dwell, and the place where your glory abides, (Psalm 26.8 NRSV). David wanted to experience the loveliness or the beauty of the King of kings and Lord of lords. *Psalm 27.4 One thing I asked of the LORD, that will I seek after: to live in the house of the LORD all the days of my life, to behold the beauty of the LORD, and to inquire in his temple.* NRSV. For the opening of a church that

---

[270] Psalm 41.10 But you, O LORD, be gracious to me, and raise me up, that I may repay them. NRSV

he had pioneered William Bullock wrote the hymn, "We love the place Oh God wherein thine honour dwells." He was quoting Psalm 26. David knew the presence of God in his life and in a place of worship too. It was not goose pimples down his back, but a sense of holy awe that the majesty of God would come to him even when in all his weakness and need. He wanted all that loveliness to brush off onto him too. This beauty or loveliness of God is almost a touchable thing, see the psalm of Moses. *Psalm 90.17 And let the loveliness of our Lord, our God, rest on us, confirming the work that we do. Oh, yes. Affirm the work that we do!* GNB.

"Come," my heart says, *"seek his face!" Your face, LORD, do I seek,* says David in psalm 27 NRSV. He did not just expect God to come to him he went after the Lord. It was the deep longing within his heart that he might come close to the Lord, *"But it is for you, O LORD, that I wait; it is you, O Lord my God, who will answer,"* Psalm 38.15. NRSV What testimonies he shared, he had a new song put in his heart, David was delivered from enemies from pits and from the mire.[271]

---

[271] Psalm 40.2,3 He drew me up from a desolate pit, out of the miry bog, and set my feet upon a rock, making my steps secure. He put a new song in my mouth, a song of praise to our God. Many will see and fear, and put their trust in the LORD. NRSV

95

The Charge to Solomon
1Chronicles 28.9

What a charge! See the charge to Timothy. A commission, a command, but much more a handing over of responsibility.

1Chr.28.9 *"And you, my son Solomon, know[272] the God of your father, and serve him with single mind and willing heart; for the LORD searches every mind, and understands every plan and thought. If you seek him, he will be found by you; but if you forsake him, he will abandon you forever.* NRSV

1Timothy 6:12-14 *Fight the good fight of the faith; take hold of the eternal life, to which you were called and for which you made the good confession in the presence of many witnesses. In the presence of God, who gives life to all things, and of Christ Jesus, who in his testimony before Pontius Pilate made the good confession, I charge you to keep*

---

[272] *yādaʻ*: A verb meaning to know, to learn, to perceive, to discern, to experience, to confess, to consider, to know people relationally, to know how, to be skilful, to be made known, to make oneself known, to make to know. The simple meaning, to know, is its most common translation out of the eight hundred or more uses. One of the primary uses means to know relationally and experientially: it refers to knowing or not knowing persons (Genesis 29:5; Exodus_1:8) Word Studies

the commandment without spot or blame until the manifestation of our Lord Jesus Christ, NRSV

It is a charge that should be given to every Sunday School teacher and every deacon and every worship leader and to every parent and every grandparent.

We will know more than we know now if we get to know Him!

He said Know the God of your father, David seemed to know God better than his parents, better than his contemporaries, better than his peers. And better than his superiors! So often the phrase "God of your fathers," (plural) is used. Unfortunately, we know that Solomon never achieved the relationship with God that David had. Compare Solomon's songs to David's songs. David knew God.

"God of our fathers be the God of each succeeding race," says the hymn writer. David had slip-ups in life. Solomon was side tracked. One allows you to get back on course the other means you drift further away!

Every son should want to be like their father. One child wrote; "Dear God, I want to be just like my Daddy when I get big but not with so much hair all over." - Sam

Some of the past generation have been great Christians, we knew them but we must know their God. Mr Leith, was a former missionary to China he and his wife would often let me stay at their house. They had suffered much when the Japanese invaded China, but the fire of God was in them still. Pastor Oldfield from Lancashire was built like an ox. Before his conversion he would fight from one end of the village to the other. When became a minister he would take many of us young people on evangelistic trips to the continent. These were lives filled with the love of God. We must know that their God is our God.

To know God meant to be intimate with him. To have a close relationship, are we more than just casual friends? My father knew God well; he was often talking to Him. I wanted to know Him to. I want all my family to know him as well. David wanted Solomon to know God. J.I. Packer said: - A little knowledge of God is worth more than a great deal of knowledge about Him.

Someone once asked evangelist Dwight Moody how he managed to remain so intimate in his relationship with Christ. He replied, "I have come to Him as the best friend I have ever found, and I can trust Him in that relationship. I have believed He is Saviour; I have believed He is God; I have believed His atonement on the cross is mine, and I have come to Him and submitted myself on my knees, surrendered everything to Him, and gotten up and stood by His side as my friend, and there isn't any problem in my life, there isn't any uncertainty in my work but I turn and speak to Him as naturally as to someone in the same room, and I have done it these years because I can trust Jesus."

Paul said to the Philippians "That I might know him and the power of His resurrection." You have to take the good with the bad. Peter & disciples took the good but they had a problem with the bad. Paul included "the fellowship of his suffering."

Someone said, "To know Him is to love him and to love him is to serve him."

When you know him you can serve him, it was not a case of David serving his country it was a case of serving God first. When Prince Charles and Dianna married one of their songs was, "I vow to thee my country" it was written by Sir Cecil Spring-Rice, the last verse starts with, "And there's another country I've heard of long ago." That other country must take priority. If you have made a vow to God first, you can serve your family or any other calling you may have. I serve God and as a result I serve the local Church.

Some years ago there was a terrible tragedy on the London underground. A train ploughed into the buffers at full speed. The only reason they could think why it happened was because the driver was going to buy a new car when he finished work and so hadn't got his mind on his job, the money for it was in his pocket. There must be singleness of purpose and our heart and mind of the plan of God for our lives.

Some Ugandan Christians each had a place of prayer in the bush, and you could tell if one wasn't so regular in their prayers because the pathways soon became overgrown! What a charge David gave Solomon, what a challenge? God gives us a charge too. An order that has responsibility, it might be to our family or to our friends to our community or to the world. Jesus gave a charge to the disciples, "Go!" It was a command with responsibility.

At my old Bible college, they established an annual prize. It was named after a tutor who had recently died. It was to be given annually to a high achiever, but I knew the tutor, and I knew he was not concerned about academic achievement but a person's spiritual depth. They used the name of the respected tutor but they did not honour his preference for godliness over intellectual accomplishment. Knowing God is to know how he thinks and to share in his conversation and the measure God uses to gauge our real achievements.

The final comment about David must therefore be left to the statement which God made. In spite of all his faults, failings, and his sins. God spoke of him as, "A man after my heart."

96

The Writers and their message.
1Chronicles 29.29

Now the acts of King David, from first to last, are written in the records of the seer Samuel, and in the records of the prophet Nathan, and in the records of the seer Gad. NRSV

There have been many suggestions as to who wrote the history of Saul and David. These include Solomon rewriting the story of his father, or individual courtiers in support of the two kings. The Bible states it was not the court recorders or the royal biographers who wrote the history of Saul and David, it was some of the prophets. In addition, there is the mention of another book, the "Book of Jashar," (2Samuel 1.18 & Joshua 10.13). This book covers a century or two, was Jashar a prophet from the past who also kept records? If so they would have added to it over the years. It makes sense for these people to be the journalists and historians of their day. They would be courageous and truthful in comparison with any recorder of court details, they were recording objective truth.

In every age and every nation there must be men and women who write the truth without fear or favour. Whole nations have had their history adapted to suit their current politics. Nations have had their histories coloured by centuries of inaccurate and biased records of the past. This has not only happened with politics and national history it has happened within the history of the Christian Church.

Behaviours that are often considered excesses in modern revivals have been despised or enjoyed as the case may be. Yet the detailed original notes of revivals of hundreds of years ago in such denominations as the Presbyterians also exhibited similar phenomenon. They were often ignored because the official biographers considered such things best not mentioned.

Very often the history of the Protestant reformation has been taught from one side or the other without the full story being told. If we were to consider the whole, we might discover some saints were not very saintly. Impartiality is almost an impossibility for us, so Jesus said that we should leave the judging to him. Later kings were able to have their own recorders.[273] Gad, Nathan and Samuel made sure it was an unvarnished history. Many have sought to excuse and almost exonerate David because of his psalms all we can do is read his life and marvel at the grace and mercy of God. If you are going to question the morality of some modern hymn writers and feel that you cannot sing their songs, remember psalm 23, the author of that song was not perfect either.

We struggle with the imprecations in some of David's songs, but we marvel at his understanding of the nature of God and the faith he had in knowing that God would hear him and see him through all his troubles. We must leave his cursing to one side, just as we leave the bones of the fish we are eating on the edge of the plate, and enjoy all the wonders of the Psalms.

---

[273] 1Kings 11.41 etc.